MW01517843

Wind, Sand and Hope

Joseph Schackelman

Also by Joe Schackelman

God Lives

Stories of extraordinary
spiritual experiences...

Acknowledgements

My mother always told me to, "Keep good company." So---Suzanne, my love—you are the best company I ever found.

The pages that follow, would never have been written were it not for you and your patience with me. The many blocks of time that you gave me for this book, were deeply appreciated. They made all the difference.

You made all the difference.

Thank You.
Thank You.
Thank You
Joe

Contents

Chapter One
The Invitations

She rushed up to him. "How did you do that?" she said. Her eyes were wide.

"Do what?" he asked.

"Get that gal in the brown jacket to take one of those invitations. You know, one of those flyers you're handing out today!"

"Oh, that. Usually I can tell which people will be interested," he said, "It's a gift. You could call it discernment."

"But she walked in with six others. All of them were in a hurry. And you just went up to her and gave her one of those flyers." She turned and waved toward the back of the store. "She's over in aisle three looking at the cover right now. How could you know she was the one out of those seven who would take it? What's your gimmick?"

"No gimmick. I just told her she might be interested in a new book club starting here next week. Anyway, I'm Dave Jackson," he said extending his hand.

He was a slightly overweight man in his mid-thirties. He was wearing a dress shirt with khaki slacks. He had the start of a full beard.

"And I'm Midge Fisher," she said, shaking his hand.

She was a slender blonde woman in her forties. She was dressed in a black business suit.

"I know," he said. "When I asked for you at the counter a clerk pointed you out as 'Midge the Manager'."

"I guess I'm the manager," she smiled. "But sometimes it's the store that manages me. Like when I came in this morning and read your message I thought my assistant had it all wrong." Her smile faded. "I couldn't believe you only asked for five flyers." She took a step back from him. "I mean do you want to start a book club here or not? I've been managing this bookstore for six years and we average 600 people a day through those doors. So--I was ready to have about 500 printed up for you."

"I don't want too many in the group or the discussion gets all watered down, so I figure this will be perfect."

"Really," Midge said. "Well anyway, are they alright? These five flyers? I suppose I should say four flyers now. I didn't use any graphics or your picture or anything." Midge edged slightly closer to Jackson and together they looked at the papers he held.

The printed message read:
You are invited to join the X-Treme Book Club

Starting at 6:30 pm Tuesday, March 29 in this store. We will discuss the novel *Wind, Sand, and Hope*.

.

The discussion leader will be Dave Jackson.
Important: Read the first two chapters and be
Prepared to discuss them. Bring your imagination.
And a copy of the book with you.
There will be no charge.

"You don't need them to pre-register or anything?" Midge asked. "I mean how will we know how many people to set up for?"

"These flyers are just fine. Set up for a total of five, and I'll need a large blackboard."

Midge smiled. "We don't use blackboards anymore."

As Jackson stood watching more people entering the store, Midge made no effort to hide her expression of disbelief.

"Let me get this straight," she said, both hands still on her hips, "You expect to get five people to join the book club-- by giving out five invitations?"

"No sense wasting paper."

"No sense expecting miracles either."

A middle-aged man with pale skin and black hair entered the store. Without looking up he passed in front of Jackson and Midge. With two steps Jackson moved to the man's side.

"A new book club will be starting here next week. I believe you'll find the material quite interesting."

Midge stood, arms crossed, watching from a slight distance.

The middle-aged man took one of the papers and said, "Book club? Really? What's the book about?"

"Mostly it's about wars."

"Wars?" The word came out loudly. "I have enough of that right at home." He attempted to give the invitation back to Jackson.

"There are different kinds of wars," Jackson said as he stepped back and out of the man's reach. "There are killing wars and there are spiritual wars. The book we'll be discussing is about both."

"Thanks anyway," the dark-haired man said as he folded the paper, stuffed it into a pocket and walked away.

The door flung open then as two women came in together. The older of the two seemed to be in a hurry. The younger one trailed slightly behind her and looked up at Jackson as they passed by him.

"Check out our brand new book club here next Tuesday night," Jackson said to the girl as he offered her a flyer.

Without taking a flyer the girl instantly looked away and took several quick steps to catch up with the other lady.

"In taverns and book stores," the older women could be heard, "that's where the crack-pots hang out..."

Jackson walked back to stand next to Midge.

"And how many signed on the dotted line so far?" Midge asked.

"Did you see how red that girl's eyes were?"

"Is that a new question to avoid an answer to my question?"

Jackson was not smiling. "That girl is not off the screen yet. She just has to get away from her mother for a few minutes."

"Oh? Looked to me as if 'Red Eyes' simply walked away from you. Actually, she sort of *ran* away from you. Would you call that a malfunction of your discernment, or what?"

As the entrance door opened again the sounds of an argument carried deep into the store. Two teen-aged boys entered. Both were dressed in baggy pants and jackets. Whenever the shorter, louder boy spoke, smoke came out of his mouth.

"There's a cigarette butt somewhere just outside the door," Midge said.

"Either that or he's been nipping on very hot barbeque sauce."

The taller, thinner boy walked slower than his companion. They stopped arguing as they glanced around the store. When they saw Midge and Jackson looking at them they strolled over to face them.

"You guys giving out some kind of coupons?" It was the taller boy who spoke. "Like tonight's freebies or something?"

"No," Jackson said. "But I do have an invitation for you."

"An invitation? To a party?"

"No. To join a new book club starting here next week."

"Sounds good to me," the boy said. "Book club, huh? With cake and wine during the lecture?"

"No wine or cake," Jackson said. "No lecture either. Just ideas."

"Just ideas? Neat."

"We'll be talking about the book, *Wind, Sand and Hope*. I think you will enjoy the discussions."

"Never heard of the book. What's it about?"

"It's sort of about wars. Different kinds of wars--."

"Hey! Haven't we had enough of wars?"

Jackson smiled at the teen. "That's exactly the question this book asks."

"Well, is that question answered in the book? Or is it only asked?"

Jackson and the boy looked at each other for a drawn-out moment. During the silence the short boy nudged his companion and walked away.

Jackson spoke first. "The question you asked," he said, "is answered in the book."

"Hang on there mister. That windy-sandy thing has the answer to doing away with wars? Is that what you're telling me?"

"Yes."

The teen looked at Jackson for an instant and blinked several times. "Can I have one of those invitations?" he asked.

"Of course."

"Copies of the book are in the fiction section," Midge said.

I'll pick up a copy and check it out," the boy said. "I've never been in a book club before." He turned and slowly walked away.

As the teenager disappeared between the shelves of books Midge looked at Jackson. "Isn't 'discernment' sort of a gift?

"Something like having an extremely clear, or godly, judgment about certain people or situations?"

"Yes Midge. That's a fair definition. Very good."

"So, you think inviting that kid to join the group--that was your discernment?" Her hands were again on her hips. "You think he will add to the literary discussions? You invited him based on your discernment, or godly judgment? Not that he'd consider sitting in on a live discussion group anyway."

"My dear Midge, give him time. Sometimes a little time will produce great changes."

The lady in the brown jacket walked up to Jackson. She was carrying one book. "I've read the invitation you gave me a few minutes ago. Are you David Jackson?"

"Yes. May I help you?"

"Jackson, the discussion leader?"

"Yes. Do you have a question for me?"

She had a look of concern. "I have to be at work very early in the morning. So I was wondering how long the weekly meetings last?"

"Good question," he said. "I think we can wrap everything up by seven-thirty. If someone wants to stick around to shoot the breeze I can stay for a few extra minutes. But when you need to leave you are free to go anytime. Okay?"

"Okay. Sounds good. Thanks." She turned and went to the check-out counter.

Midge moved up to stand beside Jackson. "Five flyers printed, three handed out and one book sold," she said. "Good thing you are not on commission."

"Aha!" Jackson said. "If you're keeping score, here comes Miss Red Eyes and her mother."

The two women walked past Jackson and Midge without looking up. As they neared the door, Midge laughed. "How old are you?" she asked.

"Thirty-six," he said. "Why do you ask?"

"Because I think you still have a lot to learn."

"Such as...?"

"Those two were shopping--somewhere else. They breezed in here just to visit the ladies' room."

"Oh, I believe you," Jackson said. "But the daughter was in the right place at the right time anyway."

When the two women reached the door the older woman stopped and waited for the other to push the door open and hold it for her. As the older woman passed through, the younger one called out, "Meet you at the car." Then she turned and walked back to Jackson. She glanced up at him and looked quickly away. "I didn't mean to be rude when we walked past you before," she said. "May I have one of those papers now?"

"Of course. These are invitations to check out a new book club starting right here next Tuesday. We'll have an interesting book to talk about. I hope you can make it."

The young woman took the flyer and read it. Without looking up at Jackson she said, "I'll think about it. Now I better get going."

Midge, who had been standing slightly behind him, moved up to his side. "Four flyers given out. Are you okay with that?"

"Oh yes. I have an idea about this one."

"Well, I have to get back to the office. Good luck with that last one. It's been good talking with you," Midge said as she started walking away.

"Wait," Jackson said. "I want you to have this last invitation."

As he handed her the flyer he smiled. "I believe the book we will be reading together and the discussions we'll have… it could be a real source of joy for you."

Midge took one step back to him. "I put in 50 to 60 hours a week here. Every week." She stood with one hand on her hip. With the other hand, still holding the flyer, she gestured. "And you expect me to take an extra couple hours every week to sit in on a program that produces almost nothing for the company?"

"You never can tell what this program might produce. Could be more than you expect or imagine."

"Oh, really? And what do you expect of it?"

"For now, I expect you to keep the flyer," he said. "It's a reminder of our club. I expect you to stay open-minded about it and eventually join us."

"You know what I expect? I expect you to be the only person here next week for your first meeting. I also expect that there will never be a second meeting."

"Well don't make any decision right now. Maybe wait 'til next week," Jackson said. "Just consider it every once in awhile."

One corner of Midge's lips showed a slight smile. "I'll keep the flyer. And I'll consider the book club every now and then," Midge said. "But next week--please don't wait for me. You would have to wait for a long, long time. "In that case, he called after her. "Have the space set up with only four chairs. And a large blackboard."

Chapter 2
The Trial

"You can't kill me." he mumbled.

"Speak up," commanded an obese major seated with four other officers at a long table. "And stand at attention."

"Yes sir," the prisoner said. He stood between two armed sergeants facing the seated officers. His uniform was wrinkled and stained. All the signs of rank had been stripped away. "I said you can't kill me." His voice was still a soft mumble and he had not come to a position of full attention.

"Son," the youngest officer said, "Do you know you are on trial for treason? If found guilty you'll face a firing squad. You understand what I just said?"

"Yes sir," The prisoner said. "But you can't kill me because I already died. Do you understand what I just said?"

There was a moment of silence. The room suddenly smelled of cigar smoke.

"Why do you say such things?" the major asked.

"Because I know," the prisoner said. He straightened up then and in a slightly louder voice said, "I know because there's not much of me left to kill. Everything inside of me died months ago. Up in the villages. The north side of Solidad."

"And you think we can't, or won't, execute you?" The major squinted at the prisoner. "We'll see about that right now."

The major glanced at his fellow officers. "Gentlemen," he said, "let's not take much time on this one." He sighed and with considerable effort, he turned to a corporal seated at a small table behind him. "Who is this prisoner?"

"Llanos, Sir. Federico Llanos. Rank is Private. Joined the Revolutionary Army in June of 1941 at the age of 18. His current age is 22. He has served four years as a marksman. Sir."

"And the charges?"

"Suspected of being a traitor, sir." He was reading from a sheet of yellow paper. "Private Llanos served as an exceptional marksman for several years. However, according to his commanding officer, a Captain Ronoldo Ortega, during the last six months Llanos has become ineffective. Private Llanos had been commended for his ability to pick off Nationalist officers positioned 100 yards behind their own lines, which, on occasion, had the effect of starting a panic in the enemy ranks." He paused as he turned the page, looked around the room then continued reading.

"According to Captain Ortega, about six months ago Private Llanos turned into a poor marksman. He fires when ordered but he has not killed or even wounded any enemy in those last six months. Even at close range. Captain Ortega has no explanation for this transformation. End of report, sir."

The judges turned back to the prisoner standing before them.

"This is a military tribunal," said the youngest officer. He was at the end of the table. His dress uniform was slightly large for him. "Private," he said loudly, "can you explain this? Do you think you need glasses? Is that it?"

The prisoner seemed to be thinking. There was a pause. He said nothing.

The young officer continued. "I have heard about you. They call you 'the long-range sniper.' Just before a battle would begin, you would take one shot and blow a hole in one of their officer's chests." He smiled slightly as he spoke. "And it would panic their troops." He continued to smile at the prisoner. "Psychological warfare. Good work."

"But now everything has changed," the major said. "You have the ability to fight and help win the battle, but you miss." He bent low in an attempt to look into the prisoner's eyes. "Have you become a traitor?"

"No sir," said the Private. "To be a traitor you have to be in league with the enemy. I don't think of the Nationalists as enemies anymore. In this war how do you know who the enemy is? Maybe you can tell me."

The major glanced at the officers on each side of him. "I think I've heard more than enough." He lowered his voice slightly and said, "Gentlemen, are we ready to pass judgment?"

"No, wait-- Sir." It was the young officer in the large uniform. "We haven't had any answers yet and I think Private Llanos might be willing to help us." He turned to the man standing before them. "Private, do you see yourself as a traitor?"

"No sir."

"Good," the young officer said. "But you do know that you have changed?"

"Yes sir."

"That's good. Now, can you tell us what it was that happened to you those six months ago? What do you think changed you?"

The soldier looked up at the faces of this accusers. He was tall and slender. His eyes were deep set. "I guess I just became tired," he said.

"You're not on trial for how you feel," shouted the major. "You're on trial for treason."

"Private, be honest," said one of the older officers who had been silent up to that point. "Treason is punishable by death. You could be facing the firing squad if we find you guilty here today. So speak up soldier. You went through this war without injuries. But now you want to die? Why? You are still young. The war will be over soon. Perhaps in a few weeks or maybe in only days. Yes, our country is small. Just two mountains and the desert between them." He looked into the distance as he paused. Then his eyes opened wide as if he suddenly remembered where he was. He continued, "Yes, our country is small but it has a future. And you are young. At a time like this, why would you wish to die?"

"Private," the young officer said, "you do understand the seriousness of this situation--this trial-- don't you?" The officer leaned forward. "You changed from one extreme to another. For over three years you demoralized much of the Nationalists army by killing one of their officers just before a battle would begin. That was excellent work. You probably saved the lives of many of our men. And then you changed. How do you explain such action?"

"Gentlemen," the prisoner sighed and pulled himself back up to full attention. "Certainly you remember what happened six months ago. It was our victory. We took the Capital city of Santa Rosa. Remember? Remember that dawn? Half the Nationalist army was guarding the gate of Santa Rosa and the other half was around the President's mansion. We spent much of the night creeping up on them.

"Then it came--our moment," the prisoner said. "Right after dawn. We stood up. We shouted, 'Justice--Equality--Prosperity'. We shouted it over and over. And there were twice as many of us--men and rifles-- as there were of them. And suddenly they all converted to our revolutionary philosophy. They joined our side! The Capital city of Santa Rosa became the Revolutionary city of Santa Rosa. Not a shot was fired!

"The combined army of Revolutionaries and former Nationalists took over the city and the President's mansion. We marched in side by side. We woke Él Presidente and questioned him--."

"Ah yes, yes, yes," interrupted the major. "I remember. I was there that night. The old president died during the questioning. I think he fell down a stairway or something. It was a glorious morning."

"It was the beginning of the end of the war," another officer said.

"Private Llanos," the young officer said, "We had nothing but victories after that. How could that change you?"

"Everything changed," the prisoner said. "The Capital was ours. So we went out into the little villages in the mountains. Hundreds of villages--three or four of them every day. I was in a squad of eight riflemen, one officer and a thousand rounds of ammunition. We traveled in a two and a half-ton truck. It was called a 'mop up' operation.

"We would park the truck just outside the village. Our officer-- Captain Ortega-- would march us into the village and point out any of the civilians he said had been suspected of having sympathy for the Nationalists." The prisoner looked up at the five officers. His eyes met theirs. "Then we were ordered to shoot them," he said. "But see, there weren't any battles to be fought." he swallowed and added, "because there weren't any enemies left."

The major slammed his hand down on the table. "That's treason right there," he shouted. "Gentlemen, what more do you need? Are we all ready to pass judgment?"

"Wait one moment," the young officer said. He turned to the prisoner and said, "Tell us more Private. Tell us more about why you changed. Tell us exactly what you saw -- what you went through. I think everyone here needs to know. Speak up."

"Yes sir. You asked. I'll tell you!" The prisoner spoke louder now. "In some of those villages the people knew so little about war that they cheered when we came down their main street. They believed we were somehow bringing them the first wave of justice, equality and prosperity." The prisoner looked directly at each of the officers before him. He said, "Then we shot them. If a man looked at our Captain angrily he would be pointed out and we shot him."

The prisoner's position of attention returned to his former posture of exhaustion. "It didn't take us long to figure out the Captain had his orders. He had been ordered to have at least one man killed in every village. It had nothing to do with suspected sympathizers. It was designed to rule the people through fear. I believe it worked the other way; it produced more hatred than fear.

"Why did this change me, you ask? It changed everything. There is a big difference between firing at the middle of a uniform at 100 yards and going into a village and shooting innocent civilians at close range. They are your

23

countrymen. They are unarmed. They could be relatives," the prisoner said, "and we turned them into bloody piles of meat.

"That's what happened to me six months ago." The prisoner seemed to shrink in height as he spoke. "When I was ordered to fire, I shot. But I shot trees. I fired into the air. I couldn't point my rifle at any of the villagers. I shot -- but I could no longer kill."

"That was disobeying a direct order," one of the officers said.

"I didn't think those were reasonable orders," answered the Private. "Captain Ortega kept getting more and more angry as the weeks passed. He was in some kind of rage after a while. It kept getting worse."

"How did it get worse?" asked the young officer.

"Worse. Full of anger," the prisoner said. He swallowed and continued, "I remember one village very well. Too well. It was on a late afternoon when we entered the central square. It was crowded because there had been a futbol (soccer) game. We marched in just after the game ended. The home team looked sad -- as if they had lost the game. They looked sad except for one boy. He was a mentally retarded kid. You know, short, fat -- but smiling. His team must have let him play for a couple of minutes because he was holding a pair of muddy, cleated shoes in his hands and he looked so pleased to be there.

"Seven of the boys from the team plus the retarded boy were on one side of the street and looking at us. The sun was right in their eyes. Captain Ortega must have thought they were scowling at him. He ordered them to be separated out of the crowd and lined up against one of the buildings." The soldier stopped speaking momentarily and looked up at the five judges. His hands were trembling.

"Then the Captain -- the Captain ordered them to be shot. All of them. They were children. Many of their mothers and fathers and grandparents were there for the game; they screamed and watched. The retarded boy held on to his cleated shoes--as if someone had maybe told him not to lose them. He started to run but I saw him get shot in the back. The bullet must have hit his spine because he went down on his face. He tried to crawl. His legs would not work anymore. He had to use his hands and arms to drag himself. Then another shot hit him in the back of his neck and blood spurted all over the place. He bled to death. He had only crawled a little distance." Llanos looked at each of the officers and slowly said, "But he dragged those shoes with him. With his last movement that kid pulled those shoes under his body. I suppose to protect them."

The Private cleared his throat. "That night," he continued. "The Captain called us together and said that whenever we leave a village, it is good to hear the women weeping and wailing for their sons and lovers. The Captain said it is good because that village will then always be able to find money somewhere -- to pay their government taxes. Captain Ortega talked to us for a long time that night. I think he wanted to make himself feel better. I don't think it worked. I didn't listen much. I just kept thinking about that retarded boy -- paralyzed from the waist down -- but trying to crawl -- and never letting loose of those muddy, old shoes."

The major frowned at Private Llanos. "All village executions were carried out by order of General Emanuel Garcia, now President Garcia, to assure the longevity of the Garcia plan. And that plan is for the reconstruction of the nation of De La Rosa." Without hesitation he added, "Now gentlemen are we ready for the vote?"

"Sir." the young officer said, "May we take a few minutes for the private to summarize his position? Can't we give him that? I know I'm swimming upstream, but I don't see any guilt here. This man served valiantly for nearly four years. Then he became battle weary. Is that so unusual? Or so wrong? Can we put him to death for having a different sense of duty -- or morality?"

The young officer turned and looked directly at the other four men. "We are all familiar with the rules of war that came out of the Geneva Convention," he said. "No unarmed civilians are to become victims of combat. You know how I interpret that? It says to me that Private Llanos stands here as a hero. He's the only one who followed the rules. He should get a medal -- not the firing squad!"

The Chief Justice looked back at the young officer. "The Geneva convention?" he said with a sneer. "What do the Swiss know about war? And what do they know about controlling the people once the war ends?" He turned back to the other officers at the table. "No more talk of the Geneva convention!" he said. "We have nine more trials this morning and I am not allowing any 'summarization' of the prisoner's position. So now, gentleman, the vote!"

Immediately three officers slapped their right hands -- palms down -- on the table. The young officer waved his hand in silent dissent. Then the Chief Justice slammed his fist down on the table. "Private Llanos," he announced, "You have just been found guilty of treason by this tribunal. This is a capital offence during time of war. Is there anything you wish to say before sentencing?"

"Guilty?" asked the prisoner. "Guilty of what?"

Four of the officers were now leaning back in their chairs. Each pulled a cigar from his breast pocket. The young officer did not move. He seemed to be still sitting at attention.

"Can't you see?" the prisoner asked. "What is treason? How could I shoot a man who is my fellow countryman?"

The four officers with cigars were busily biting ends off the cigars and spitting the ends on the floor. One was licking the outside of his cigar. Another had produced a lighter.

The prisoner drew himself up to his tallest height Then, with his voice for the first time very loud he said, "*La gente de los pueblos no sabe de guerra!* " (The people of the villages know nothing of war!)

The major brought his hand down on the table again. "Let's not waste firing squad bullets on this traitor," he said. "Let's have him hung in the prison courtyard." He smiled for the first time. "And leave him there for three days."

"Yes," agreed a member of the tribunal. "Feed him to the rats."

The Major nodded and added, "But, let's leave him in solitary for a few days before the hanging. We don't want our rats getting fat."

Four of the officers laughed together. The young officer stared down at the top of the table. He said nothing.

The two guards each took one of the prisoner's arms and turned him around. The air over the tribunal table became clouded with cigar smoke.

Private Federico Llanos was led away.

Chapter 3
Panzon

Federico heard shouting from the prison courtyard. Angry voices repeated, "Ballet de la Morte" (The Dance of Death). Federico went to his small window and pulled himself up to look at the courtyard. A prisoner stood in silence surrounded by shouting guards. He waited motionless while the guards kept moving around him. One guard ordered him to stand up straight. That guard then measured him with a length of rope. As soon as he had the man's height marked on the rope he climbed up the steps of the gallows platform and measured from the noose to the closed trap-door in the center of the platform. He repeated this action several times as the other guards shouted, "Ballet de la Morte".

This was the third day, Federico was in solitary confinement.

The next morning Federico was awakened by a new sound. The sun had not yet completely risen, yet somebody was playing a drum in the courtyard. The drum would beat one, slow drum roll and suddenly stop with a solitary staccato beat. The sound was followed by ten seconds of silence. Then there would be another drum roll.

Federico pulled his bucket over to the cell window. He balanced on the rim of it so he could see into the courtyard. An entire squad of guards stood at attention at the base of the gallows platform. The drummer, who appeared to be a boy, stood on the other side of the structure.

Drum roll. Silence. Drum roll. Silence. Then an order was shouted and the squad of guards that had been at attention relaxed. They stood or leaned against the gallows platform and all of them started to smoke cigarettes.

From the squad room, two more guards appeared. Between them was the prisoner who had been so carefully measured the day before. His hands were tied behind his back and he was stripped down to only a pair of short pants. Every rib showed through his pale skin. His feet were bare.

Federico stood on his waste bucket and watched. The guards shouted obscenities at the prisoner who was being lead up to the gallows. Federico thought, it is just after dawn and the guards are drunk already. Then Federico recognized the man leading the shouting and swearing. It was the guard with the large stomach -- the guard who steals the food.

The prisoner was not blindfolded or given a hood to cover his face. He was lead to the center of the platform and the noose was put around his neck and tightened. Then he was forced to step up on an ammunition box which was on its side so that it elevated the prisoner by about five inches. "Those animals," Federico said out loud. "They are not going to execute him by breaking his neck. They are going to strangle him."

At that moment one of the two guards who had lead the prisoner up the platform kicked the ammunition box from under the man's feet. The gallows rope stretched a bit so that the prisoner's toes barely touched the floor below them as the prisoner attempted to raise his body to lessen the pressure of the noose around his neck. His movements were quick and light and the guards who had encircled the platform laughed. The heavy-set guard called out, *"Ah, Ballet de la Morte!"* Within several minutes the prisoner's toes were bleeding. His attempts to elevate his body became more and more desperate. With each effort his feet tired so that his body dropped and the gallows rope became tighter around his neck. His face became strangely pale.

Then his feet could no longer support the weight. His body did not relax. It twitched for a long, long time...

Federico stepped down from his cell pail. He thought, those guards look at us as insects -- like cockroaches that children drop on hot stove lids to watch them dance until they are dead. Then thoughts -- frightening thoughts -- began to race through his mind. Justice, equality, prosperity -- where is the justice today? How we reach out for one more breath of air before we die! How is justice served when such guards live and eat our bread and laugh at our deaths? If a man cannot die with dignity then what has life prepared him for? How we struggle to live! Where is God when such executions are allowed to go on? Soon I will be on that same platform.

Still, as terrible as death can be, waiting is worse. Strangulation is a very, very slow death.

For three days and nights the body of the executed man hung in the courtyard. Most of the remaining prisoners could see it from their cell windows which faced the courtyard. During the day the body would bloat as it swayed in the sun. At night large rats would come and fight each other as the climbed up the man's legs to eat the enlarged stomach area. One of those nights as Federico watched he thought he saw the body moving. As he recoiled from the sight he lost his balance on the waste bucket and fell backwards on the cell floor, the contents of the bucket splashing over him. For a long time Federico did not move. After what he thought may have been an hour, he slowly sat up and was surprised to find that he had been crying. "I know that I'm starving", he thought. "If the guard brings me something to eat today, I must ask for pen and paper. I must write a letter to my mother while I can still hold a pen."

Around midday a guard brought Federico a cup of cold coffee. The guard was the heavy-set one. He was chewing as he let himself into the cell. It was the same man that had led the other guards in shouting at the prisoner being executed.

"Where's the bread?" Federico asked.

"Gone." replied the guard.

"I need a bit of bread," Federico said. "There was no bread yesterday or the day before."

"What do you want bread for?" asked the guard. "You are going to die soon. Does it matter whether you starve or hang?"

"What is your name?" Federico asked.

The guard looked at the prisoner and said, "They call me Panzon."

Federico thought, ah -- he is called the Fat One. No surprise. Then he said, "Can I have a pen and paper. It is to write my mother."

The guard said, "Maybe," as he pulled the cell door shut behind him.

That afternoon the guard called Panzon returned and slipped a single sheet of paper, a pen, and an envelope under the cell door.

Federico called after him, "Friend, will you mail my letter if I write it?"

"I'll do what I can," answered the guard, "but I am not your friend."

For the rest of that day, Federico worked on the letter.

Dear Mama, these are the most painful words I could ever write, but I must let you know. I did nothing wrong. I always honored you and what you went through to raise me. And I was always faithful to the Church. And I am not a traitor to the Revolution. But a military court has the opinion that I am guilty of treason and has sentenced me to die. Waiting for my day of death makes me very sad. But I was sad even before the trial. One of the judges believed me, but there were five judges and four believed I was a traitor. Dear Mama, please do not be sad. I remember how you sacrificed for me as you raised me without a husband. I remember how you had to save pesos, and I love you for the kind of mother you always were to me. Thank you.

Do you remember the story Padre told us about the battle of the angels? How they fought in heaven and the battle was so fierce that it sounded like thunder. And only when Archangelo Miguel beat Lucifer did the good angels defeat the bad ones. Then millions of bad angels fell from heaven. You remember that story? After the battle was won, God looked around heaven and saw there was so much empty space and he said, it is my nature to create beauty -- not empty space. So I will create a new form of life. It will fill heaven once again. And in seven days there was a new world with animals and abundant food and a perfect garden and people. People!!! So remember, Mama, when we die we will go to heaven. Not like the guards in this prison. They are going to hell. But then we will be part of God's new creation -- to replace the fallen angels. You will be even more beautiful because you will be a spirit and your spirit is pure. And I will be there before you to welcome you into our new home.

This is the knowledge that has come to me from within the dark of this prison. This is what will give you the strength to go through the days that await you.

A great sadness has come over me. I look at death not as a thing to be feared but as an event that will carry me beyond this world and all the pain of this world. Mama, I have had enough sadness for both of us. You rest and find peace. We will be together in heaven. In the name of the Father, the Son, and the Holy Ghost. Your son, Federico.

Federico re-read the letter several times. Finally, he folded it carefully and put it in the envelope.

"Guard," Federico called. "The letter. It's done. You can get it now."

"Stinks worse than ever in here," the guard looked at the envelope. "I know your village. I live near Santa Rosa," the guard said as he entered the cell. "Give me the letter." Rosario is just up from there.

"When they brought me here I had shoes," Federico said. "Shoes and a small gold ring. You can have the shoes -- for the letter -- getting it sent out. The other guards took my shoes and ring. They are in a paper bag in the office. The shoes are yours. The ring is mine?"

The guard looked at Federico for a moment. He sneered. "There are no shoes in the office. No ring. No paper bag. You have anything else for the executioner so that he springs the trap-door instead of using the ammunition box. Will you tell him for me?"

Federico was surprised. "Are you sure?"

"It stinks worse than ever in here," he mumbled as he slammed the cell door behind him.

Soon after the guard called Panzon left, Federico heard a voice. It was Panzon's voice coming from the guard room. It sounded like he was giving orders. Federico heard the voices of the other guards. They were laughing. Then Panzon loudly spoke again. More laughter followed. Soon Federico recognized his own words. Panzon was reading Federico's letter out loud to the other guards. He would read one sentence and stop. The others would laugh. Only when they had stopped laughing would he continue to read. Federico's words to his mother seemed to take a long time. The guards laughed at the end of every sentence. Eventually he heard Panzon read, "Your son, Federico." There was no more laughter. The only sound was the paper being crushed.

It was two days later when Federico discovered a pain in his lower back. He could no longer lie on his back but only rest by turning from side to side. His chest was covered with sores. Each morning he tried to feel all over his body for changes. He knew his eyes had sunk further into his head. His chin was covered with a bristly beard. His knees were always bloody from falling. There's not enough blood getting to my brain, he thought. Sometimes I don't want the guards to see me crying. Then, an hour later I cry whether they are watching or not. And the next time Panzon eats my bread, I hope he chokes on it.

Federico could not recall when it happened. Sometime during his solitary confinement he lost track of the days. He developed a fever. I can feel it in my bones, he thought. Maybe because I can feel all my bones now. He slept lightly day and night and had dreams that were strange, wonderful -- and painful. In one recurring dream, Federico found he had been transformed into a mountain lion that walked into the courtroom and mauled four members of the military tribunal. In other dreams he was lifted up and transported back to his home, his mother, his friend Olivia, his neighbor Guilhermo, and there was meat and fresh bread on the table and large pitchers of cool water, dark red wine, and small cakes with pieces of chocolate melted into the dough.

Late one cloudy afternoon a voice came to Federico during one of his dreams. "Private Llanos," it said. Federico couldn't tell whether it was the voice of God or the voice of his executioner. Then he awoke to see his cell door open to allow a grey-bearded padre to enter. The door was pulled shut behind him.

"Pax vobiscum," murmured the padre. "I have come to hear your confession and to bring you your last Holy

Communion." One of the old priest's eyes had a nervous twitch.

Federico had trouble sitting up. When he tried to say 'Hola' his throat was too dry to allow any sound to emerge. Federico worked at clearing his throat for a long time. At last he was able to say, "What do you want?"

"First I'll hear your confession," said the priest. "Then Holy Communion and then I'll pray for you." As he spoke he unwrapped a small loaf of bread and a bottle of wine from a yellowed cloth that appeared to be as old as the priest.

Federico saw only the bread and wine. "Let me have some of that," he said and then started coughing.

"First I'll hear your sins and a sincere act of contrition."

"Listen you old fool." Federico's voice was suddenly loud. "I'm dying from starvation and lack of water. Forget sins and absolution. Give me something for my gut!"

The priest took a step backward and broke off a chunk of crust from the loaf of bread. He offered it to Federico who snatched it from the priest's hand. Federico took one bite, chewed and stuffed the rest into his mouth. As he chewed, Federico growled something at the priest who quickly offered the wine bottle. Federico pulled the cork out with his teeth and in one motion drank half of the contents. He chewed slower then and looked at the priest. "Does your visit here mean that tomorrow is my execution day?"

"Yes, my son."

A silence fell over the two men. Federico continued chewing for several moments. Then he swallowed and drained the wine bottle, tipping it up to get the last drops. "It doesn't matter," Federico said. "I died a long time ago." Then he took the remaining bread from the priest. He tore a soft inner portion of bread from deep inside the loaf, stuffed it in his mouth and chewed slowly. After a time he said, "I've been dead in my spirit for a long time. Tomorrow will mean nothing to me."

"Oh no, my son," the priest said with a smile. "Do not despair. I have a plan."

"Listen old man, I'm not your son and I care nothing for your plan."

"No, my son," the priest smiled. "Hear me out."

The bread made Federico's stomach hurt less and the wine began to warm him. He blinked at the old priest and saw the man more clearly. It was as if some fluids began to return to his dry body. "I didn't mean to turn into an animal," he said, "but I've been alone for a long time with almost nothing to eat or drink -- waiting for death. I gave up on life. Can you understand? I surrendered my spirit." He paused for the right words. "Because living became the burden." Federico looked down at the loaf of torn bread in his hand. "After you feel death," he said. "Feel the starvation taking over your body, feel your brain never getting enough blood, waking up in your own blood where you fell -- the instinct to live leaves you."

Federico kept blinking trying to clear his vision as he spoke. "You reach a point where you no longer want to escape death," he paused again, "you know it will be a blessing."

"But my son," the priest interrupted, "my plan..."

Suddenly a wave of nausea seemed to flow through Federico's body. He felt tired in a way that he knew was close to physical death. "You don't understand old man," he said. "I am dead already. I feel nothing. I stopped thinking -- living -- being! I gave up!"

The priest smiled patiently and said, "Just let me tell you. You see I'm going to pray with you. I will pray that tomorrow the executioner's rope will break. Then he will have to give you one more day of life. It's a tradition here in Santa Rosa. And tomorrow night I will pray again for the rope to break. It will be a miracle. You'll see..."

In that instant a wave of heat surged through Federico's body. He moved quickly, not a motion was wasted. He hurled the empty wine bottle against one wall. It splintered into many small pieces of dark glass.

Then Federico took the remaining loaf of bread in his hands and broke it into two pieces. He threw the smaller piece at the wall behind the padre and the larger chunk he hurled with all his strength at the priest himself.

"Are you turning down God's assistance?" the priest shouted.

"I'm turning down hope. I gave up hoping long ago. I want nothing to do with it -- or you. Get out of here. Let me finish dying without your help. Guard," he called. "Get this old fraud out of here."

Before dawn of the next day, Federico heard shouting coming from the street outside the prison. Soon after, a church bell started ringing. Then another bell rang out, and both kept ringing. The shouting continued and came closer to the prison. Federico heard voices entering the prison office. A siren started screeching, probably an ambulance but the sound was not moving, Federico thought. The ambulance must be parked with its siren turned on. Then he heard a guard coming down the hall -- a guard with keys.

"There is wine flowing in the streets and women running around like wild deer," said the guard. "Young women too."

"What is happening?" asked Federico.

"It's over," shouted the guard. "The shooting has stopped. Come on out of there." The guard was unlocking Federico's cell door. "We're going home. We are all going to go home."

"Is this a cruel joke? This is my hanging day. Is this how you get people to pay attention to it?"

"Oh no my friend," the guard laughed. "The war is over. Four years and thousands of deaths and it's finally over. They have surrendered -- just as we knew they would. All shooting has stopped."

Federico stepped back into the shadow of his cell. He thought, if the war is really over, does that mean that all prisoners are to be killed, silenced forever, shot during attempted escapes?

"Don't you understand?" The guard wore an expression of extreme pity. "All of you are free. Take my word for it. All cell doors are open." He motioned for Federico to come out of the cell. "Now we are all brothers again. So go. Vaya! Vaya con Dios!"

Federico did not come forward.

"Vamos!" the guard shouted. "Presidente Garcia himself sent a message. It said to empty the prison of all living things. So take your freedom before El Presidente changes his mind."

Federico thought, "He doesn't understand the message". A shiver ran through him then as he thought, "that message meant this celebration is the perfect time to execute all who disagree with the president. Empty the prison -- sure: Dispose of the bodies.

Then the guard said, "Your cell door stands open. I'm leaving to join the celebration in the streets. And when I have had my fill, I am going home too. Live well, brother. "Then he paused and brought his hand to his chin. He smiled and added, "Now go and shave your face before you go out into the street."

Federico touched his cell door. It moved several inches. He pushed it again and it opened into the dimly lit hall. Another prisoner and a guard were laughing. They waved and went out the door together. Federico could not make out the words they were using. "If I stay here I might be hanged", he thought, "or I might not. If I leave I might be shot in the back. Either way I'm dead, so I have nothing to lose." He stepped slowly out into the hall. It was empty now. He walked to the guard office. It too was empty. "Could it be?" he thought. Federico walked through the office and opened the door to the street.

It was a moment of intense sensations. Each started painfully and then slowly turned to joy. The smell came first. Federico's eyes would not adjust to the light but he was amazed by the sudden memory of clean air. There was no sweat odor, no stink of toilet pails, and no stench of aging vomit. Now it was clean, lung-filling, pure mountain air. The memory was becoming a reality.

Then came the sounds. Noise was on all sides of Federico. He could hear voices of children and old women. There was music coming from a band near him, but the music was not a patriotic march; it was dance music with a rhythm of exuberance and joy.

Only after the fresh air and the barrage of sounds had registered did Federico's eyes adjust to the sight of the celebration. He remembered this street, remembered how the citizens and dogs ran out of his path as he and the armed guards hurried down this street that lead to the prison. This was the same street but now everything has changed! It was like the midway of a gigantic carnival. Movement was everywhere. There were hundreds of people and not one was still; all were running or dancing. The street was littered with bits of papers. Music was coming from a brass band furiously blaring out a peasant dance. People were throwing money at the feet of the musicians. Federico thought, "Are my poor eyes deceiving me? The people of Da la Rosa are throwing money into the street? Everyone is rushing; where are they going?" Those who were dancing held wine bottles, and as they spun around, the wine splashing on others who laughed at the new red splotches on their white clothes.

Federico cringed at the sounds and the movement and he thought, "I must leave this place -- this place that has become strange. I, who had given up on ever having freedom, now I feel as if freedom is too much for me. My spirit is being overwhelmed by sounds and motions. I need to find silence and solitude. I have become accustomed to being alone. I cannot think, or feel, when I am in the midst of people rushing around. This frenzy, this madness -- it is not for me."

Federico began walking. People ran past him. Dancers bumped into him. Federico kept his head down and walked on.

"*Free wine at Del Monico's*," a girl said.

"Imported cervasa. Imported just for this celebration," a shopkeeper called out. "Half price for you. Enjoy, senior."

Federico walked on. Far ahead he could see the city gates and he knew that just beyond that point were some fields. He felt the sun on his back. It was hot and dry.

"I don't see any veteran in these crowds," Federico said out loud as he walked. "Where are the men who fought the war? They are the ones who have a right to celebrate. These children running, girls dancing, and old women shouting -- were they in any battles with real bullets coming at them? Were they in prisons? Ah, but maybe they were in their homes praying during the times of the shooting. Or maybe the veterans are dead." Then Federico thought. "So I talk to myself now? Is this what I have come to? How long have I been doing this? Enough walking. Now I must find some food." He saw a bakery and entered the front door.

The shopkeeper looked up at Federico and announced, "We are closing for the day. There is nothing left. A gang of boys came in and stole everything."

"What kind of boys are they to steal from you?" Federico asked.

"With most of the soldiers gone to their homes there is no law in the streets. Gangs of boys can do whatever they think of doing. It's the celebration you know."

"Yes, the celebration," Federico said. "But can you find something for a veteran? We are celebrating but I am starving. Is there any sense to this? Can you find some little thing, some scrap of crust, anything?"

The shopkeeper looked at Federico with disgust. "Oh yes," he said. "Today you are starving. So I give you crumbs. Tomorrow I'll be starving. The shooting has stopped but our people keep on dying. What's the sense of that?" He walked into his back room and was gone for a long time. He re-emerged with a small paper bag which he handed to Federico. "These are half of the crumbs that my assistant has just swept together from the bottom of the oven. You'll have to pick out the burned pieces because they taste bad. My assistant has the rest of the crumbs. He has a wife and two children. I am sorry I cannot give you more."

"Gracias senior. This is good and I appreciate it. This is a good time for the sharing -- even crumbs."

Federico did not leave the bakery. He stood and ate crumbs from the baker's paper bag. He ate the burned crumbs and he ate the perfectly baked crumbs. He ate rapidly.

With angry, watery eyes, the baker watched Federico eating. "These are bad times to have a bakery," he said. "Before the war the people had no money. They blamed the Federalist government. And they came to me and wanted all the bakery for free. Then came the war and again the people had no money. They blamed it on the war. The came to me and asked for all bakery to be free. Today, for the first time in many years, the people are spending money and a gang of youths came in here and, before I could drive them out, stole all the bakery I had made."

The baker watched in silence as Federico ate one or two crumbs at a time. "What we need," he said, "is fewer dreamers and more people who will pay for what they eat. Now go veteran! Do not come begging back here tomorrow. Do not come back here -- ever!"

When Federico left the bakery he came to a water fountain in the street. He drank some of the clear, mountain water from his cupped hands. "My hands," he thought, "they seem to have minds of their own and how filthy they are." Then he saw, and thought, how they tremble.

When Federico straightened up from the fountain he looked at the sky. He thought, "I have forgotten the sun. How could I have forgotten that?" He continued to gaze at the sky. It was midmorning and only a few clouds were overhead. "That sky," he thought, "is a shade of blue I have never seen before. Everything has changed. The air is so clear and the clouds are whiter than before."

He searched his mind for the moment that brought about the changes he felt within himself. "Was it being set free from prison? Or was it getting some bits of bread in the stomach? Is it these wine-drinking dancers," he asked himself, "because theirs is the dance of life ... and I had been prepared for the dance of death?"

As Federico neared the city gates he came to a bench placed under some trees. He sat and continued to ask himself which of the incidents had changed him the most. "It started with that guard" he thought. "I had not seen that guard before. He called me brother. He unlocked my cell and said, 'Go with God.' Was he an angel? Certainly I was transformed by him… from being a prisoner to being a free man. From a caged animal to a man who can go anywhere. Yes," Federico thought, "that was the beginning. Being set free. Being given a new life. Yes, that must have been how Lazarus felt when Christ called him out of the tomb and he simply walked back into life -- one step at a time."

Federico continued to sit on the tree-shaded bench. "How full life is" he thought. "I went from being starved to finding that burned bread crumbs taste sweet on the tongue. And very soon just outside the city gates, I will come to a river. Somebody once said, 'Where the river flows, there is life.' I will bathe in the river, find some clean clothes, shave, if I can borrow a razor, and take the road north. I will take small jobs to pay for food and a pair of shoes. And I will take the road heading north. I will walk to my home."

Federico stood and resumed walking. As he passed through the city gates a group entering the city pushed past him. One man swore at him to get out of the way.

"No," Federico called back to him. "I can go anywhere I wish. I have been set free." He smiled and thought, "How strange it feels to smile."

Then he was through the gate and outside the city. He walked straight ahead. The sun was high and warm on his back.

"Yes, oh yes," Federico thought, "an angel spoke to me and I have been changed. Everything has changed."

"I can live on crumbs and clear water," he said aloud. "I can live on air. I am alive."

He squinted into the distance. Ahead he could make out a bridge, and he knew it was near. The river was near. And beyond the river, the road north.

Chapter 4
The First Meeting of the X-Treme Book Club

If you travel to the upper Midwest of The United States you will usually travel by one or more of the major airlines. This means you will fly into Chicago's O'Hare or Milwaukee's Mitchell International airport. If you look out of your window shortly before landing, you will see a multi-laned highway (Interstate 94) which connects the airports to each other as well as the states of Wisconsin and Illinois.

Halfway between Milwaukee and Chicago on Highway I-94 you will pass Racine, Wisconsin. Should you take the highway 20 exit to Racine, you will see a string of retail stores just off the highway. The sign says, "Edge of Town Mall, Established 2010." The largest building of the complex is a massive steel and glass bookstore. Inside the front doors you will see a placard stating, "You are invited to visit the X-Treme Book Club meeting here tonight. The group will be discussing the novel, *Wind, Sand, and Hope*. Discussion leader will be Mr. Dave Jackson."

Halfway down the store's center aisle you see an open section with a carpeted floor and large stuffed chairs. Four people are seated in the chairs while one man stands at a table. Behind him is a blackboard on which one word is printed: "Jackson". The man turns to the group, smiles and says, "Thank you for being here tonight. My name is Dave Jackson, and I will be serving as moderator during our weekly discussion meetings. Now, may I see a show of hands? How many of you have been in a book club before?"

Two of the four raised their hands.

"Thank you. For your information, this club will be different -- different from any other book club that I know about. This is the X-Treme club -- with a capital 'X'."

The younger of the two women raised her hand, "How is this club going to be different?" she asked.

"Good question. I'm going to ask you all to invest more of yourselves than other book clubs ask. You see, other clubs urge you to read more as they teach you how to enjoy literature. Their bottom line," Jackson said, "is to sell more books. But I'm not an employee of this store. I'm a volunteer who could care less about book sales. My goal is to help you understand our book at a deep level."

"If you are volunteering here," the same woman asked. She was smiling now. "Then what do you do, professionally?"

"I teach literature at the University," he said. "And I'm working on my doctoral dissertation."

"Aha," blurted the youngest member of the group -- a teen-aged boy. "So we are part of the research for your PhD. Like we are your guinea pigs, huh?"

"Don't worry," Jackson said. "We don't allow any guinea pigs in here. However, I am looking for examples of how literature can change lives. So I will ask you to do more work in here than any other club. But I promise you it will be much more rewarding than other groups. I believe you will learn more about literature -- and yourselves -- and through that understanding go on to have more enjoyable and productive lives."

"I wouldn't mind helping you with your research," said the teen, "but I don't need any more school work or assignments. Okay?"

Jackson looked at the boy seated before him. "Actually I do need to give you an assignment for some homework." Quickly, he added, "It will be quite worthwhile. Don't worry. It will be fun work."

"Oh, sure fun for you," mumbled the boy. "For me, the words 'fun' and 'work' don't go together."

Jackson ignored the comment. "Names," he said. "Let's do our introductions now."

"I'm Emma," the younger woman answered with a smile. She was in her early 30s and slightly overweight. She squinted as she spoke.

"I'm Laura," said the other woman. She was in her late 40s, well dressed and strikingly beautiful. Even seated, she had the poise of a fashion model.

"We'll keep it on a first name basis," Jackson said. "So -- gentlemen?"

A high voice said, "I'm Jerry." It was the teen-aged boy. He was wearing blue jeans and a jacket that was too large for him. He wore a baseball cap nearly down to his eyes. On the floor by his feet was an overloaded backpack.

"I am Clayton," said the middle-aged man. He sat straight up in his chair. He had jet black hair and was wearing grey slacks with a dark blue blazer and a light blue shirt open at the collar. He did not smile.

"And I am Dave," the moderator said. He was in his early 30s with a closely-cropped beard. "I believe this group will come up with a nice range of ideas."

"What?" Clayton snapped. He looked at Jerry "What did you just say?"

Jerry returned the stare. "I told Emma here that I think you dye your hair." Then he added, "So—do you?"

"That is none of your business," Clayton said.

Jerry turned back to Emma and in a stage whisper said, "I told you he did." Then he looked back at Clayton and said, "Dark brown would look more natural."

"Alright you, alright," Jackson interrupted. "Let's all stay focused on the book. Okay? Okay."

Without looking up from under his cap, Jerry asked, "What time is this class over?"

"We'll start at 6:30 every Tuesday night. You'll be able to leave by 7:30," Jackson said. "Or you can stick around longer if you wish. By the way this isn't a class; it's a discussion group." Jackson paused and looked at each of the four people before him. "You each have read the invitation, and you were told to read the first three chapters for this meeting. So, do you each have a copy of *Wind, Sand and Hope* and have you read the first three chapters?"

Each member of the group nodded.

"Good," the moderator said. "I do ask you to keep up with the reading which is usually two chapters a week. It is best for our discussions if we are all on the same material." He took a breath and said, "Well then -- let's begin."

Jackson held up his copy of the book. He looked directly at Jerry. "I wish I had read this when I was high school," he said. "I had to be at the university before I even heard about it. Now I guess it's big on campus." He grinned. "Imagine that. The collegiate crowd is reading it - even those who aren't taking any literature classes." Then Jackson's smile faded and asked, "What do you say is the main theme -- so far?"

Jerry looked up at the leader and said, "Aren't you supposed to be telling us what the theme is?"

"Let me rephrase the question. You are all reading the novel *Wind, Sand and Hope*. What's it about?"

Silence.

"Anybody? Yes, Emma."

"I could be wrong," she began. "See, it's kind of early in the book for me to tell for sure." She paused and squinted up at the leader. "But could it be something about power? See, I read how the revolutionaries chanted 'Justice, Equality, and Prosperity' as they marched into war. Was that supposed to be irony? I mean, so far it looks like one dictator was deposed…"

"And killed," added Laura. "All on the same night."

"Same morning you mean. It was after midnight," Jerry said.

"Okay. Now we all know you read it without skipping too many paragraphs."

"Hold it," Jackson said. "Emma, finish your thought."

"Well, one dictator is thrown out of power -- yes, even killed -- but the people who took over -- I don't see that they are any better." Emma looked around the room as she chose her words. "Like power produces violence. What good is it for a man to even have power if he gets killed for it? I don't know where the plot will take us. But if we're going to get something to really think about -- like possibly an alternative to power -- by the end of the book, well I think that would be great. Oh, I don't really know but I thought the theme might be power."

"Excellent Emma," Jackson said. "Anyone else care to contribute or add something to what Emma said?"

"Question for Emma," Jerry said. "What gives you the idea that the author will give us an alternative to power? I mean, I'm really interested in just what that might be. And could an alternative to power also come out like an alternative to war? This world could use that."

"Good question," Jackson said. "Emma, care to answer that?"

"Sure," Emma said. "It's an idea I had as I read about Federico. See, the author has him talking about transformation. He uses the word over and over. It just seems to me that's a promise -- or maybe a hint -- from the author that by the end of the book Federico will be changed and the readers will have something to look at and consider. Am I right?"

Suddenly Jerry sat up and said, "I sure would like to see an alternative to war. Especially if Congress reinstates the draft. Right guys? See I'm graduating from high school in six weeks. It would be just my luck to turn eighteen, graduate, and the next day get drafted into the army."

"Okay, good. Good," Jackson said. "Keep those thoughts in mind as we all read on. We're talking about the central theme of the novel. Emma says it might even include an alternative to power. Jerry caught that idea and ran with it saying an alternative to power might also be an alternative to warfare. Those are all good ideas. Now let's shift gears for a bit. Did you identify with our lead character so far?"

In a soft voice, Laura said, "I thought that Federico comes across as a bit of a snob."

"Hey, where did you get that from?" Emma asked. "I don't see that at all. I like him."

"Naw. I thought he wanted to be just better than everybody else," Laura answered.

"Yeah," Jerry said. "Like maybe he's over-compensating. Probably to hide an inferiority complex."

Emma quickly turned to face Jerry. "We all have inferiority complexes," she said.

"Sure we do. No big deal," Jerry said. "When we're in high school. But we'll all get over them once we graduate. Right?"

"Maybe you boys get over them," Emma said. She frowned and added, "But guess what happens to us girls. Ours keep getting worse."

"No way. It's just a matter of time," Jerry said. "When the right guy comes along he can nurture you out of those problems."

"Hold up guys," Jackson said. "We're drifted into psycho-babble -- the curse of every discussion group. Let's get back to the question."

"What was the question?" asked Jerry.

"The question is -- can anyone identify with our lead character?"

Clayton leaned forward, raised his hand and said "The lead character of the book, Francisco…"

"Federico!" It was a group correction.

"Okay, Federico. It sure was dumb to put in his letter to his mother that the guards were going to hell. That blew any chance he had of having his letter sent. I could never identify with that level of stupidity."

"No, I thought it showed that he wasn't sucking up to the guards," Jerry said. "I liked him for that."

"I was thinking something different," Laura said. "I thought that part of his letter showed that Federico really believed he was soon to be executed."

"How did you figure that?" Emma asked.

"Well, he was thinking about heaven and hell. As if that prison wasn't enough of hell for him."

"Okay guys," the moderator said. "As long as you brought up prison, did you catch the irony -- that he was a prisoner of his own side?"

"Was that in there?" Jerry asked. "Are we reading the same book?"

Both women turned to confront Jerry. "Sure. Federico was in the revolutionary army," Emma said.

"And once the revolutionaries were winning the war, and Federico saw no need for more killing, he was put in a revolutionary prison." Laura added.

"And he was condemned to die by a revolutionary jury -- or tribunal," Emma said. "You've been skipping some important parts."

"Ah, the jury," Jackson said. "How about that jury? Did you like their sense of justice?"

"It was a travesty," Clayton said.

"Well sure," said Emma. "They were in power. Of course they wanted to stay in power. And they had the power to execute anyone they thought might question their power.

We all know that power corrupts and absolute power corrupts absolutely."

"Wow!" Jerry said. "So is this kind of writing irony -- or realism?"

Jackson smiled at Jerry. "Both," he said.

There was a moment of silence while the discussion leader glanced around the room. "So," he said, "do you like Federico?"

Four voices answered, "Yes!"

"Unanimous. That's good. Now comes a tougher question. Why do you like him?"

"He wasn't really a traitor."

"He wasn't even a revolutionary."

"He was a humanitarian. He saw the evil of war so he stopped being a part of it. He stopped killing. You have to admire him for that."

"He stood up to authority."

"Yeah man," Jerry said. "At his trial he asked the judges if they knew who the enemy was. He asked them, 'In a civil war, who is the enemy?' That was so neat."

"Good Jerry," Jackson said. "Anything else?"

"Federico stood up to all authority," Emma said. She spoke with great conviction.

The moderator looked at Emma. "You care to explain what you mean by that?"

"Well, he stood up to the authority of the Church when he threw the communion bread at the padre and ordered him out of his cell."

"And do you see any symbolism in that scene?"

"Maybe," answered Emma. "See, I suppose Federico was throwing away his last chance. He was refusing the 'Bread of Life.' Christ is sometimes called the 'Bread of Life'."

"Oh wow," Jerry yelled. "Standing up to God. Man that's really being a revolutionary. Power to the people!"

Suddenly Emma thrust her hand up.

"Yes Emma?"

"It just dawned on me. Maybe Federico wasn't rebelling against God at all," she said. "Maybe he was symbolically standing up to a symbol. Can I say that? Does that make any sense? See, if he believed he was going to die in the morning -- then he must have given up all hope. So he couldn't face the pain of having hope revived. He had passed over already and couldn't go through it again. He couldn't. It was already a done deal. The communion bread meant nothing to him."

Jackson smiled at Emma. "Quite a perceptive idea."

"Mr. Teacher," Jerry interrupted. "Can we back up a bit? I mean this may sound really stupid and all but, what does the title mean? Is there hope in this book? What was Federico doing by throwing that bread? If he had been in our school system he would have been ordered to take some anger management counseling."

"Okay. First of all it is never a dumb question to ask what the title of a book means," Jackson said. "So look at the situation. Here's this 22-year-old soldier who knows more about death and dying than the old padre. So Federico was angry. Angry yes. But what else? Guys? What was Federico going through?"

"Depression," said Emma. The others nodded their agreement.

"Exactly," Jackson said. "Big time."

"But he perks up once he's out of the slammer; right?" asked Jerry.

"Sure. In my mind Federico came back to life."

"I think what Jerry is asking," Clayton said, "is will this book be positive? Like, where does the hope come in? By the end of the chapter we know Federico recovers. But does he stay depression-free?"

Jackson looked from one person to another. Finally he said, "You'll know the answer to that when you finish reading the book. You ask is there hope for Federico. I say, we'll see. Maybe a better question would be, is there hope for the readers of this book? Can they expect some reward for reading it?"

"Can't you just tell us?" Jerry asked.

"You wouldn't learn much if I just stood here and told you the story," Jackson said. "I want you guys to learn from it. Consider this: learning is a self-inflicted punishment but it is also a worthwhile effort."

Jerry pulled his cap off and scratched his head for several moments. "I ask for answers," he mumbled. "And all I get is platitudes." He put his cap back on and pulled it as far down as it would stretch.

"At this point," the group leader said, "maybe we should get one important definition down. So let me ask, how do we define literature?"

There was a long moment of silence from the group. Jackson allowed it to go for several seconds. Then he jumped away from the table he had been leaning against and turned to the blackboard. "Copy this down," he said.

Three members of the group pulled out notebooks and pens and sat waiting. Jerry tapped Laura on the shoulder and asked, "Can I borrow a sheet of paper?"

She tore a single page from her notebook and said, "You're in high school and don't remember to bring paper to class?" She handed him the paper.

"I'm not a brain like you. I'm a jock." Then Jerry added, "So do you have an extra pen or pencil I can borrow?"

Slowly and in large letters, Jackson wrote on the blackboard: *Lit. = writing having excellence of form or style and expressing ideas of permanent or universal interest*. When he finished he turned back to the group. All of them were bent over writing. He waited until they stopped writing and asked, "What is the key word in this definition?"

There was no sound. No movement. Not a hand was raised. Jackson turned back to the board and underscored the "ideas." "Ideas, ladies and gentlemen, Ideas. Literature tackles ideas and communicates them."

"Do we have to memorize that definition?" Jerry asked.

"Sure," he said. "It will be good for you. But I also have an assignment for you. This is what I call real homework. It is to talk about *Wind, sand and Hope* with your friends and families. Jerry, for you, it means talking to your parents. Don't be a pest but whenever you can, talk to them -- about what?"

Emma squinted up at Jackson. "The ideas in the book."

"Thank you, Emma," he said. "If one of your parents wants to read some, or all, of the book, so much the better. What this assignment really is, is learning how to communicate ideas."

Jackson stopped speaking then and looked at each member of the group. He leaned forward and in a low voice he said, "Ideas -- rebelling to authority, facing death, living through depression, acting out our own inner convictions, what it's like to face your execution while believing you are innocent, civil war, what it must be like to kill your fellow countrymen, are there possible alternative to war and what do they look like?...yes, Jerry?"

"Mr. J. that's all way too deep for my parents. No way could I talk to them about things like that."

"Wanna bet?" snapped Jackson. "I have a hunch your parents will be pleased that you are thinking about real ideas -- as our definition of literature says: ideas of permanent or universal interest."

"Come on Mr. Moderator," Emma said. She had stopped squinting. "What you are asking is risky business. If I started talking about war to my friends at work they would think I came in high. It's way too different for me."

Four people sat looking up at their leader -- looking for an answer. There was a moment of silence. Then Jackson walked away from the blackboard and stood close to the group. "I'll tell all of you a little secret," he said. "This is how you can get along with parents, co-workers, and bosses -- even enemies. Ready for this? One word: listen." He looked at each of the four. Jerry had his hand over his mouth stifling his laugh. Clayton was looking away with a bored expression. The two women were looking up into Jackson's eyes.

"Once you bring up a topic or a question." he said, "ask their opinions. And then -- listen. Most people think they know how to listen. And most of them are wrong. Listening can be work. It means biting your tongue. Ask for their opinions and then sit there in silence while they answer. Look at them. Don't contradict -- at least not while they are talking. Listen -- and you will have the beginning of communication and understanding. Then what follows is the back-and-forth flow of ideas." The teacher looked at each of the four and added, "And once in awhile -- when you bring about agreement -- it can be a pretty special moment."

"Yea, a real Kodak moment," Jerry mumbled.

"Don't judge it until you've tried it," Jackson said. "Jerry, you brought up the idea of the draft being reinstated. Emma, you figured out Federico rejected the 'Bread of Life' -- or the symbol of it. You guys are talking national politics and classical theology. Major, major issues. So take it home or to the workplace and talk about it with those closest to you."

The moderator stepped back then and looked over the heads of the group. "You think -- why is this so important? It's because, in a figurative sense, ideas can come alive." Then his voice became very low. "Ideas can come alive with meaning and importance. They become alive like a part of you -- like of your life -- like a part of your thinking. Take those ideas and hold them gently in your mind. Give them attention. And communicate them." He paused then and his voice returned to normal. "And next week we'll take a few minutes to talk about how you did."

"Just for clarification," Jerry asked. "Do you want me to discuss -- or listen?"

"What do you think?"

"I suppose both."

"Well, there's your clarification."

"In all honesty Mr. J., I'm not trying to get out of the assignment. I'm just afraid I won't be able to get either of my parents into it."

The teacher looked at Jerry and asked, "You remember the movie, 'Field of Dreams'?"

"Sure."

"What was the main theme of that movie? How was it phrased?"

"Easy one," Jerry said. "Build it and they will come."

The discussion leader smiled back at the teen-aged boy and said, "Good. So here's a variation on that phrase. Listen -- and they will talk. Got it? Listen -- and you will have no problem. And remember, two more chapters for next week."

"Right."

"Okay."

"You got it."

"Hey man, no promises."

Chapter 5
Home

"Which side were you on?" called the farmer.

Federico quickly answered, "For the people. I'm for De La Rosa forever."

The farmer was sitting beside the road. He had a basket with him. Federico had just walked through the night. The man looked at Federico in silence. After a long moment he asked, "Where are you headed now?"

"The war is over. It no longer matters which side anyone was on. This is a time for going home," said Federico. "And I am on my way home!"

"Like that?" asked the farmer. Federico had on only a khaki shirt and pants. He was without a hat or shoes. "Are you a deserter?"

"No," said Federico. "I thought about it many times but I didn't think I could get away with it. Even so I spent the last four weeks in a military prison. They took everything I had. Even my shoes. If I would have had a gold filling in my teeth they would have taken that too."

"And what were you in prison for, that is if you don't mind my asking," said the farmer. He stood up as Federico crossed the road to him.

"You can ask," Federico said. "Nothing violent. I got tired of war. I could not face any more of it. I did not want to see any more death. One of my friends, Corzon, took a bullet in the face. I was right there – with him." Federico thought in silence for a time and then said, "After that I had the crazy idea that if the war went on long enough – everyone would be dead. Crazy huh?"

"You thought you might be next?"

"Yes, I suppose. Or maybe not. I no longer know what I thought except that I had enough." Federico spoke slowly. He thought he might cry if he went on about his feelings. "You are a farmer, yes? Could you use a hard-working man who would work for some old clothes and a meal a day?"

"You are too weak to work," the farmer said.

"They starved me in prison," Federico said. "One of the guards ate most of my food before it got to me. But I'll be strong again."

The farmer silently gazed at Federico. Then Federico thought he should straighten himself to look taller and stronger but the thought came to his mind that he would also appear thinner. After a moment of silence Federico simply said, "Por favor?"

For the first time the farmer smiled. "There's a mission house just up the road. I'm taking these sausages there now. They have clothes for the poor. Maybe they'll give you some eggs and a bite of meat. They have plenty of eggs and clothes. Take whatever they offer. I'll wait for you outside the gate. Then you will come to my farm with me. I have work to be done. And my name is Paciano. How do they call you?"

"My name is Federico. Graci."

Paciano smiled and said, "It is good. Now let us get you some clothes and a hat. We'll be working in a tobacco field before the day is over."

For three weeks Federico worked side-by-side with Paciano. They cut tobacco and hung it to dry in the sun. They ate together but seldom talked to each other. Paciano said he was saving Federico's pay for him and would give it all to him when he wanted to leave. However, after the tobacco was harvested Paciano accused Federico of killing and eating one of his chickens. Paciano claimed his chicken was worth more than the savings Federico had earned.

Federico thought Paciano wants to argue. He acts as if he wants to fight. "I will not argue with him and I will not fight." Then, as Paciano yelled at him, Federico stood up and, with one shirt, one pair of pants, shoes that did not fit – and with a sigh, Federico left the farm.

Though Federico did not have any money, those three weeks had brought some healing. During the long hours of laboring in the fields Federico thought only of the future. The war was over and, Federico thought, I am going home to see Mama. I will hug my mother. I will see her smile first – then she will laugh – then laugh and cry together. It is she who loves me no matter how thin I am. She loves me no matter how many men I have killed. She loves me no matter if I have money or not. My old room will be there in her house. She will give me rice and beans and coffee. She will say, Federico you were gone for four years so now you stay until I fatten you up. And then, Federico thought, I will hear her singing in the kitchen.

Federico also thought of Olivia. She lived two houses down the road from his mother's house. Federico and Olivia grew up together. She had been his best friend, and when he joined the De La Rosa army they were beginning to be more than friends.

Olivia was a gringo. She was a Kryger – a Dutch name. Her parents came to the village from some northern part of the U.S. They said they were artists and were paid by a foundation to study the native art of small villages. They took many photographs. Some of the villagers thought Olivia's parents were spies. Her father was a giant of a man. Most of the men in the village only came up to his chest. After several years most of the villagers agreed Senor Kryger was indeed a spy.

Olivia's mother Tina, was small with large, blue eyes. She liked watching futbol games. All the girls of the village were jealous of Olivia – blonde, blue-eyed Olivia who grew up looking like a Hollywood actress. She knew all about art and futbol and, best of all, Federico thought, she likes me. How good it will be to look at her again, to talk, and to hug her again.

When Federico left the tobacco farm, he took the road that would bring him home. He walked by night and hitched rides during the day. He did not get many rides as his mission clothes were too large for him. From a distance he appeared to be either an old man or a man with a terminal disease. Progress was slow and Federico's village of Santa Rita was many kilometers from Santa Rosa. Most of those who gave Federico rides were farmers taking produce only to the next town or village. To Federico, the journey which took five days, seemed to take a very long time.

The closer Federico traveled to his village, the happier he became. The war is over, he said to himself. Mama – I am almost home. Do you have any wine? Mama, does Olivia visit you often? Can the three of us sit up into the night and talk of the last four years? I wrote you Mama but the letter didn't get sent. Damn Panzon! Olivia, you are so beautiful! You were a girl when I left and now you are so beautiful. Such a women! I cannot take my eyes from you. Ah, don't look at me. I will fill out these clothes after a few weeks of Mama's cooking. Yes – it is good to be home.

Federico knew he was only a few kilometers from his village. He had walked through the night and he was tired but he walked on. I could run the rest of the way he thought, but I would rather walk and sing. So Federico smoothed his clothes as best as he could. He patted down his hair in back and as he walked he sang. He did not know many songs; the military did not teach songs. Still, he recalled the comic song he and Olivia had sung together. "Un hombre con joroba no puede ver su propis joroba." (The man with a crooked back cannot see his own hump.) When I come walking up the street of her house, he thought, she will hear my voice and remember our funny song. Then she will look out of her window and see me. But I am so thin! Am I bedraggled? I must look nothing like a returning hero! But we did win the war. Can I explain being imprisoned by our own side? Has she filled out as a woman? Are her eyes still such a bright blue? And this is my village. I might never leave. Why should I leave when everything I want is right here? There will be work here and I will grow strong again. Will she marry me? Would the children have brown or blue eyes? Maybe the boy will have dark brown eyes and the little girl blue eyes like her beautiful mother. My future is spread out before me, he thought. I know who I am and what I'm going to do. The morning is beautiful. Birds are singing along with me I will have breakfast with Mama.

Then Federico's thoughts were interrupted by the sound of barking. Three of the village dogs came charging at him. They barked and slowed down as Federico kept walking. He talked to the dogs and they, in turn, tried to smell his shoes. They continued to bark "Ah, you don't recognize me," Federico said aloud. "But you will. I'll be with you for a long, long time." Then he was inside the village. "I am here… Wake up you citizens," he thought. "I am on your road."

Then he turned the corner to his home…

Change! Everything had changed! The road was the same but one house --- his house – was torn apart. Federico looked at his mother's house and had to stop walking. There was no longer a building. It was barely a frame – only a skeleton remained of what had been a house. All of the outside boards were gone. Many of the windows had been removed – frames and all. The front door was gone. From a distance you could see into the house which was as bare inside as outside.

Federico ran up to the house. He stopped in front of it and looked in stunned disbelief. It was stripped of all the exterior siding. Most of the interior was bare. No furnishings remained. In Federico's mind, what he saw only partially registered. He did not know how long he stood and looked at the naked frame.

Eventually a man came up the street. "Is that you – Federico Llanos? Federico! Can it be???"

"Yes, it is me. You are?"

"Guilhermo – cousin Guilhermo. Federico – we didn't know if you were dead or alive…"

"Tell me Guilhermo, what happened here? Tell me now."

"Here," Guilhermo nodded at the shell of the building. "You know how the people are. Nobody wants the bank to take back a nice property. So, at night, some people take what they need. The siding peels right off. Once the door is gone, the furniture walks off by itself."

"Yes, yes. I know. But that's only when the place has been abandoned," Federico said. "This house was occupied by the same woman – my mother – for twenty years."

"Your mother?" Guilhermo was surprised. "You do not know?" he whispered.

"No," said Federico. "That's why I'm asking."

"Tu mama se murio." (Your mother is dead.)

"You say my mother is dead. From what did she die? Do you know?"

"It was, as they say, from a broken heart."

"No, no," said Federico. "People don't die from a broken heart!"

"She did. The whole village knew about it. Did the army not notify you?"

"I can't believe this," said Federico. Tears began to fall from his eyes. "How did it happen?"

"It was very soon after your friend came to tell her."

"To tell her what?"

"That you had died – in combat. He came right after the armistice. Here in the village we were still celebrating. That's when he came with the story of your death. Many of us listened. We stood right here. He told how he was there and held you in his arms."

"But Guilhermo, I was never wounded. Not a scratch."

"But he told us it was a hero's death. It was what turned the final battle in our favor and won the war. He even told your mother she was to receive a ten thousand peso government insurance payment."

"Lies!" shouted Federico. "It's all lies. How could she believe him?"

"He said he expected to be able to tell her all the details over a few days and he needed to stay at her home during that time. He said it would take him that long to tell her what a hero you were and that he also believed it was his duty to comfort her. And he kept telling her that she was a wealthy woman because of the insurance. He even brought her a bottle of wine."

Two older men joined Guilhermo. "Es verdad." (It is true) said one. The other man nodded and added, "Every word."

"How can this be?" asked Federico.

"Oh, mi amigo, it was a disaster," Guilhermo said. "She was crying and kept saying, what good is money without my only son. And he kept saying they must talk inside the house – just the two of them and not the entire village." Guilhermo stopped speaking and looked at Federico. Both men stood with their hands hanging down at their sides.

"Then the most amazing thing happened," Guilhermo said. "They began to argue. We were all surprised. Your comrade became furious and changed his story. He told everyone that you died by being hanged inside a military prison. Guilty of treason he said. He said you were a skinny traitor."

"Dios!" said Federico. "It was Panzon, the snake. He threw the letter away and kept the envelope. Comfort her, huh!" Federico looked at his cousin and asked, "Was he a big man?"

"Yes, yes." And he said you were thin and died like a coward."

"Big stomach hanging over his belt?"

"Yes. That's him."

"He said you gave him her name and address. He even told her to check the handwriting on the envelope. We didn't know what to believe."

"And what of Mama?"

"Ah, Federico, it was too much for her. She cursed your friend. She said she didn't want any insurance money; she just wanted her son to come home."

"Yes, go on."

"Then your comrade told her there would be no insurance money because you were executed. He said you died a dishonorable death without any burial service. He shouted at her. It was something about a Ballet de la Morte." Guilhermo paused and looked at the tears running down Federico's face.

"Go on."

"Well, she went inside the house. I don't think she was listening to him anyway. And she came out with a big butcher knife and ordered him to leave." Guilhermo stopped speaking for a moment. Then he said, "Federico my old friend, do you want a kerchief?"

"No. Just go on with your story."

"She wanted him to leave. He wanted to keep yelling at her. That's when several of us men went up to him. He was big. It took several of us. We took his arms and walked him out to the street." Guilhermo again stopped speaking. He looked away from Federico. "Your Mama," he said, "she had her hand over her heart. She became pale and collapsed right there on the front step."

Federico did not wipe the tears from his face. "Was she in pain?" he asked.

"I believe so," Guilhermo said. "It was a heart attack. She only lived two or three hours after that. Yes, she died that afternoon." Guilhermo suddenly looked up into Federico's eyes and said, "It was a wonderful service for her. There was much weeping from the old women. The two men who were standing next to Guilhermo nodded. One of them said, "Wonderful service with much weeping." The other man added, "She was a saint."

"Can this all be true?" Federico asked

"Si. Every word. I am so sorry."

"I wish I had died in that war," Federico said. Then he looked into the distance and for the first time, noticed Olivia's house. It was the largest house on the road. Olivia, Federico thought, might be there. Maybe I still have someone. I might not be completely alone. There will be no joy in this day, he thought, but if I can see Olivia there might be some scrap of hope. For now the heaviness that fills my chest seems like more than I can stand. But if I can see Olivia, there may be some reason for me to live. There may be some future – some hope…

"Guilhermo, does Olivia still live there?"

"Oh, my dear cousin," Guilhermo said, "that family moved out of the country three years ago. Olivia's father was a spy from the U.S. They all left one night. No new address. But they cleaned the house before they left. We heard rumors that they went back to Chicago or Holland. Nobody really knows. They probably have different names and I am told they left no tracks. If you know what I mean."

"You sure?" Federico asked.

"Sure. They left without telling anyone their plans. People used to talk about them. But they were just guessing. Nobody really knew." The two men who were with Guilhermo nodded their agreement.

Federico turned from the three men and walked to the street. From there he turned on to the road. He walked slowly and in silence. He felt his mouth clenched tightly so that his jaw hurt. He felt his body moving slowly in a bent over position. Federico thought, this feels as if I am on a patrol in enemy territory. That thought took over his body so that his eyes darted from side to side. He felt adrenaline rushing through his muscles. His body told him, it is too quiet here. That means the enemy is close. This air is too still. I can sense the presence of danger.

Then Federico's mind suddenly began to race and it was filled with thoughts. They were thoughts that argued with each other. How can there be enemies here? I am home. But no, there is no longer any home. With no home, is this then enemy territory? Then what did the war accomplish? Why did Corzon have to die? Corzon, my only friend during those four years. Did we lose that war? I don't remember winning. Or did both sides lose? Then where is the hope? Can a man have hope when his mother recently died? Is that what makes a man? Then I want no part of it. She died thinking I was dead. She died in great pain. Why God, did you allow such pain? No person was ever more filled with goodness than she. Of all the enemies, all the hatred, she had love in her heart. And one person is responsible for her pain and her death. Panzon. There is the enemy – Panzon. Maybe he is the only enemy. If I can destroy him there will be far less evil in this world .I must get a rifle. I will track him down and put one .30-caliber slug through his fat stomach. And another through his fat, lying mouth and another through his stupid brain, his ugly face and his chewing mouth.

I am no longer on patrol, Federico thought. I am alone. I will always be alone. And there is only one enemy. The Panzon – the fat idiot. I will find him and watch him die. Mother is gone Olivia is gone. My home is gone. Panzon is my last reason for living. I will find him. That will be my only course of action.

Federico's lips turned down at the corners. He thought, I have a new purpose for my life – to give great pain to Panzon. To see him bleed. Panzon was the cause of mother's death. It will be a life for a life. Hey, Panzon – you will pay.

Chapter 6
Pilgrimage

As Federico traveled, he ate little and drank only small amounts of water. He was on his pilgrimage to the village of Rosario – to kill Panzon.

Federico hitched rides when he could. Travel was slow. Many of his rides took him only short distances along the main road, leaving Federico off at intersections where other trucks would not stop. Still he moved on. He hitchhiked during the days and walked by night.

When Federico was picked up he spoke very little. He was thinking.

Much of his recent past swirled through his mind. He was physically fatigued and his thinking was disorganized. It seemed to him that every series of thoughts ended in questions. He tried to focus on his goal of getting to Rosario and finding Panzon. It seemed to him that finding Panzon was now the only thing of which he was sure.

When I kill Panzon, Federico thought, I'm sure to be caught. And when that happens I will be executed. So, is my goal to kill Panzon or is it the wish for my own death?

But how can that be when I am dead already? I died in the villages. Still, now I travel from village to village. *Where is death taking me?*

The Captain told our squad that we were preventing another revolution. But we were the revolutionaries! It was our revolution that we fought. And won. We were told that the executions in the villages would preserve the peace. Yet, we were doing the killing so what form of peace were we preserving?

Ah, but Panzon – he must die. That is certain. That I know.

When he told Mama that I had died he knew that it would kill her. I was her only child. Such pain that Panzon caused her. He hoped she would share her house and her food with him.

And her bed.

Ah, but instead she came out with a butcher knife. Fat Panzon, with his chewing mouth. I must shoot him where it will cause the most pain and a slow death.

Yes, yes Federico thought, a gut shot could take two or three days to bring Panzon to his death. He will get just what he deserves. Two villages, Santa Rita and Rosario – one the home of my Mama, and the other the home of Panzon – two villages with no value in either one. Rocky, sandy, soil. Freezing at night and burning heat during the day. No value in either. The land, too thick for anything to take root and grow.

That snake Panzon! Federico's mind raced. Panzon knew he would be passing through Santa Rita on his way home. Yes – one bullet through his intestines and after two days he will beg me to finish him. He threw the letter away but kept the envelop. He planned to stop at Mama's house – it was my house too – to fill her mind with his lies.

That one bullet will make him stop eating. And stop chewing!

He insulted Mama in front of the entire village. Maybe it is better that Olivia had already gone. Why did she have to go?

So I am alone, Federico thought. My village does not have a home for me. My home has been stripped. Mama has died a painful death. This is more alone than I have ever been before.

During the war I thought I would have a future when I returned. Panzon took it all away. Four years, in and out of battles. Killing. We were told to get the job done and go home heroes. It would have been like that – except for Panzon. He took away my future. Soon I will take away his. His pain must match mine. That will be the only pleasure to be left in my life.

How could I know? If I had written to Mama as soon as I was out of prison, my letter would have made her safe from Panzon. But how could I know that he would go to our village – our home? Mama worked her entire life away. In the fields. It was all sacrifice and no reward.

I was not her reward.

Her death was partly my fault. I share in the guilt of her death. Am I any better than Panzon?

What is the meaning of it all? Certainly life is about more than military victories? But that was all we had for four years. Still, it all comes down to nothing. We were revolutionaries to overthrow the dictator. Then our general became the new dictator. We were all killers. How many men did I kill? Twenty – twenty-five? What good did it do? Was my commanding officer pleased—or promoted? He was the one who reported me for not following orders. So – was it all vanity?

Vanity is a poor reason to kill.

So much of our thinking seems to be off base. Where is the foundation on which we can build? We need a level foundation which is unchanging. There must be that one place that cannot be destroyed by men's ego or greed.

Or must we be realistic? Was Mama's life the path for everyone?

All sacrifice and no reward?

If life is so difficult and so disappointing, Federico thought, why do we all go on? Go on for what?? If there is no place upon which we can build that can be safe, secure—some place that we can call home—then why must we all keep looking? Why do we work so hard—for a lifetime—just to die? *If every life simply ends in death than what is the value of life?* What was our war for? What difference did it make? How many men bled to death on those fields? I walk, and I walk. I question, and I question. But where are the answers?

One morning, As Federico walked down the narrow road, questioning God, himself, and the world in which he lived, he came to a sign that read, "Rosario".

The sign brought Federico to a fully awakened state of mind. "So this is where I am to reach my goal," he thought. "After these many days of walking and riding—Panzon will lie to no more women. His blood will soak into the sandy earth of Rosario. Will this bring my mother back? Or Olivia? No. These things will never be. But killing Panzon will give me pleasure. I was trained to kill the enemy. I was told to look at the enemy as if he was an insect. But it was fat Panzon who looked at me as if I were the insect. He starved me day after day. But he was the cockroach. He was the fat bug chewing my food, swallowing in front of me. For what? It gave him no pleasure. I never saw him smile.

Federico walked toward the village. The houses were far apart with fields between them. Several dogs slept curled together as he walked past them. I must be too thin, Federico thought, for the dogs to be interested. Another reason to kill Panzon.

Several children walked along the road. They saw Federico and looked away. One of our patrols must have been here, Federico thought. Didn't the villagers cheer loud enough?

Two elderly women were also on the road. They looked defiantly as they passed by Federico. I have been sleeping in the fields, Federico thought. I have not shaved in days. I am thin as a skeleton. I must look like a mad man. *Perhaps I am a mad man...*

Federico came upon an old man sitting in front of a small farm house. "Hola amigo," Federico called out. The man did not reply. "Is this really Rosario?" Federico asked.

"Si. And who are you?"

Federico answered, "I am back from the war."

"Si. Which side were you on?"

"The revolutionary army."

"Si," answered the old man. He spat on the ground by his feet. "Your comrades came through here only days before the war ended." He spat again. "They made the nationalistas look like angels."

"I know. I know," said Federico.

"They killed three of our boys; the boys were just standing there when a company from your army came through." He spat again as he said, "They shot them. One minute the boys stood there taking a break from the field work. The next minute they were all dead."

"That was probably one company that didn't understand their orders," said Federico.

"But it was the company that came through here," answered the old man.

"I am sorry," Federico said.

"We were better off under the rule of the nationalistas."

Federico waited several moments and asked, "Can you tell me sir, if there was a man from this village who was in the revolutionary army. Did he return here yet?"

"Big fellow?"

"Stomach hanging down to here."

"Chacho? Yes. He came back. He claims he was in the battle that won the war. Says he was an advisor to General Garcia."

"Of course," Federico said. "And he eats a lot. Is that your Chaco?"

"He keeps chewing even when he's not eating. Right?"

"That's him. Chacho eh? Can you tell me where he lives?" Federico asked.

"So you know him? He doesn't look like you. He still wears his uniform when he comes into town," the old man said. "He lives right over the next hill. He has a small house and a few chickens. He shovels chicken dung all day and comes into town every night. He thinks he is our town hero."

Federico looked at the old man and asked, "He lives alone?"

"He lives alone. Yes. He smells like chicken crap. Who would live with him?"

Federico said "Thanks" to the old man, turned and walked to the hill. As he reached the top of the hill he looked down at a tiny farm house with about twenty chickens around it. Federico watched the scene for several minutes and said aloud, "Only fifty meters."

Federico returned to the road and walked toward the village until he came to a house with a sign by the road. It said, "Surplus Store; blankets, guns, ammunition."

As Federico entered the store a small man with a black beard looked up at him from behind a table. "Good morning," he said. Federico knew the man was not from Rosario. "Can I help you?"

"Yes, please," Federico said. "I'd like to see your newest thirty caliber rifle. Nothing too beat up. It has to have a telescopic sight. Do you have something like that?"

The small man looked at Federico for a long time. Finally he said, "I have a nice Springfield here. It wasn't in the war. I think some officer had it in his house." He bent over and came up from under the table with a rifle. He laid it down with great care. Then he looked again at Federico and smiled.

Both men stood silently over the rifle. Neither touched it.

"You have some ammo for this one?" Federico asked.

"Sure. You need a full box?"

"No, just enough for the clip."

The clerk again reached down into a box on the floor. He stood back up and placed five .30 caliber shells on the counter next to the rifle.

In one quick movement Federico had the rifle in his hands with the bolt open. "Does this go in here?" It seemed as if Federico was talking more to himself than to the clerk. Then he chambered one shell and slammed the bolt forward.

"Don't load that in here," shouted the clerk. His face was turning pale.

"A small can of oil and a few patches of cloth too," Federico said. "This rifle needs a cleaning."

"Please, sir. Put that piece down. I don't have any money here. I haven't had a sale all day." He placed a small can of oil and a package of cloths on the table. He was now extremely pale.

"I need to borrow this for a day or two," Federico said. He took the oil and cloths with one hand and the rifle in the other. "I'll bring it all back," he said. "If I had any money, I'd give it to you. Maybe by tomorrow." As he walked out of the store, Federico noticed a telephone wire leading from the roadside pole into the store. He walked on the road until he was out of sight of the store. Then Federico left the road and walked into a wooded area. He sat down and watched the road. Soon two police cars sped past. After a few moments they slowly drove by in the opposite direction. Federico did not move. The cars kept going until they were out of sight.

Deep in the woods, Federico sat down with the rifle. He opened the oil, took out the cloths and broke the rifle down into its parts. Slowly he wiped off the excess. Then, with great deliberation he reassembled the weapon. "I have only five shells," he thought, "but one shot is all I need. There is great comfort in holding this rifle, sighting down the barrel and holding it against my cheek. Is it a feeling of control or of impending revenge?"

With the rifle at his side, Federico closed his eyes and thought of his mother. He could see her eyes and her hands. Her eyes, in his memory, were very large, soft and deep brown. They were warm, he thought—the only warmth I have experienced. Must a man be doomed to have no more warmth in his life—no more than that? Panzon's fault. Fat, chewing beast! Slug of a man. Maybe one shot through Panzon's heart will bring warmth to my heart.

Then Federico thought of his mother's hands. He tried to remember them as pale and graceful with long, slender fingers—the hands of a lady. Instead, his memory rejected the fantasy. He saw again, her hands as they had been, blackened by field work with calloused and mangled fingers twisted by arthritis and heavy work. They were not the hands of a lady. They were hands that showed all the signs of many years of labor. The image that came to Federico's mind was of roots. The roots of a tree that had been uprooted. They were like black, mangled, dying roots of an old tree that had been torn out of the ground by a vicious wind.

A slight chill ran through Federico's body. He looked up and saw that the sky had become cloudy. He stood, stretched and said, "It's time to feed the chickens."

Very slowly Federico walked to the top of the hill. He felt his heart beating faster in his chest. At the peak of the hill Federico stopped and looked down at the farm below. He saw a small house and a flock of chickens spread out for some distance. He waited. Then a figure emerged from the house. Despite the clouds overhead Federico could see the person clearly. He was wearing the wrinkled khaki pants of his army uniform but now he was wearing a poncho on top to cover his massive stomach.

Federico sprawled down on the ground and placed the rifle against his shoulder. "I will cause Panzon no pain," thought Federico. I will not let him linger and have time to think.—do not give him the chance to make an act of contrition. One bullet through the center of his chest—and he will be in hell   Everything Federico had learned from being a sniper returned to him then. Fire down on your enemy. Take your time. Keep the sun to your back. Stay out of sight. Pick your target. Check the wind. Do not rush. Try for a clean shot. Breathe in. Everything is calm. Breathe out. Check the wind one more time. Adjust for the wind. Focus on your enemy. He is not anything human. He is your enemy. Enjoy your kill.

The scent of fresh oil on the rifle smelled good. It would be a clean shot. No wind. The rifle fit perfectly in his hands, Safety off. Federico took aim. The rifle felt good against his cheek. He squeezed the trigger…

Chapter 7
The Second Meeting of
The X-Treme Book Club

As Jackson neared the meeting place for the X-treme Book Club he could hear voices. Two of them were arguing.

"Everybody knows vengeance is the strongest motivation there is." It was Clayton's voice—unusually loud and firm.

"But what about self-preservation?" asked Emma.

"That's temporary," answered Clayton. "As in, 'keep me alive until I can have revenge.'"

Clayton and Emma were on their feet facing each other. Jerry was sprawled in one of the over-stuffed chairs glancing from one person to the other. He was smiling silently.

Laura was also seated. "You guys are talking about emotion," she said. "Heat-of-the-moment motivations. But the thing that drives us year after year—that's life. That's what keeps us going."

Jackson walked into the meeting space and said, "I see you have started without me. Mind if I join you?"

"We were talking about the book," Clayton said, "and I said I look forward to the part where Federico puts a bullet thought Panzon's chest. And Emma here said that Federico is going to learn how not to kill because that will give value to his life."

Clayton and Emma sat down on opposite ends of the meeting place.

"You two remind me of my folks," Jerry said. "They can argue about anything." He looked from Clayton to Emma and then spoke directly to Jackson. "Obviously, it's a gender thing. Women want to keep the nest as a warm safe place for raising their young with everybody loving each other. But men want justice. And justice requires laws and laws require punishment in order to have any clout." Jerry looked at the other club members and added, "I'm a man and I believe that revenge is sweet."

"You have it so easy—all of you," said Clayton. "You are sound and young and you think you have been observers so you know so much. But you have not seen life and death as I have."

"Are you a combat veteran?" Jackson asked.

"No," Clayton answered. "I am a doctor, and I have spent many weekends in the Emergency Room at St. Mary's. And I have seen a man with five bullet holes through his chest, lungs, and neck. He clung to life. And he lived. And how did he do it? He wanted to kill the man who shot him.

He wanted revenge on his enemy before the police could find his enemy and put him safely in prison."

"But is that motivation—or anger?" asked Emma.

"Come on—what's the difference?" said Clayton. "The guy's lungs were filling up with his own blood. He had to be restrained from getting off the table and running out of the ER to buy a gun of his own."

"So what happened to him—the guy with the bullet holes in him?" Jerry asked.

"He went into surgery that night," said Clayton. "We removed one bullet from his left lung. It was close to his heart. The other bullets went right through his body. The surgery lasted well over an hour. He needed a lot of blood. And he was critical for a couple of days. After that he was a mean patient." The doctor smiled as he recalled the wounded man. "I think he checked himself out of the hospital after two weeks. Three nights later there was a series of shootings downtown. Two men were killed and another seriously injured. Police ballistics reported it was all by the same gun—which was never found. The newspaper editorialized that there was a vigilante in our midst and the police weren't doing enough to stop it. My patient might have been questioned," Clayton said, "but he was never arrested. I guess he didn't know which man shot him in the first place so he shot three to make sure he got his enemy." Clayton smiled as he concluded, "It was literally 'over-kill' with him."

"Okay people," Jackson called out. He signaled "Time out" with his hands. "This will be a good time for each of us to re-introduce ourselves. It will be sort of a short exercise to draw us together." Then he mumbled, "Which we obviously need."

The group went silent. They looked up at Jackson standing in front of them.

"We know each other's names," said Clayton.

"But not much more than that," said Jackson. "Tonight, I want to hear what your occupations are. And hobbies, if you have a hobby. And—why you want to be in this book club. I think it will be interesting."

"This will all be in confidence, right?" asked Emma.

"Yeah," said Jerry, "Like 'what happens in the book club—stays in the book club,' right?"

"Right," said the group leader. "And anything you don't want to bring up—well, you are always free to pass."

Jerry raised his hand and sat up straight. "I'll start," he said. "I'm a high school senior. I don't know yet what I'm going to do after graduation but if the draft is reinstated I will move to Canada. For a hobby, I love books, that's why I'm here every Tuesday night. I like printing presses and well done books—the kind printed on heavy enamel stock with four-color pictures." Jerry paused, looked solemn and added, "And I take very seriously my role as class clown."

Emma and Clayton both laughed. Laura, very softly, said, "A little more class and a lot less clown might be a big help."

Clayton glanced around the group and said, "I'll go next to give these lovely ladies a bit more time to think what they are going to say. As you now know, I am a doctor—a surgeon at St. Mary's hospital. My wife and I have teenaged children. Boy and girl," Clayton turned to Jerry and said, "So I am quite used to wisecracks at all times. I play golf, and I would like to eventually collect several of the older sport cars. For now golf is the only thing I have time for. Nearly every Friday and Saturday night, I am called back to the hospital for ER duty. Stabbings mostly and some gun shots. One night a man came in with his arm almost hacked off by his girlfriend. She had used his Japanese ceremonial sword. But that's another story."

"And your reason for joining our little group?" asked Jackson.

"I'll pass," Clayton said. He looked away quickly.

"You sure?" Jackson asked.

"Yes. No. I'm not sure. You see, I don't understand her thinking." Clayton said. "It's my wife. She wants me to be here. She has a problem." The doctor slowly looked at each of the others in the group. In a very soft voice he said, "My wife says I'm too logical..."

"Hey Doc," shouted Jerry. "Speak up. We all want to hear every word of what's wrong with you."

"My wife" Clayton said loudly, "says that I am too logical. I guess that's her tactful way of saying that I'm not very considerate of others. I don't know. Anyway, she insisted I join this book club because she heard that our book becomes quite 'sensitive' after a few chapters. So, I guess I need more of what you call getting in touch with my feelings—or maybe just finding my feelings. She—my wife— wants me to enjoy being around people. She wants me to change. I really don't much like people. Is that so bad? Well, that's why I'm here.

"Sometimes I think her—my wife—is jealous of the esteem I receive at the hospital," Clayton said.

"And why do you think that?" asked Laura.

"Well, as a surgeon I make a great deal of money for the hospital, and she's just a stay-at-home-wife."

"Pardon me!" Laura said. The phrase came out like a shot. "Did you say 'just' a stay-at-home-wife?"

"I'm merely trying to be factual," Clayton said.

"Really. And do you like being a surgeon?" asked Laura.

"Yes, I do," Clayton said. "Something wrong with that?"

"And in the OR," said Laura She sat without moving, yet her eyes had narrowed, "there is only one general. Right?"

"What do you mean?"

"Only one person," said Laura, "giving the orders."

"The surgeon, yes, of course."

"And all the other people are sergeants or privates—so there is only one general. Right?"

"Well…in a manner of speaking," Clayton said, "I suppose you are right."

"And everyone in your OR salutes you?"

"What are you getting at?"

Very slowly, Laura said, "It's not that way at home is it?"

"Well," Clayton said, "She—my wife—has her own way of doing things…"

"And I suppose," Laura interrupted, "her ways are not always your ways of doing things. Right? And by the way, does your wife have a name or do you always call her 'she'?"

"Is this some kind of attack or something?" Clayton asked.

Jerry laughed out loud. "Don't you get it, Doc? Your hide is being nailed to the barn door," he said. "And she's using your hammer."

Clayton's shoulders became stiff. His cheeks were red.

Jackson said, "Hmm." Then in a low voice he added, "this little exercise was supposed to pull the group together."

The doctor looked down at the floor and mumbled, "As if I care what you guys think. I was asked to share my feelings. I did, and now… I get bush wacked for speaking out!"

"Whoa, Doc!" Jerry said. "Weren't you just telling us that it's a cold cruel world out there? So, then you finally see it as it is and right away you want an exemption from it. I know you are a doctor and all that, but does that make you special? Like has the Pope given you some sort of dispensation from reality?"

"Very interesting," the moderator said. "Perhaps dealing with the truth does mean facing it—accepting it and then going on and living with it."

"You guys know what," said Clayton. "I don't think any of this does any good. My being here may have been a mistake from the beginning. I suggest you move on with this meeting! Okay?"

"I agree," Jackson said. "We move on. So who's next?"

Emma smiled and cleared her throat. "I am a medical records transcriptionist, and I'm at St. Mary's too. I am single with my own apartment and an answering machine that has hundreds of calls from my mother." Emma squinted as she spoke. "That's my life. Now why am I here? I guess, I want to meet interesting people."

Jackson looked at Emma. In a soft voice he said, "That's part of your life—but I believe there is a lot more to you than you have told us. Is there more you would like to say tonight?"

"No. Pass for now."

"Okay. Laura, how are you doing tonight?"

"Fine, Mr. Jackson, fine," she said.

"Wait!" said Clayton. "Before you tell us your occupation, let me guess. You either are, or were, some sort of athlete, right?"

"Why do you say that?" Laura asked.

"Because you are always so still," the doctor said. "You are very observant, but you also conserve your energy—dramatically. Like an athlete. Am I right?"

Laura laughed. "Sure, I conserve my energy. Know why? It's because I am usually tired out. I work in a bakery... I get up at five A.M. six mornings a week. I am single, but my daughter and grandson live with me. I'm here because I no longer want to read romance books or mysteries. I am a Christian, and I want to be productive with my time. And my pastor recommended 'Wind, Sand and Hope'."

"Thank you, Laura. And I am Dave Jackson graduate student at the university working on a dissertation tentatively entitled, 'The Role of Contemporary Literature in Society.'" He stopped speaking and looked at the group. "I think this will be very helpful. Now then," he suddenly announced, "are we all keeping up with our reading?"

"Well, you did pick a funny place to stop," said Clayton. "I mean, we are left hanging."

"You can read ahead anytime," said Jackson. "It might be fun. I won't hold it against you. We just have to agree on some stopping place for the convenience of our discussions."

Jerry raised his hand and said, "I really liked that part where Federico is talking about war and he says what's on his mind. He says something like, I had this crazy idea that if war went on long enough, sooner or later everybody would be dead." Jerry paused and glanced up at the leader. "Why can't our politicians and world leaders understand that?"

"Good thought, Jerry," Jackson said. "And it's not a crazy idea at all. It's outside the box---sure. But crazy? No way."

Emma was bent over her book. She paged rapidly as she spoke. "I really liked that part where Federico is going home—or going where he expects home to be." She turned several pages and said, "Here. He's going to see his mother and Olivia. Olivia who has the potential to be his wife someday. Here it is. He's thinking, 'My future is spread out before me. I know who I am and what I'm going to do.'" Emma looked up and added, "He was so, so on course. That was so moving. I felt like this is one, decent, humble man. And what happens two paragraphs later?"

Finding no response from the group, Emma continued. "Federico sees that his home is destroyed. His mother is dead. Olivia is gone. It was so much in such a short time. The siding is stripped from the house. The furniture is gone. When Federico asks Guilhermo if his mother's death was painful, Guilhermo answers, 'Yes.' It was all so cruel. Nobody protected Federico. How could those people do that?" Emma stopped then and looked around the group. Again she waited for an answer.

"I believe Federico made a mistake," said Laura. "He put all of his hope—in temporal things."

"What's temporal?" asked Jerry.

"Those are the things that are limited by time," Laura answered. "They are things that fade or disappear—that can be taken away or lost."

Emma asked, "Don't we all do that—to some extent?"

"Yeah," Jerry said. "Like all those 401K's that devalued in 2009. They disappeared into thin air."

"I had hope in the stock market," the doctor said. "I'll never do that again. But Laura, give us an example of the non-temporal thing."

"Sure," answered Laura. "For Federico to get through everything that hit him right there, he needed faith in the heavenly Father and the hope for eternity in heaven." Laura smiled as she spoke. "Those are the eternal things, things that last – the things that a person can cling to."

"Oh," Clayton mumbled, "that stuff." He looked down and away.

"The group leader scanned the club members. His expression was one of surprise. "Well then, Clayton, what is your reaction to Federico in the last chapter. What are your thoughts?"

"You know," said Clayton, "I didn't have any use for Federico at first. I thought, just another little-boy-lost story. But in the last chapter we read for tonight, I could not help but identify with Federico. It seemed as if Federico took me back a few years—to a time when I still asked the important questions. Those philosophical questions that mankind has probably struggled with for thousands of years. But what got me," Clayton said, "was that so much of what Federico was asking—well, those were all questions that I've asked myself many times too. It made me feel like he had been there before me, you know? Something like he asked his questions at the right time," he said.

"It all made me feel extra sorry for him." Clayton's voice became soft and he said, "Still—it somehow made me feel hopeful for myself."

"That's interesting," said Jackson. "Would you care to take your idea a bit further?"

"Sure," answered Clayton, "If I can. It was right after Federico learned that his mother had died. Not just died, but was publicly humiliated and died in great pain. He's grieving of course, he recalls his mother's hands. He wants to remember her hands with long, slim fingers—the hands of a lady. But reality takes over and he remembers her hands as they were in real life. They were the evidence of a lifetime of labor. Worn, calloused, arthritic hands. Hands like I have seen many times on patients-worker's hands."

As he spoke, Clayton sat looking down at his own hands. "And then, in his grief Federico asks, do we work so hard for a lifetime—just to die? And that leads him to another question. If every life simply ends in death then what is the meaning of life?"

Clayton smiled. "I don't know," he said, "it just made me feel anxious. Anxious—and hopeful. I realized that over the years I've stopped asking those questions. But Federico will keep on asking—and maybe he'll find the answers. And then maybe he'll share those answers with us—before the end of the book. Hopefully in some form that we can understand."

Emma sat up and pretended to fan herself with her hand. "Are you guys reading way more into this story than is really there? Clayton you feel 'hopeful'? That part of the book is totally depressing. Totally. I'm no brain like some of you. So, for my sake, can we get some definitions here? I've been listening to this and strange as it is—Jerry makes more sense than anybody else."

"Ah," Jerry said smiling. "At last, recognition for my brilliant insights."

"It's easy to understand Federico," Laura said. "He was in shock, and he was depressed as well as grieving. Sometimes, when you are down in the deepest hole, you ask the deepest questions."

"So, Federico asks, does death detract from the value of life?" Laura said. "In other words, does a person's death wipe out some, or all, of the value from that person's life? Or—is Federico's question something like, does death take away from the 'meaning' of life? And now Emma has asked us to define the terms. Glad you asked Emma. If you wouldn't have, I would have. I can define the meaning of life, but I'm not sure of the value of life."

Jackson looked at Laura and said, "This is tough material."

Laura suddenly leaned forward. "Unless…" she blurted out. "Unless," she repeated, "meaning has to do with the purpose of the individual's life. Like what he or she feels he must accomplish in that lifetime. So then value—well, that could mean the success he or she had in accomplishing that purpose." Laura glanced over at Emma and asked, "Does that help?"

Jerry interrupted, "Doesn't do a thing for me."

Emma looked puzzled. "That's too simple. Clayton said that Federico's questions gave him hope. So, I thought, there must be some underlying question. You know what I mean?"

"Sure," Laura said. "The underlying question is how do we produce that value—each of us—in our own lives. Clayton's hope comes from the implication that the answer will be found in Federico's life."

Jackson looked at his watch and an expression of surprise crossed his face. "Alright guys," he called out. "We're going to have to wrap it up very soon. Okay? So, is there anyone who would like to summarize tonight's meeting for us?"

"I could summarize it in one word," said Jerry. "Disaster."

"How can we end the discussion now?" asked Emma. "We have only just formulated the question—the question we all want answered."

"Ah, excellent point," the leader said. "But isn't that the perfect place to stop? It gives each of you a week to think about the answer. A week to consider all the answers you can come up with and sort through—until you can find the one, best answer for you."

"But aren't you supposed to have the answers?" Emma persisted.

"Not really," Jackson said. "You come up with the answers, and I'll tell you whether you are right or wrong."

Clayton looked angry. "What kind of deal is that anyway?"

Jackson answered, "If I give you my opinion—you will probably accept it and stop looking at your own ideas. And you'll learn nothing. But this way gives you each a week to work out new potentially creative efforts. Chip away at it every day. You may come to enjoy it."

Emma mumbled, "I don't even know what I'm looking for."

Jerry called out, "Hey Doc, does this help you to change your life around and start to like people now?"

Jackson said, "Read two more chapters for our next meeting and be prepared to discuss them. And remember the words of the Delphic oracle: 'unless a man first seek the answer, he will find it not'."

Then Laura said, "Christ phrased it in the positive when He said, 'Seek and you will find.'"

Chapter 8
The Mist

Federico squeezed the trigger ever so slightly. The cross-hairs within the telescopic sight were fixed on the center of Panzon's chest. Federico squeezed harder—and—Panzon turned white! Everything inside the sight became a pale misty white. Federico lifted his head and looked around the sight. The rifle had not fired. Federico took his finger off the trigger, blinked—and looked at his target. Panzon was now enveloped in a wispy, grey-white mist.

"Am I blinded?" Federico said. He looked at other objects, the tiny farm house, individual chickens, and the shovel leaning against the house. All were distinctly visible. He looked back at Panzon and saw a cloud of white. It was nowhere else in that entire farm except around Panzon.

"There is something between the Panzon and I," Federico said. He spoke to himself as had been his habit in prison. "But am I really seeing it or imagining it?" He closed his right eye and looked around the sight with his left eye. "No, the left sees perfectly—but I can't aim with the left. The problem is my right eye. I can see perfectly with my right—except for Panzon. Is it fear of being caught and executed?

No. I am ready to finish dying. I am dead already—ever since the villages."

Then Federico put the rifle down and looked at Panzon. He could see him clearly. Quickly, Federico picked up the rifle and aimed—and Panzon was again hidden behind the cloud of white.

"This is not my imagination. Whatever that thing is, it's wrapped around Panzon. There is a third party here," Federico said. "I can't get a clean shot off. It's a living thing. It moves with him. The grey changes to a pale blue at some moments. Can it be there to protect that beast from being exterminated? I have shot many men but never have I seen anything like this. The Panzon is protected by a covering. It absorbs my vision when I aim this rifle."

"Let's try that again," Federico said. He put the rifle up to his eye and saw the grey cloud covering his target. He put the rifle down on the ground, blinked, and saw Panzon clearly. Black hair, moustache, stomach under a poncho. Federico moved several meters to one side. He could see Panzon perfectly. Then he knelt down on one knee and aimed at a chicken. His view was unobstructed. He aimed at a corner of the farm house. He had no problem seeing it clearly. Then, he aimed at Panzon only to find him covered by a grey mist.

Federico ejected the cartridge from the rifle. "What just happened here?" he thought. He sat on the ground and rested the rifle next to him. I have just seen something new—

all new. "I don't know what it was. I don't even know if I really saw it," he thought. "But yes, I did see it. It was real. It was as real as this rifle; as real as I am; but with different qualities, different physical characteristics than the things I normally see.

Federico tightened the telescopic sight on the rifle. "Perhaps," he thought, "my eyesight has suddenly expanded to include another level of vision. Or has my mind shifted to include a new level of insight? And what other things are out there that I have not seen before? It seems that whether I have seen them or not—there are other things in this existence.

"Ah, Panzon's mother," Federico thought, "Had she prayed for angels to protect her son? No! Panzon could not have had a normal, human mother, and it was not angels that I saw. It was like a smoke-screen except that it was not smoke."

"I can see him," Federico said aloud. "Now Panzon is going to walk into town. He will trade a chicken for some bread. Stuff the bread in your fat mouth Panzon," Federico said. Then he added, "Choke on the crust!"

"I only saw that cloud of white whenever I tried to kill Panzon. Am I infected with some pity for that beast?" At that thought, Federico jumped up, rifle in hand and looked down the hill. Panzon was walking away from his house. "I am very tired," Federico said, and sat down.

Federico awoke suddenly. It was late afternoon. He stretched as he looked around the area. Then he thought back at the events of the morning. "I cannot kill Panzon today," he thought. "Perhaps another time. Maybe never. Let him live with himself; what worse punishment could there be? Hunger! I must get some food and water. There is no light in the farm below. Panzon is in town. While he is trading chickens for bread and wine I will kill and roast one of his chickens. Tonight I eat. Tomorrow I will get more food, some water and go to a place alone. I must think. I must get away from people. During my solitary confinement I grew accustomed to thinking alone. Tomorrow I will go someplace where I will find answers to my questions."

Federico walked into the surplus store and placed the rifle on the table. The clerk was not to be seen. "Hola," Federico called. "Anybody?"

The clerk emerged from the storage room, took one step, recognized Federico and stopped. "It's you," he said.

"Yes, I'm back," answered Federico. "Here's your rifle."

The clerk looked from Federico to the rifle and back to Federico. "It looks like a different rifle."

"I hand rubbed the stock," Federico said. "With that oil. Here's a freshly killed chicken to pay for the oil I used."

The clerk took several quick steps to the table and picked up the rifle. As he picked it up he passed the tip of the barrel close to his nose. "This hasn't been fired," he said.

"No. I didn't get to take my shot," said Federico.

"So—good," said the clerk. "What were you hunting anyway?"

"A man who deserves to die."

"Were you in the war?" the clerk asked.

"Yes."

"And you killed other men?"

"Sí. Many."

"And killing your enemies—does it do any good?"

"I used to think it did. Now I don't know anymore."

The clerk looked at Federico for a long moment before asking, "And what path are you on now?"

"I don't know," Federico said. "I only know that I have to be alone. Everything is changing. I don't know what I want anymore. I need to think things through."

"Have you considered walking the desert?" the clerk asked.

"The desert?" Federico looked at the man, an expression of surprise on his face.

"Think about it," answered the clerk. "A nice little walk. About thirty miles across. Maybe two days and one night. Alone under the stars. Silence and solitude. Good for thinking. It helps you to think things through. The desert makes a person choose."

115

"Choose what?" asked Federico.

The clerk looked at Federico and said, "To live life or to throw it away."

"What do you mean," Federico aside, "To live life— or to throw it away?"

The clerk smiled at Federico. "You take two large canteens of water, a little food, a good hat and jacket, and you walk alone," he said. "The answers come easier in the desert. No distractions, so you can choose. In the desert, if you stay long enough, you either choose God..." he stopped speaking then and looked away.

"Yes you choose either God or what?"

"Or you go mad," the clerk said.

"That's some choice," Federico said.

"But that's life," the clerk said with a smile. "That's the bottom line."

"Interesting," Federico said. "I know I want to choose life, but I'm not sure that I know how."

"Listen to me..."

"Why," interrupted Federico. "Why should I trust you?"

"At least hear my advice. Consider it. Maybe you'll see some wisdom in it."

"You talk of life," Federico said. "Most of me is dead already."

"I know," the clerk answered.

"But I still want to choose life."

"Si. Good idea. Now consider walking the desert."

"Tell me why," Federico said.

"Because you have killed many men—you know about death. But what do you know of life? Perhaps your path to wisdom is only now beginning."

"Then Federico felt a strange sensation. He felt muscles—small and weak muscles—beneath his eyes. They were pulling upward from his cheek bones. "Am I smiling?" asked Federico as he thought, "Have I forgotten how to smile? Strange feeling."

"Yes, you can smile," said the clerk who was also smiling. "You see some messages come to us with a voice of thunder. Other messages have only an incessant murmur. But the message which is the message to live—that comes to each of us in a still, small voice.

"Go out there. And listen. Listen to the stillness. You will either choose good—or El Diablo. You walk out into the desert one person, and you come back a different person."

"You sure?"

"Oh, yes." The clerk smiled slightly. "Often in the desert the air is unusually clear. So you can see, in a way, see so far ahead that you can choose your future." The clerk smiled again. Then he added, "You'll see."

Federico stood silent and motionless.

"Thank you for returning the rifle," the clerk said. "Wouldn't it be good to never again depend on guns and bullets? To choose a better way?"

Federico nodded.

"I have been taking orders for so long, so long," Federico said, that it will be wonderful to make my own choice."

The clerk looked into Federico's eyes. "I do believe," he said, "that you will choose life." Then he pulled a wallet from his hip pocket and took a stack of paper money from the wallet. "Use this to equip yourself for the walk," he said. "There is enough here to take you across…"

"No-no. I couldn't," Federico stammered.

"Take it. Choose well," answered the clerk. "And you'll see…"

Chapter 9
The Desert

"I must walk across this place," Federico repeated. He had been walking for most of the day.

"Keep your eyes on the mountain," the shop keeper had told him. "Because crossing that desert alone requires you to keep focused on old Solidad."

As he walked, Federico shook both canteens. He knew one was still full and the other partly full. Still, he liked reassuring himself that he brought everything he was advised to bring. In the distance, on the far horizon, stood the dark pyramid of the mountain—Solidad.

"Just keep looking toward that old lady," the shop keeper had told him. "Solidad can't come to you. You must go to her. And just beyond the north side of that old girl you will see the edge of the desert and the first signs of the other side."

Federico obeyed. "I will keep glancing at the mountain," he said. Speaking out loud helped him to feel less alone. He repeated, "I will keep walking toward that black mountain. Walking to Solidad. Keep walking."

As he walked, Federico's mind went back over the last forty-eight hours. "You have a hat?" the two clerks at the supply store asked him. "You must have a good hat—and sunglasses," they said. "Those are your two most important pieces of equipment." Federico smiled as he remembered the clerks.

"They tried so hard," he thought. "And it worked. I bought everything I needed there. Then, to the expanse of the sky and sand, Federico added, "Keep walking toward Solidad."

He had asked one of the clerks why the mountain was named after a woman.

"I think it is because she stands alone," the young clerk replied. "She is not part of any range. She is a loner—like Solidad."

"So Solidad was a person?"

"Allow me," said the older clerk as he pushed the junior clerk out of the way. "Solidad is the name of the mythic woman from centuries ago," he said. "Of course, every village has its own version of the story, but Solidad was a lady of mystery and sadness."

"Mystery and sadness?"

"As my father told it to me, and his father told him, Solidad had many children. Mostly boys. First, her husband was murdered by some men of the next village. Then her children left her one-by-one. Each one went into the world. None of them ever came back. She waited. None ever returned. Yet she still waits." The older man cleared his throat dramatically and continued in a softer voice.

"It is said that on dark nights, when the desert wind is especially strong, you can hear her crying." As he spoke the old clerk looked directly into Federico's eyes. "Some call it an echo," he said. "Some say it is only the wind." He leaned so close to Federico he could smell the old man's breathe. "But those who have heard it swear that it's the wailing of a woman's voice weeping for her lost children, and she weeps as only a mother can."

"I must keep walking toward that mountain. Keep walking," Federico said. "Focus. Walk."

Then Federico's thoughts returned to the clerk in the gun store. "He gave me money," Federico recalled. "For the food and clothes. A strange man. I stole from him. But I brought it all back. And he talked to me about walking the desert. So keep walking. He must have thought that I was strange too. It was obvious that I needed to be outfitted if I was to do what he advised me to do—so he paid for it. Reached into his own pocket. Strange man. What motivates a person to do that? But I must keep focused on the mountain. I will walk toward Solidad. I will keep focused on the mountain. I will walk toward Solidad. I will keep walking. What did that man really mean? What did he want?

"Panzon is still alive. I should have not taken the rifle back to the store. I wish I could kill him but—I don't know—I don't think I can do it. Was it because I returned the rifle that the clerk gave me the cash? How many people are there like that who give away money—to strangers? Money and advice. Was he simply showing me that he was sincere? Money and advice. But with just one look he knew I needed cash. He knew I wouldn't have lived through one night in the desert without food, water, and clothes to cover me.

"This is such a cruel place. Such an expanse of nothing. It goes on and on. There is no beauty here. No beauty; only wind and sand.

"I don't seem to be getting any closer to the mountain.

"There have been no birds for hours. The sky has only dark clouds. Hard to focus. Tired. Hungry. Some clouds are black like smoke. Some are grey. *Keep walking to the mountain!* Ahead is Solidad. She looks dark blue. It is getting harder to see her. She is like a woman of mystery: sometimes I can see her—sometimes I cannot. Is she friend or is she enemy?

"*Keep walking!* How frustrating it is not to be heard—by anyone. I have a need to communicate, but no person can hear me. Except maybe the dead. Do the dead hear?

"Sudden fear! I am not sweating anymore. Bad sign. How long has this been going on? Must stop and take a small drink. Stop walking so as not to spill any. Two sips. Basta! Resume walking.

"But why am I doing this? Am I punishing myself? I was not a reward for my mother. Is this walking the desert going to help me stand taller among other men? Will this free me from those memories that plague me? In this wind? The sand? The base of Solidad?

"Can I make is across this dry place? Keep walking. I'm dead if I don't make it. What's the difference? I'm dead now. Nothing lives here. It's all death. Wind, sand—and death.

"How long have I been walking? Some sort of stupor has come over me. I lose track of time. Heat stroke? Dehydration? The clerk who gave me the cash said that out in the desert you either find God—or go mad. Am I mad? I must be because I have not found God. In this place there is no God. But this is no time to worry about God. Stay focused.

"I am close to the mountain. Now I can take off the sunglasses and hat. There are black clouds overhead. Straight ahead—the mountain. I will rest at the feet of Solidad.

But again—it happened! Walking without looking up. Wake up! Eyes burning with sand. Stay awake. My name is Federico Llanos. I was a private. I shot many men. I am guilty. I deserve to be punished. Can God hear me? Or is self-punishment what the desert is for? Solidad has to be close. How long was I stumbling along? It is going to rain out here in this desert? No. But the wind is strong. Will the wind keep me from reaching Solidad? Keep hydrating. Eat later; not now. Lady of mystery. Keep walking to her. The wind makes the sand burn into the skin. Stay awake. Keep walking.

My eyes are so filled with sand that I cannot see ahead. Where is the mountain? Have I turned around? Am I mad? Is there nothing else for me other than this emptiness—this dead space—this loneliness? The wind is stronger, and louder, by the minute.

A house; that's what I dreamed about in the army. A home with a family, maybe Olivia and I would take the kids to a soccer game on Sunday afternoons. That was what I wanted.

"Look for Solidad. Where is she? There. Keep looking up.

"I joined the army to bring justice to my country—to bring my people together. My people were my goal. But I am walking at the speed of a snail.

"I was not raised to be a killing machine for General Garcia. That was never what I wanted. I didn't know what war was like—or the extent of the death and destruction

"As long as I can keep walking, I am alive.

"And there were others who were unlucky enough to be marksmen too. We were ordered to begin each battle with that first shot. Ordered to start the killing. When we joined the revolution we didn't know what it would be like. We wanted to be the bringers of justice for all. Where did we all go wrong? The blood of our victims is on us, on us all. So much guilt. We killed so many, but we ended up *not* hating them. That's it. They were disorganized. And we were a machine. We felt sorry for the Nationalists. They were no longer the enemies—*we* became the enemies of justice—of our country. We were the enemies because in the end there was no longer any good reason to kill. But we were a killing machine. We kept on and on. For no reason. And then our killing machine developed feelings. Feelings of sorrow—and guilt.

"To kill for no reason—what sin was that? Does that sin have a name? Can any priest forgive such a sin? Can any penance ever be enough? If I die out here, it will be no loss. It will be relief.

"The wind is stronger than I am. It has worn me down. It has filled my ears with sand. It has burned my skin and blinded my eyes. I can feel the strength of the wind. It picks up the sand and hurls it across this flat desert. It has a force that tries to push me down. Is it alive? It seems to behave like a furious animal, an animal that has been disposed from some other territory—some ancient and evil territory—uses the sand to punish and to burn.

"If I die here I will be alone in my death. No one will remember me.

"Walking. The mountain. Yes—to Solidad. This is now a major wind storm. The scarf over my nose and mouth does very little. The driven sand works its way inside the cloth. It burns the skin; fire inside my clothes and fire outside. And the howl of the wind is deafening. It tries to hold me back. Keep walking. But why? Of all the places on this earth, why am I in this one? Wind, sand and nothingness. Have I come here to die? Death won't be so bad. Maybe I will find rest in death.

"Why? Why didn't I stay on the other side of this desert? Was the other side the safe side? Is there a safe side? What is my destination? The other side? Is the other side a destination? No. I have no destination. That's good to know. Then why am I here? Why am I on the earth? This desert is a waste of earth. And I am a waste of a human being. We belong together. Maybe it is my destiny to die here...soon.

"Where is Solidad? Is she that black giant in the midst of this pain? Does it really matter? Can't walk much further. Where would her north side be? Which way is north? Can a man trust a mountain? Can a man trust himself?

"The enemy is the wind and the weapons he carries can kill me. The wind is laced with broken bits of cacti, thorns, slivers—and now something more deadly—small shards of rock that have been sheared off the surface of the mountain. All these piercing, stabbing, vicious elements tear at my exposed face and hands.

"I can walk no further. My face feels as if my skin has been torn and burned away. Eyes no longer produce tears. They are full of sand. So little air to breathe because the air is thick with sand. Can't get a deep breath. Lungs seem heavy. No strength left. I am empty. I have disappeared. I am a depleted being—an emptied vessel. Now there is nothing here in this desert but wind and sand.

Then the wind came upon Federico. It swept over the miles of flat desert, gathering waves of sand. The sand hit the sheer cliff face of the mountain's north wall, and the sand plunged down on him. Federico hunched against the falling sand. It crashed over his head and back.

"What more do you want of me" he called. "No! Madre! Dios!"

At last, blinded by the sand, deafened by the wind, weak from hunger and thirst, Federico's knees slowly unhinged beneath him and he dropped, kneeling, into the cold and burning sand. Federico's knees slid out from under him, and he fell on his side. Quickly, the darkness enveloped him and he slept.

In his sleep, Federico heard his own voice saying, "Solidad, you have been my guide. The way to you has been painful, dangerous, and exhausting. This is a sad and lonely place. Still, I am close enough to hear your voice. I am so close I could reach out and touch you. I am cold, thirsty, and near to death. Still, I am not alone. I am near Solidad."

In his dream Federico then heard another voice. Whether it was the sound of the wind or the spirit of the mountain. It slowly spoke in a woman's voice. She said, "Wanderer, do not come any closer. You have lost faith in your fellow man. You have lost faith in yourself. Now you want to renew your life. Do not come close to me for I am darkness. Because I am of nature, I am the bringer of death. If you seek life, you do not want me. There is no life in me. I would only betray you with death. You want life, freedom from guilt and you even want eternal life. Do not come any nearer to me for I am of the darkness."

Then the voice had an echo. "Come out of the darkness. Seek the light." The echo of the voice said, "...the light." And the voice said again, "Seek the light." And the echo repeated, "The light—the light—the light..." Then the voice faded away until even the echo was gone.

Federico could sense the brightness of the light through his eyelids. He blinked himself awake. He could feel soreness in his legs and back. The arches of his feet hurt from walking in the sand. He tried to spit sand out of his mouth but had no saliva with which to collect the sand. So he blew out what he could and rinsed with water from a canteen.

When he was fully awake he sensed that something was missing. It was the wind. The air was still! He blinked his eyes again and saw that the black clouds of the day before had given way to show a pure, pale blue, radiant sky. He took another drink from his canteen. The water was still cool from the cold night air.

Then Federico stood up. Everything hurt. His head ached from the pounding of his pulse in his ears. When his eyes adjusted to the light. He saw that he was at the base of a cliff. Dark rock jutted above him in a vertical mountain face. This was Solidad and in the distance Federico could see a small cluster of buildings. "Ah," he said, "that first trace of civilization that had been promised to me."

Resting in the sand were six buildings. They were low, white buildings with red tile roofs. One of the buildings had a bell tower with a cross on it.

"That's better," Federico said to the still air. He took another drink of water. "I can get there before the day is half over," he thought. "They will take me in. In their courtyard they will have a well with fresh water. There will be men to talk with. Food. Rest. Safety from the wind and sand. A monastery is a very good place to have dinner tonight. I'll stay for a day or two and recover my strength."

He thought, "I have survived. I am alive. This empty vessel may be refilled. I will see what waits ahead."

Chapter 10
The Third Meeting of the
X-Treme Book Club

Jerry leaned forward and asked, "Okay, can you guys explain that mist thing?" He sat back in his chair. "I know, I know—Doc over there will probably call it a psychological aberration. Somebody else will call it a form of hysteria. But see—putting a label on it does not explain the action for me. You know what I'm asking?"

"Okay, Jerry," said Jackson. "You're halfway there. You mentioned hysteria. Well, hysteria can cause temporary blindness of a specific object or person. That's a simplified definition. But—is that really what was going on? Anybody care to add to that? Anybody?"

Jerry raised his hand and said, "Federico thought the mist, or the cloud or whatever, was a separate entity. He even thought that it had a mind of its own. Like it wasn't *his* mind. Like it had a will of its own."

"Maybe that was the author's way of telling us that Federico could not control the mist. See, to him, it felt like it was something separate from him," Emma said.

Clayton, who was seated next to Emma, said, "So, the mist that kept Federico from shooting Panzon—that mist was in Federico's brain. Is that it?"

"Or maybe it was in Federico's heart," Laura said.

Jackson looked at Laura and said, "Would you like to clarify that for us?"

Laura appeared to be in deep concentration. She sighed. Then she said, "I think that when your will and your conscience are in conflict, things like a mist appearing—such things happen. And if you're not a sociopath, the conscience wins out."

"But that's not what was happening to Federico," Jerry said. "He wanted to kill Panzon no matter what his conscience told him to do or not to do."

"Oh, I agree," said Laura. "That's what his brain wanted to do. And that's what his gut wanted him to do. But his heart stopped him. It was the work of his conscience stopping him from killing again. And it did it in a way that Federico could handle. He was able to save face. Like the decision wasn't Federico's fault. His heart made it easy for his conscience to comply."

Suddenly Emma blurted out, "My mother says men don't have consciences!" Her announcement was followed by a moment of absolute silence. Then she continued, "Men do what they want and can rationalize anything. What looks like a conscience is only their fear of getting caught."

"There's more than that in sociopathic thinking," said the moderator. "A true sociopath sees no wrong in what he does whether it's betraying his country for a million dollars or killing his wife for the insurance money but that's not the point today. Right now the question is, did Federico have a conscience?"

"My mother," Emma said, "says that all men are conscience-free when they are between the ages of 15 and 50."

"All men?" Jackson asked, a surprised look on his face.

Clayton said, "A lot of guys over 50 are the worst ones."

"Oh, Lord," said Emma, "there's no end to it."

Jerry held up his hand and asked, "What's a sociopath?"

Emma turned to face Jerry, "Duh. That's someone without any conscience. His decisions and actions are only to benefit himself—even when they are at the expense of others," she said. "Sociopath equals no conscience."

"Would that like include a guy who lies to girls to get his own way?"

Laura leaned forward and said, "Of course, Jerry. That's what Emma's mother is worried about isn't it? Now, are you worried that you're a sociopath?"

Jerry appeared to be confused. "Well, is there any such thing as a part-time sociopath?" he said.

"He's worried," both women said together.

"Probably for good reason," Emma added.

"And he can switch it on and off," Laura said. "How convenient is that?"

"No. Wait!" Emma said. Her eyes were dark with emotion. "You can make your point any time. I need to finish making my point right now!"

"Sounds important," Jackson said. "Go right ahead"

"My point was that all men are sociopaths," she said. "All men—as in right from the beginning. The very first man, Adam betrayed his wife Eve just to avoid a scolding..."

"Is that in the book we're reading?" asked Jerry.

"Not now Jerry," the leader said. "Emma has the floor."

"When God caught Adam," Emma said, "eating the forbidden fruit, Adam lied to save his own skin. He told God, 'The woman gave me the fruit of the tree.' Adam shifted the blame on to us girls; he betrayed his wife; he lied to avoid punishment, and he let the woman take the blame. Those traits have all been passed down from fathers to sons for millions of years. From the first man on. See what I mean?"

Emma stopped speaking then and looked at each of the club members. "I know what your point will be. Federico had a conscience. I know. It happened when he saw the boy dragging his soccer shoes with him as he died. But see, Federico had already shot twenty-five other human beings. If you call that a conscience, I'd say it was too little and too late. Federico may be the main character of this book, but you can't call him a hero. He's just another example of what I was saying; men do not have consciences." Emma's voice became soft then. She added, "I suppose my mom has lots of good reasons for telling me what she thinks about men. And she may be only partly right. And I'm only half her age so what do I know… but, so far, I have found her to be pretty accurate."

"Very interesting," the leader said. "And is Emma right or wrong?" There was a silent pause. "Guys?" Another pause. "Anybody?" Again a silence until finally, "Yes. Laura. What do you think?"

"It's dangerous to generalize about people," Laura said. "Especially men. There are some good men and some stinkers," she said. "I suppose there are even some who can go both ways, but you can't say *all* men are without consciences. It wouldn't be fair—or correct."

"Thank you," Jackson said. "I was hoping *someone* would come up with that bit of common sense." Jackson appeared to be thinking. Then he smiled slightly and said, "The trouble is, the fact that there are some good men makes it much easier for the few who are bad to get away with their immorality."

"Now we're into immorality," said Jerry. "I think you are beginning to take the fun out of it. Just tell me, how does a guy know if he might be a sociopath—or not?"

"Fair enough, Jerry," the moderator said. "So let's tackle that—with two definitions. Okay? We have already partially defined a sociopath as a person without a conscience. Now let's define the word conscience. In my dictionary, conscience means knowing right from wrong regarding one's conduct—coupled with a sense that one should—or must—act in accordance with what is right?"

"What about speeding?" asked Laura "We all do it…"

"You have to find out what's top clock when you are behind the wheel," Jerry said.

"Like I said," Laura continued. "We all do it, and it could be dangerous for pedestrians or cyclists on the road."

Jerry sat forward with a look of surprise on his face. "Oh, no!" he said. "When I drive over the speed limit, it never makes me feel bad later. Does that mean I don't have a conscience? And If I had been pulled over I would have tried to lie my way out of a ticket. How bad is that? How bad am I?"

"If I may," Clayton said as he stood up. "Let's take a different example." He stood next to the leader and looked down at the other book club members. "Jerry, what is your life's dream today? If you could have anything—what would it be? Answer right now."

"Lead guitar and lead singer, Doc," answered Jerry "In an acid rock band."

"Okay," Clayton said. "Say you are in a club on a Saturday night—not a school night, of course, and the band is really good. So this guy walks up to you. Just then the band takes a break. So this guy says he can teach you to play guitar better than the one in the band. And he says he'll make you into a much better singer than the singer in the band. And then he says he can give you the band. It will be yours. You can give it any name you think up. You would be interested, right?"

"Right on, Doc!"

"So then this guy says to you, 'Let's go out to your car and talk it over.' The two of you walk out, and there is a stretch limo at the curb. What kind of car would it be Jerry? Caddy? Mercedes? Lincoln?"

"Make it a Rolls-Royce."

"So this Rolls is sitting there idling, chauffeur behind the wheel. You and this guy jump in back. Of course, there's caviar and champagne on the built-in bar..."

"I don't like caviar," Jerry interrupted.

"At this point, I wouldn't complain," Emma said.

"Yea," Clayton said. "Shut up and eat it." As he spoke, Clayton turned back to the table behind him and picked up four 3 X 5 index cards. He looked at several and put them back. He held one as he said, "The chauffeur turns around to look at you. She takes off her chauffeur's hat and a bushel of long, hair drops down around her shoulders..."

"Wow, Doc," Jerry said. "Your secret is out now. You're a hair man!"

"She's drop-dead beautiful," Clayton continued. "And she asks 'Where to?'"

"Boy! Boys!" Laura said loudly. "Does this adolescent male fantasy have a point?"

"Never mind her," Jerry said. "This is cool. Go on, Doc."

"So the guy you're with," Clayton glanced at the card he was holding," he says, '349 Maple street'."

"Hey, that's my address," Jerry said.

"And the guy sitting next to you, hands you a 9-mm Glock pistol." Clayton said, "And he says: 'Everything around you is yours—if you will kill your parents.'" Clayton looked directly into Jerry's eyes and said, "You have five seconds to tell the guy yes or no. So, what will it be?"

Immediately Jerry answered, "No way. This is silly. I would never agree to that."

"But why not?" asked Clayton.

"This is stupid," Jerry answered.

Clayton leaned forward until he nearly touched Jerry. "Why not?" he persisted.

"A thousand reasons," Jerry shouted. "But most of all because I love them. And they love me. And it would be wrong."

"So--" Clayton was smiling. "Now you think you have a conscience, right?"

"Yeah, I think so. You can't make me do something I don't want to do."

"Don't be so smug, Jerry, What if the guy next to you shows you his ID, and he's from the CIA. He tells you about two men in the next house. Our government knows they were responsible for the attack on the World Trade Center. But—lacking hard evidence, they will go free and return to their country as heroes and will work to bring more terrorists back here—unless they are stopped. Our government can't do it—but you, Jerry—you can bring justice to the free world." Again Clayton leaned in toward the teenager. "Now what do you say?"

"I guess I would call the President and suggest that he send in a squad of US NAVY Seals with 'crowd buster' automatic rifles you know, like Obama did to get Osama bin Laden out of the way."

.

Clayton smiled and said: "Would that make you happy?"

Jerry said: "You're messing with the rules of debate. You're twisting everything around. Know what? It makes me think I'm not a sociopath but probably you are."

"Ladies! Gentlemen! Guys!" called Jackson. "Slow down. We are getting off the track. We need to get past the mist and across the desert with Federico tonight. If we get behind tonight we'll never catch up."

138

"I wouldn't mind meeting for a couple more months," Emma said.

"So—guys, here's what we will do the rest of this meeting," Jackson said. "We'll get into the desert together and see just where we are at quitting time. Okay? Okay. I would like to begin with a bit of background on deserts. Listen up.

"The spiritual leaders—men and women—who founded monasteries were drawn to the deserts," he began. "Originally they fled into the deserts to escape persecution. After a time, they found that being desert dwellers worked for them. They had the belief that deserts were designated by God, to be used as a place for finding God." The teacher said.

"The desert in our book is probably the Atacama Desert in northern Chile. It is famous for its sudden storms with winds that include gravel, sand, and chips of volcanic rock from the Andes.

"If you remember, Christ himself went out into the desert when he wanted to commune with his Father." Jackson said, "See, the desert is wasteland. It has no value to the world because there was nothing there to be exploited." Jackson stopped speaking then and scanned the faces of his students. "You probably remember the story of Moses and the children of Israel, right?"

"Was that like in the movie, 'The Ten Commandments'?" Emma said.

"Yeah," Jerry said. "With Charlton Heston. That movie is always on TV the night before Easter. I think Heston is dead now. Right?"

"Yes, Heston died a couple years ago," the moderator said.

"He always got those movie roles that were larger than life," Emma said.

"And you always talk in clichés," Jerry added.

"Anyway," Jackson spoke louder. "The people in that story—the people of Israel—left Egypt to return to their promised land. Does anyone know how long that took them? Anyone care to guess?"

"Forty years," Laura said.

"Well alright, Laura," Jackson said. "But do you know that they could have reached their promised land in several months…"

"If old Moses would have stopped to ask for directions," Jerry said.

"Not quite. God kept them out in the desert that long so they could learn to depend on Him, to depend entirely on him."

"Wow. They were really slow learners," Emma said.

"Or maybe, it is a hard lesson to learn." Jackson said. He paused to glance around the room. "Anyway, my point is that the desert is a unique place. We could say it was designed by God as a place where men can go to be transformed."

Jerry laughed. "Where men go to be turned into women?"

"Oh so funny," Jackson said as he scowled at Jerry. "No. For the purpose of this book, the desert is where men can live as they try to be nothing but themselves. It is the place where they can build a monastery and live in poverty, in solitary lives, live in prayer and silence—and most importantly—be dependent on no one but God."

Jackson looked at Jerry and said, "I believe it means living without any ego. No lying to one's self. All honesty and transparency. Looking for God as the answer to all problems. Finding salvation only in God. Answering His call to fellowship with Him. You could call it a passage into spiritual maturity. Are you following what I mean?"

"Like those guys walking around downtown," Jerry said, carrying signs that say, 'Repent or Die!' Those fruit cakes give me the willies. Like they know the will of God or something."

"Actually, I think seriously seeking God's will is much of what it is about," Jackson answered. "And if people like that scare you maybe should try to find out why you are frightened."

"Hey," Emma shouted. "Way to go Mr. J. Finally a put-down."

"Oh yeah." Jerry sneered. "Well those inmates of monasteries, what do you call them?"

"Monks—or brothers of an Order."

141

Jerry laughed. "Monks or monkeys? I can't see that they serve any purpose. I mean, what good do they do? Who cares what they think?"

The moderator signaled for a time out. He looked at each member of the group before he spoke. "I believe Jerry's question is right on target. Even though he meant it only to be funny—it is pertinent. It is one of the themes of 'Wind, Sand and Hope'. What good are monks? What purpose do they serve? Can men meet with God? I believe these question will be answered as we read the rest of the story of Federico."

In a lower murmur Jerry said, "I doubt that."

Laura raised her hand and Jackson nodded to her. "Maybe I'm getting ahead of the story. But I have been told that whatever men seek God they will be opposed by Satan. There is a spiritual war going on you know, even if we can't see it. And simply being out in the desert is no protection from Satan. When he was thrown out of Eden he was ordered to, 'wander the dry places'—as in deserts. Right? So what has happened to deserts? The time frame we are at in our book is now the mid-1940s. At that time in our history we were testing atomic bombs in the desert," she said. Quickly she added, "Not that there is anything inherently wrong with atomic energy. It can be used for good-or evil. But where have we put our faith lately? Are we now using nuclear energy for mankind? Or are we using it to stockpile weapons? What are we choosing? And since the 40's, what have we done to our desert? Entire cities have been built around flashy casinos—and what have they brought to the desert? Gambling, organized crime, alcoholism, drug abuse, vice…"

"Sure, but, no place is perfect."

"You could almost feel the sand burning Federico's skin," Emma said. "Like if God had this old piece of furniture and wanted it cleaned up to fit in Heaven. So he had it sandblasted—stripped off the old paint and ready for the new. It must hurt."

"For a few minutes I was actually sorry for old Federico," Jerry said. "I think it was where he said, 'I am an empty vessel.' He was really, really lonely."

Laura smiled then and said, "I think the desert represented a turning point in Federico's life. Sure, he was being stripped of his old life—his former self—but he was certainly pointed toward a better life."

"In the desert chapter?" asked Jerry.

"Yes." Laura said. "What's the title of the book we are reading? 'Wind, Sand and Hope' but out there in the desert Federico said there was nothing but wind and sand. Meaning the author has to make good on the title—so, hope is straight ahead."

"Wow! That is really cool," Jerry said. "I didn't' pick up on that at all. You're the brain."

"I'm no brain—believe me," Laura answered. "But I can give you a tip. Federico's life is a parallel of Christ's life. He's going to go through a lot of what Christ went through including going out into the desert. Christ spent forty days and nights in the desert—resisting temptation—at the turning point in his life."

"Wait," called Emma. "What was the turning point for Christ?"

"Before the desert, Christ was in prayer and fasting; he worked with only a handful of men. After the desert experience, Christ became a very public person, His ministry was set in motion."

Emma raised her hand, squinted up at Jackson and said, "We know Federico is looking for his salvation. Maybe call it 'eternal life'. I see the clerk in the gun store as some sort of 'holy man'—right? That guy sent Federico out into the desert. He told him to keep looking at Solidad. But remember there are two mountains—Solidad and El Diablo. Is that whole thing symbolic? Telling us that there is a third path to salvation? Old Solidad—in Federico's dream—told him that she was part of nature that always leads to death, the other mountain, El Diablo means Satan, who leads to damnation. So, is the author telling us that there is a third way?"

"And that would be what?" asked Jerry.

"God's way," Laura said. "Federico was given his freedom of choice, but he is being lead toward the new path, which is obedience."

"That sad story of Solidad," Clayton said, "I believe it is a recurring myth found in most primitive agrarian societies. It is what parents preach to their children to keep them from running away. To keep them home on the farm—probably for cheap labor."

"That sounds like preventative parenting," Jerry said. "Lay a guilt trip on the kid before he has a chance to do anything wrong."

Jackson wide-eyed, took a step forward toward Jerry. "That's a very good insight. And probably true. Good thinking Clayton—and you, Jerry. Keep it up. Any other comments or observations?"

"May I ask a question?" Laura said.

"Of course."

"How old is Federico anyway?"

"That depends," the discussion leader said. "We're with him for about forty years of his life. In the first chapter the court recorder tells us that Federico is twenty-two-years-old. That was in 1945, just when their civil war was winding down. Then Federico's salvation experience was after he had been in the monastery for seven years so he's 29 there. And 13 years later he became the Abbot so at that point he's 42. So then he was the Abbot for 15 years making him 57 years old at the end of the story."

"Thanks," Laura said.

"It's starting to sound like a long book," Clayton mumbled as he yawned.

"Not really," Jackson said. "We only get some highlights from Federico's life. It's not a very long story."

After a moment, the leader said, "Alright. We've talked a lot today. That's good. And we've made some progress in getting through this book. But—again—I have to ask you, what is the theme that came through in the last chapter? The theme, guys. What is it about? It can be on the surface in actions or underlying as in thought, insights, and suggestions. Where is the author taking us?" A silence fell over the room.

"Not all at once," Jackson said with a hint of a smile.

"I asked what good are monks anyway," Jerry said. "Is that a theme?"

"And what part does the desert play in the journey of Federico?" Emma said.

"I was thinking something else," Laura said. Her voice was quite soft. "We know Federico is going into the monastery. But what happens to a man's hatred when he becomes a monk who prays his life away? That might be an interesting theme. That's what I was thinking."

Jackson said, "All of those ideas are good. But to keep it really simple, I'll state it in two words: The Test."

"Those are the two words I hate the most," Jerry said.

"Just watch for that theme as you read on," the leader looked at his watch. "And do read on. Two more chapters for next Tuesday. Stay caught up on your reading and the discussions will be more productive. Guys—that was good thinking tonight, all of you—keep those ideas with you and talk to others about them. Jerry, you talk to your parents about these concepts and when they talk, you listen. It will make your parents think you are growing up." Jackson smiled then, "Even though we know better."

The teacher paused as if he had more to tell the group. After another moment he said, "Maybe we're all growing up." Very quickly he added, "keep thinking. See you next Tuesday."

Chapter 11
Confession

"Bless me Father for I have sinned," Federico said. He sat on a wooden bench beside the elderly priest. They were in the monastery courtyard. Beside the bench was an old water pump with a tin cup chained to it. It was late in the afternoon, and the wind blew through the monastery walls so desert sand swirled around the feet of the two men.

"My last confession, Father Marcus, was one week ago, as you know. And my sin now is the same as it was then."

"I have an enemy who produces hatred in my heart," Federico said. "I am nothing more than a vessel full of hate toward that man He killed my mother with his lies. He nearly killed me. I want only to see his blood splattered over the sand of the desert."

"Vengeance belongs only to the Lord," said the priest.

"But Father, it has now been seven years since the Panzon killed my mother…"

The priest interrupted, "Seven years is like the blink of the eye to our Lord."

"Ah, but I must destroy him. I must do this, or my hatred will destroy me. I am little more than a vessel filled with the acid of hate. It burns in my chest." Federico hit his chest with his fist. "It rises in me and sets fire to my throat." He coughed as he spoke. "It wakes me during the night and drains me during the daytime." Federico stopped speaking.

"Go on."

"I am a vessel of acid—the kind of acid that kills."

The priest looked at Federico. He looked into his eyes. There was a moment of silence. "It is foolishness and sinfulness to hold such hatred in your heart, my son. The prophet Ezekiel knew that man needs the water of life that comes from our God. Ezekiel said, 'where the river flows everything will live.' He was talking about eternal life He was talking about the water that puts out the fires. That water washes you clean—clean enough to someday enter into the presence of Heaven."

"Yes, Father."

"How long have you been at this monastery?" the priest asked.

"Seven years."

"And how did you get here?"

"I crossed the desert, Father."

"How?"

"On foot."

"And you came from town?"

"Si."

"So, you faced a head-wind."

"Yes, Father—in a sand storm. I almost died."

"And when it was over, how did you feel?" asked the priest.

"I was burned up by the wind and sand," Federico said. "I was empty. I had become an empty vessel."

"So, you felt like an empty vessel, little brother. You were free, yes? And were you also free of your hatred?"

"Yes." Said Federico, "I was free—then."

"That was when you arrived years ago. Now, my son, tell me, what has happened during those seven year?"

"It has been my confession all those years. I slowly let all the old hatred slip back in."

"Slip in?"

"Yes, Father." Federico's voice was barely audible.

"Understand this, little brother," said the priest. "When God the Father and His Son Jesus Christ came together—long before time began—there was only a void—a vacuum. Then they created the entire universe, spoke it into existence, and saw that it was good."

"Yes, Father Marcus, I know all that."

"But understand," said the priest. "They filled the vacuum. The very creators of nature have ordered nature to refill vacuums. And refill them quickly. When you had your hatred taken away—that was when you should have replaced it with Christ."

Slowly Federico stood up. He looked down at Father Marcus and said, "What would you have me to do? Am I to go back out into the desert?"

151

"Sit down, little brother." The old priest smiled at the novice. "Now you will go on that important part of your journey…"

"Not in the desert though," Federico said questioningly as he sat down.

"No, Brother Federico. It will take place right here. This is called salvation."

"Marcus, my mentor, my friend, the river Ezekiel spoke about—where is the river? I have lived in this monastery for seven years, and I have seen no river. I have felt no river. Where is it—for me?"

The elderly priest smiled at Federico and said, "You have to invite the river into your life. That happens when you invite Jesus into your heart."

"This is a strange place to talk about a river. In this desert nearly everything dies from the lack of water. We can't raise cattle. The calves die. We can't grow corn. This desert is a difficult place to have to live."

"Yes," said the priest. "But it makes you depend on God."

Federico pointed to the pump directly in front of the two men. The tin cup chained to the pump swayed in the breeze. "We don't have any river here," he said. "Is that pump symbolic enough? Will that work?"

"Fear not. We are working with more than symbolism today."

"Oh. We are? Tell me Marcus, what else do we have today?"

"Today, we have the Father's love," Marcus said, "Christ's redeeming sacrifice on the cross—and the power of the Holy Spirit. The water is symbolic of the only real life for us—for any of us. That is the life granted to us by Christ. Comprende?"

"But what, my friend—what do you want me to do?"

"Have you read the third chapter of John today?"

"Where Jesus says you must be born again. Yes, I read it over and over."

"Then what you must do is think about what you have read."

"Yes, Father. And now, my penance?"

"You will get no penance from me. You have suffered enough for your sin." The priest sat in silence for several moments looking into Federico's eyes, "Sit here in silence and listen," he said. "Stay right here. In silence. Wait for God's leading." Marcus smiled and added, "Someday a pope will come along who will tell us we do not need priests for confession; we just need to talk with our Lord. So, Federico, you are ahead of that time. Stay here and listen. Repent. Accept Jesus as your Lord and Redeemer. Serve your fellow man. And sin no more."

"And is it proper for me to sit here in the courtyard and listen for God's voice? I mean instead of in my cell?"

"Stay here. Now do not say your act of contrition to me. Stay here and say it to God. Then close your eyes and listen. Listen with your mind—and your heart."

"Thank you my friend. God be with you."

"And with you."

Federico closed his eyes, and immediately a scene came to him. He saw before him a fire. It was a raging, angry wall of flames like an entire forest with the heat and flames devouring trees and plants. The fire was moving directly toward him.

Then a voice said to him, "Take the step. Forward." Federico saw himself stand and take one step—forward. There was a loud hissing sound, and as he looked into the flames he could see a stream of water flowing into the fire. He took another step forward and the stream turned into a river. It quickly flowed into the flames and extinguished them so a cloud of dark smoke and steam rose up into the atmosphere and disappeared. Before him a river of bright blue water spread across the ground and stopped at his feet. Federico took another step—forward—and his feet were in cool, clear water. He could feel the heat in the earth beneath his feet, but the water itself was cool and life-giving. Two more steps and he was up to his knees, and the water refreshed his entire body. He walked deeper into the water so it was above his hips, then chest high, then up to his shoulders, and he had no fear. He looked around, and the shore line was gone. He was surrounded by only water, and it was bright, blue and clean. Then he took two more steps, and he was immersed. The water was above him as well as around and under him. He could feel the pressure against his ear drums, and he was in and under a silence of blue. It was as if the waves of love were moving above and around and through him. Federico stopped walking and raised his hands above him. As they broke through the surface of the water, he saw a bright light shining down upon him. As he looked up at the light he felt each wave flowing over him.

Then suddenly everything in the world changed. The light from above turned dark. The water below became cold. It was bitterly cold. When Federico looked around he was amazed to see that the water had turned red. It was a deep, dark, red. Sudden, sharp pains moved through Federico's chest. He lowered his arms and tried to ease the pain by hugging his chest, but there was no relief. The water sound in his ears turned into a low moan, and Federico could feel his feet slowly sinking into the mud below him. Then words formed in his throat and in a mumbled, agonized voice he said, "I am sorry. I am so sorry," and the red water burned in his eyes, and his body sagged under the weight of the water above him. As he said, "Forgive me for I have sinned," he closed his eyes against the boiling river, and his burning eyes.

"Dear Father in Heaven," he said. "You know I hate myself worst of all. Because I am a sinner. Will you have mercy on me? I have carried the sin with me for years. Free me from this sin, I pray. I have tried to do it alone and I can't. So, Father, please let your son Jesus come into my heart and my life. I thank you for his blood that allows me to ask for forgiveness. And I accept Jesus as my Lord and Savior. I accept him into my spirit and at this moment I give my life over to him entirely. That is my thought, my hope, my wish, my prayer. My everything. Hear me, Father. Hear my prayer. Lord, have mercy upon me. Amen,"

When he again saw himself, Federico was walking out of the water. The river had returned to bright blue, the light from above was brilliant again, and Federico had crossed to the river's other side. He stepped up onto the dry shore and felt light and clean. He knew—he knew---the hatred that had filled him before had been replaced with peace.

"Where the river flows everything will live," the prophet had said. Then Federico thought, "I have crossed over that river. It is a river like no other river. I was buried in the blood of that river. Now the old is gone, and I have walked out and crossed to the other side. I breathe fresh air. I am on new ground. I am on this earth—but I am now on new ground.

Federico knew that time had passed, but he had no idea of how much time had gone by. He knew only that the wind was blowing across the monastery courtyard... He could feel it on his face. Then he heard a voice.

"Did you repent?"

Federico opened his eyes. The question had come from Father Marcus who was sitting several feet from him.

"With every atom of my body," Federico answered.

"And did you repent," the priest asked, "in your spirit too?"

"Like the broken, beaten sinner that I am."

"Did you feel forgiveness?"

"Father, I was washed in the blood of my Redeemer!" Federico said.

"So then you felt gratitude and accepted Jesus as your Savior?"

"Yes, Father. Oh, yes."

"And you felt accepted by Him—and loved and full of joy?"

"You know it all my friend. Were you there?"

"I was right here praying for you." The priest paused. "My prayers were all answered."

"There is so much relief, Father. Things—many conflicts—so many things are settled now. It's like a pathway has been cleared for me. It's like I am free to move on—at last. Thank you for your prayers. Thank you, Father."

"So what do you see now?"

"Well Father, you will probably think I'm crazy or something. I am so happy. So very happy…"

"But what do you see now?"

"Well, you asked; so here goes. That old tin cup hanging on the pump right there. It has a beauty to it that I've never seen before. That's what I see."

The old priest smiled and said: "But what exactly is it you see now that you have never seen before?"

"That cup is old and dull and has dozens of dents in it. And it is chained to the pump so it can't get lost. It is always there. But when the wind blows it moves back and forth and rubs against the pump so that the edge of that cup is polished."

"Yes," the priest added, "metal sharpens metal."

"Look," Federico pointed, 'that polished edge is so bright in this sun and as the cup moves in the breeze it seems to be free."

"But it is chained," said the priest.

"Yes, but it's free."

"It's chained," said the priest. "But chained to the source of life…"

"The pump. Yes—the water! Of course!"

"And the cup is used to serve. It is functioning—doing what it was created to do. To serve. And the water flows as if from the tabernacle…"

"And the water is like the presence of God."

"Exactly Federico. Exactly. You see, you understand even if you do not have words for it. Your old eyes have been put away—left behind you. You have new eyes and with those new eyes you are now beginning—just beginning to see through the eyes of our Creator."

"They seem like new eyes my Father. And this is because I see everything more clearly now. There is so much beauty here."

"Your new eyes," Marcus laughed, "feel good, huh?"

"I see you in a new light too," Federico said. "You are always so humble about having the shape of Augustine but not the wisdom, but all of a sudden I know that you know the mind of God. And Father, that's worth more than knowing all the theology in the world."

"Oh my son, leave me out of this," "said the priest. "Just enjoy this day—and this new life. Feel it and give thanks. Because you are starting to see everything new."

"Yes Father. That's what it seems like. Everything new."

"Because you are a new creation."

"What does 'new creation' mean?"

The old nature—that wants to sin—has now taken a back seat. Your vision has changed. You see potential for good where you formerly saw evil. Your spirit has shifted so you no longer want to sin. Now you want to be our Father's assistant in this world… The old is gone; now you are part of the new creation—you will be what you were created by God to be…"

"Wait, wait," Federico put his hands out in front of him. "This is way too much for my little brain."

"Don't worry," Father Marcus said. "Just follow your spirit. You see, your new spirit is one with God's perfect Holy Spirit now."

"So I don't have to memorize what you were telling me. God's Spirit will direct my actions?"

"Yes, when you listen—and obey."

"Oh, I want to obey, always."

"Not that it is always easy," said the priest. "You still have to get yourself out of God's way. You still have to make choices—choices that have consequences. You will be tested."

"Father, should I be worried?" Federico asked. "I'm not good at taking tests."

The old priest leaned toward the younger man and smiled. "No, don't worry. But know that a test is coming. It always follows the salvation experience. It's all part of the plan."

"Well Father, I won't worry—today anyway. This has been too perfect a day to have worries. But—is there anything you can tell me about the test? I want to pass it as soon as possible."

"It will be for your own good. It is designed to teach you to trust in the Father's will, the Son's redemptions and the Holy Spirit's power. So don't worry—just trust."

"You sure?"

"Have I ever mislead you?"

"No."

"I didn't say it would be easy. I simply advised you to trust in God. It will be a lesson in trusting."

"Will you be there to help me, Father?"

"No, my son. I will not be there for you, but you will have all the help you need."

Chapter 12
The Test

The door to Federico's office flew open. "I've got him," shouted Mason. His bulk seemed to take up half of the small room.

"Do you ever knock?" asked Federico.

Mason, his face flushed with victory, ignored the question. "I got the chicken thief. I caught him red-handed!"

Federico intentionally waited several seconds for Mason to calm down. When the blood began to drain down from Mason's cheeks Federico said, "I didn't realize anyone was stealing our chickens."

"Well he won't do it anymore. I got him. He's all ours now. And he's just outside. You want to see him? He's a thief and now he's our prisoner."

"Brother Mason, let's not be so quick to accuse him."

"But sir, why not?"

"If he is guilty then we will have to judge him, and we don't do that here. You learned that once. Don't you remember?"

"Well, maybe you don't want to judge anyone, but I've been watching, and every time this guy goes by we lose one chicken. So I caught him with one of our chickens. Today! He had it under his poncho."

"And are you certain it is one of our chickens?"

Again Mason ignored the question. "I forgot we do not judge here. Maybe this time we should. You want me to bring him in? I got him right outside."

Federico looked at Mason who appeared to still be out of breath. Federico sighed and said, "Sure. Bring him in."

Mason had a grip on the man's arm. He walked him straight up to Federico's desk. There were two chairs in front of the desk. Mason roughly pushed the man between the chairs and let loose of him. Then Mason stepped back and smiled as he blocked the door with his body.

Federico saw before him a man who had once been tall and heavy. He was now bent over and extremely wrinkled. He was wearing a weather-beaten poncho, peasant slacks and heavy boots. His cheeks and eyes were deeply sunken into his face.

"I am Brother Federico, the Abbot of this monastery, and I'm glad to meet you." Federico extended his hand.

The prisoner did not shake hands, He looked down at the floor and mumbled, "I am sorry about the chicken. It was either that—or starve. Your security guard took the bird back."

"Are you from around here?"

"No, I come from up north."

"There is no need to steal," the Abbot said. "Our gate is always open to help feed the hungry." He noticed the man was hardly more than a skeleton, "Would you like to clean up and join us for dinner?"

The man looked up but did not answer.

"We are contemplatives. So we don't speak during our meals, but there will be a scripture reading. I would like you to sit with us."

Again the man remained silent.

"You see we are looking for someone to help us here at this monastery. Are you married?"

"No. Never."

"Any family with you?"

"No. What kind of help you looking for?"

"We need help with our chickens," Federico said.

"I know all about chickens."

"Oh sure," Mason blurted out from the doorway. "Sure you do!"

"Brother Mason," Federico said. "Would you wait outside please?"

Mason looked at the Abbot and raised one hand for permission to speak only to see his superior make one quick hand movement of dismissal. Mason walked out of the room but left the door open.

"Please sit down," Federico said.

"No, thank you," said the man and remained standing.

"Would you be able to stay with us for an indefinite period of time? Perhaps you could help us with our flock of chickens," the Abbot said. "We sell some eggs and give some away. It's an important part of our mission work here."

The man looked intently at Federico. Finally he asked, "How many chickens do you have?"

"I really don't know. Maybe after you have been here for a while you could tell me." As Federico spoke to him, the man pulled himself up and stood at a nearly straight position. It faintly resembled the military posture of attention. Federico thought, this man is much younger than I thought. "So what experience do you have with chickens?"

As the stranger thought about an answer he made a slight chewing motion with his jaw. Federico thought, "What experience do you have with chickens—other than eating them?"

At that instant, a chill took hold of Federico's heart. He felt suddenly uneasy. Then he felt a surge of emotion inside his chest; it was some sort of revulsion; it was in his chest—and stomach. "What is this sensation?" He asked himself. As he again looked at the man, Federico's hands turned to fists. Can this be? He had tried to hide the recognition from himself. But it could no longer be suppressed. Is this Panzon? Yes. It is he. Is he being turned over to me? Yes, he is. He is mine. Is this Panzon the killer? Yes. I shall have justice. Is this the beast responsible for my mother's death? Can this be real? Yes! He is here—at my mercy.

But no! It must be my imagination, Federico thought. This ancient wreck of a man is far too old to be Panzon—an older brother maybe? This stranger has such hollow, empty eyes. He is a skeleton—like a terminally ill man. And such a look of hopelessness hangs over him like a shroud.

Still—look at him. Yes, it is Panzon—the guard without feelings. And what am I to do with him. I have hoped for this moment for years. Now, at last, he is here—on my ground. At this monastery, I dispense justice. At the word from me—Panzon will pay.

Yes. It is Panzon. How he lied to my mother! How he made her die of a broken heart! Could I kill him today and go to confession tonight? But no. I cannot kill. God would judge me—I would judge myself. But if he stays with us I could assign him to shoveling chicken crap for the rest of his life. And what good would that do? How could that help me? Ah, such cruel thoughts! What's a man of God to do?

If only Father Marcus were here—to tell me what to do.

Am I to forgive Panzon? What if I can't do that?

If I can hurt him—something that leaves a deep scar—will that help me to get beyond my hatred?

Is there any job that is dangerous? I could assign Panzon to repair the bell tower. He looks so weak that he could easily fall. Would that really help me—or him?

Panzon is a sinner—a serious, grievous, methodical, premeditating seducer and a thief. He must learn his lesson. He deserves to die!

Then Federico remembered the words of his friend and advisor, Father Marcus. It had been just moments after Federico had accepted Christ as his savior. The vision of the tin cup chained to the pump came into Federico's mind. It was brilliant in the afternoon sun, as if—as if—it was reflecting God's glory. Federico recalled being extremely joyous. Then Father Marcus told him, "You will be tested. I won't be here to help you, but you will have all the help you need."

"Is that it?" Federico thought. "This is a test? Must it be so hard? How am I to measure out justice when my veins flow with hatred? Marcus, where is the help you promised me?"

Then Federico looked at Panzon standing before him. His clothing was wrinkled; his skin was wrinkled. His eyes were nearly closed; his jaw made a chewing motion. He seemed half asleep.

Federico thought, "What would our Father advise me to do with this wreck of a man? Tell me Lord. You know he is a sinner, and he deserves to die. So—what am I to do with him?"

Immediately the answer came to Federico's mind: "You are right. He is a sinner. And he deserves to die. But remember my son, you were once a sinner who also deserved to die. Instead of death you received mercy for an eternity. Can you not be merciful to another sinner?"

Federico put his head down on his desk. His lips silently formed the words, 'I don't know. I don't know.' Then the words slipped out aloud, "I don't know."

Panzon looked up. "What?" he asked.

"I just said that I don't know."

"Don't know what?" asked Panzon.

"Anything!"

"Just two minutes ago I thought you knew everything."

Federico glared at Panzon, "I don't know what I'm going to do with you!"

The tiny, old man standing before Federico looked up and said, "Just do whatever you want. It really doesn't make any difference to me." Then he sighed, and his eyes nearly closed again.

"Mason," Federico called. "Would you come in here please?"

Immediately Mason was inside the Abbot's office. He smiled at Federico then glared at Panzon.

"Will you take care of our visitor please," Federico said. "Show him where the showers are. Get him some clean clothes and take him to one of the guest rooms. Yes, and tell Brother Lawrence to send a supper plate to his room."

"So he's staying with us?" Mason asked.

"For a time." Federico looked at Panzon and quickly turned his eyes back to Mason. "And tell Lawrence that I won't be down for dinner tonight or breakfast tomorrow."

"Doing some fasting again?" Mason asked.

"Yes. It is a time for fasting and praying."

"So—you're going to pull an all-nighter, huh?"

"You can call it that," Federico said.

"Is there anything I can do to help?"

"Yes," Federico replied. His voice was loud. His expression was stern. "See that our guest is back in this office by 10 am tomorrow."

Federico looked across the room at the fragile man. He was wearing clean slacks and shirt but wore the same boots as the day before.

Panzon sat in one of the chairs facing the Abbot's desk. He did not look up. After some time, he swallowed and asked, "Is God a man?"

"You mean as opposed to being a force...?"

"No, I mean is he a male?"

"Yes," replied Federico. "Definitely. He is a *he*—the Father. Why do you ask?"

"Because no man—no real man—could ever forgive me for all my sins. You see," he looked across the room, over the desk and into Federico's eyes. "Long ago, I crossed over the line. I went too far. Now I am beyond forgiveness."

"I think I can understand that feeling," Federico said, "but I don't agree with the logic."

"Why not?"

Federico looked again at the man sitting across from the desk. He looked at him and thought, "The Lord sees value in that wreck of a being. Why Lord?" Then Federico said to the man: "I know. I know. I know of your sins."

Panzon looked away from Federico's stare. "You say you know? I don't think you can..."

"Panzon, I was there when you were the sinner." His voice became loud, and his eyes were filled with anger. "I was one of those you sinned against."

"How can this be? Are you a ghost?"

"You were a corporal in the revolutionary army," Federico said. His voice had the sound of a growl. "It was near the end of the war. You were assigned to guard the prisoners at the military prison at Santa Rosa. When you brought them their bread and coffee—you ate the bread and drank most of the coffee."

"We had orders to starve the prisoners into a weakened state."

"And did you also have orders to steal their shoes? Or steal anything of value they had? Or take their final letters and turn them into guardhouse jokes?"

"Who are you anyway?"

"And were you part of the company of soldiers that executed those prisoners? Remember 'Ballet de Morte'?

Those prisoners were fellow countrymen, and you treated them like insects—instead of breaking their necks you let them slowly strangle to death. I was there, Panzon. I was there and saw it all—and I saw you!"

"Then you were one of those prisoners. But how is it that you did not die?"

"The war ended before I was to do the 'Dance of Death'. God spared me," Federico said.

"But sir. You know all these things. Then you understand that God cannot forgive me. I am guilty. I went too far. Now it is hopeless."

Federico looked directly at Panzon. He looked into his eyes for a long moment. Only after Panzon looked away, Federico said, "I killed twenty-five men." He paused but continued to look at Panzon. "And he still forgave me."

"This is true?" asked Panzon.

Federico sighed and answered, "He is a merciful God."

"Ah, then," said Panzon. "Maybe God will forgive me. I am glad he is so merciful. But sir, with all due respect, can *you* ever forgive me?"

Instantly, Federico stood up so that his chair scraped across the concrete floor. "I have a monastery here. Work to do. This place doesn't run itself you know."

"Yes, sir. It must be a very big job."

"So come back here by mid-morning tomorrow," Federico said. "I don't have any more time for you today."

"I'll be happy to come back tomorrow," Panzon said. "See. I remember something about Christ saying, 'Whatever you bind on earth will be bound in heaven'. Maybe you can explain that to me tomorrow? Yes?"

Federico looked at the man standing before him. A moment passed. Then Federico shouted, "Mason. Come in here now. And get this chicken thief out of my office!"

Again the two men sat in the room. They did not sit together. They sat across from each other. They sat in silence.

In that silence, a voice came to Federico. It could not be heard by Panzon but only by Federico. It warmed his heart when he heard, "Do you remember the cup?" Federico knew—it was the voice of Jesus.

Federico answered in his mind and his heart. "Yes, of course. It was chained to the pump."

"You saw that cup—as if for the first time."

"Yes. That it true."

"Remember that you saw it through new eyes. You saw a very old and worn out thing become beautiful."

Federico smiled with the memory. "That is true. At that moment it was the most beautiful thing I had ever seen. That vision has stayed with me. Thank you."

"Those eyes of yours that saw such beauty—and purpose—with those same eyes, look at Panzon."

Federico looked up to see Panzon sitting, silently pulling some chicken droppings from the bottom of his boot. Instantly, Federico looked away.

Then Federico again heard the voice that had entered his heart. It said, "Do you love me?"

"Yes I do."

"Then look at Panzon." With a split-second glance Federico looked up to see Panzon making a chewing motion with his jaw. Again, Federico looked away.

After a moment of silence Federico heard the words, "do you really love me?"

"Yes Lord, I do," said Federico. "You know I love you."

"Then—look—again!"

Federico sat up straight in his chair. Slowly, he raised his head, and he saw Panzon. Federico looked past the space that was between them and, as he had been commanded, he looked at Panzon.

Federico saw a man utterly broken. He saw Panzon humbled by a lifetime of losses. Before him sat a fragile man who had become nothing more than a grain of sand being blown in the wind. He saw a man completely powerless to control—or even understand—the forces that had taken over his life. Federico saw a man who had given up all hope for a marriage, family, security, and happiness. He saw a man who cared not whether he lived or died. As he looked, Federico saw a man shrinking in the shadows—a man who had never stood in the light of grace.

"How can I feel this way?" Federico asked himself. "Panzon is a murderer. How can he deserve my sympathy? And yet—I feel such sorrow for him. My heart is filled with compassion. But is it my heart that has produced these feelings? My heart was filled with hatred. Where has all that hatred gone? What has changed everything that was in my heart?"

Then Federico thought, "It is in my heart that I sense your will, Lord. You are telling me that it is Panzon that I must help. That is the thing I must do. This is not my will, Lord—but yours. Still—everything has changed. One moment ago it was not my will. Now it is. It is exactly what I know I need to do. This is from you, Lord. Yes—I know. Alright my Lord. I submit my will to yours, I thank you."

At that moment Federico sensed a great peace flowing over him. It was a peace that he could not understand, and which he did not try to understand. It was inner-sensed. As he looked at Panzon he saw something far beyond humanity. It was a soul capable of salvation. It was a being moving toward a form of perfection. As Federico looked at Panzon, he saw a man full of promise, and he saw the face of a saint.

From across the desk, Panzon looked back at Federico. Panzon had a puzzled expression. It was an expression of deep wondering at what was to be.

"Pure compassion runs through my veins now," Federico thought. "I am your servant Lord, and Panzon will be my project. Yes, your will is now my will. They are as one. It will be done."

Suddenly, Federico realized that it was he, himself, who was changing. He no longer felt any need for revenge on Panzon. There was no feeling of hatred. It seemed to Federico that now two men were on paths of healing. Federico saw Panzon as a spiritual being rich with potential. "Bringing him to God would be the answer," he thought. "The permanent solution. The restoration of his hope. Panzon's despair could be replaced with hope. This is God's will," Federico thought, "and who am I to disagree—when obeying feels so good? Give Panzon friends, decent food, honest work, the promise of Heaven and even—the joy of the fellowship of Jesus."

Federico looked up at Panzon. He looked into his eyes. In a soft voice he said, "Now I forgive you—for everything."

Oh Lord, Federico thought, I see what you are doing. You have set Panzon and me on parallel paths. His path is to be out from the shadows and into the light, while my path is to know the release from hatred by feeling your compassion.

You showed me compassion produces forgiveness and true forgiveness leads to love. So then, my work is to be your obedient servant. I am to help him emerge from the

176

shadow of the tomb and stand in the light of eternal salvation.

Then Federico understood at a far deeper level of seeing and knowing. He realized the Lord told him to look at Panzon—and he obeyed. He looked, and during those moments he received the gift of seeing through the very eyes of God. As he saw one of God's own creations he understood that the Creator loves the thing he has created. In that intense moment of knowing, Federico was filled. He saw—and was filled with knowledge and peace—and change.

"If I stayed here would I confess my sins to you?" Panzon asked.

"Yes," Federico said. "I am not a priest, but I am a Christian who hears the sins of others often."

"Then can I get to know you first? Would you tell me a little about yourself?"

The primary thing you need to know about me is that I am a Christian because I accepted Christ as my personal redeemer." Federico said. He smiled and added, "Since then there have been moments when I have been allowed to see things."

"You see things?" Panzon asked. "What sort of things? Angels? Visions of the Holy Mother? What?"

"No, nothing miraculous. Nothing like that," Federico said. "They have been things that were quite ordinary. Or they *were*_ordinary until I saw them again. But then I saw them, for just a few moments, as I had never seen them before. I saw them with incredible clarity." Federico paused.

"So that's it?" Panzon asked. "Incredible clarity?"

"Oh no. It was much more than that." Federico said. "Along with the amazing clarity, there was a feeling that came over me. First it warmed my heart."

Panzon smiled. "Warmed your heart—like heart-burn—indigestion?"

"Hey, be serious. What I am describing are some of the most important feelings of my life."

"Okay, then tell me about those feelings."

"It always starts with a warmth in my heart and my heart beats fast. Then there is this mysterious sensation of being free. Being so light and clean. New and pure. Free of the past."

"Wait!" interrupted Panzon loudly. He lifted his hands over his head mimicking a military surrender. "You are going too fast for me. What things did you see at those times? Apostles? The gates of Heaven? The parade of the Saints?"

Federico looked surprised at the question. "Like I told you. Ordinary things. Common things."

"Yes, yes. I know that. But can you give me specifics?"

Federico was silent for a moment. Then he looked at Panzon and said, "Oh, the shape of a tree. Or the shadow of that tree at dawn. Or an ordinary drinking cup that became brilliant in the sun light. Once it was a tiny red flower such as I had never seen before. It was in a field in the midst of a two year drought, and it was in full blossom. It was gone the next day, but the – perfume of it remained in the air."

Federico looked away from Panzon before he continued in a softer voice. "These things seem to happen when I am alone with Jesus and in prayer. Sometimes I see them when I am literally talking to Jesus. But most often when I am listening."

Panzon looked away from Federico and said, "You must be some kind of a holy man, huh?"

"No. But I have been blessed."

"So you know about sin?"

"Everyone has sinned. Only Jesus was perfect. I was one of the worst sinners ever. I am just thankful that we have a merciful God."

"But you do not look, or sound, like a sinner."

Federico smiled at the comment. "That's because I try not to sin anymore. Yet, once I was bad..." his voice trailed off.

"And what sins did you commit?" Panzon asked.

"I was in the Revolutionary army during the war. You know all about that. I shot and killed twenty-five Nationalists."

179

"You were a sniper?"

"Long-range."

"You shot officers, yes?"

"After the first two, I shot only officers. That is correct."

"Ah, so you were one of our heroes."

"No. After some time, I couldn't fire anymore. So I was court martialed and sentenced to be executed."

"And which was the sin—that you killed twenty-five men that you couldn't kill any more than that?"

Federico glanced up at Panzon. "As the war was coming to an end, I was part of a squad that was sent up to the mountain villages. We shot and killed at least one man in every village so that all the villagers would remember to pay their taxes. That's when I stopped shooting at people. I shot at trees or into the air. The killings made me sick." Panzon lowered his eyes to avoid Federico's gaze.

"But I kept sinning," Federico said. "Sins of omission you see, I never tried to talk my comrades out of shooting civilians." His voice trailed off. He gazed out the window.

"How old were you then?"

"Oh, twenty-two," Federico said. "But I knew better," he added. "I had four years of combat. I should have tried to talk to them. Our squad must have killed about two hundred men—and boys—in those villages."

"And I suppose you never pointed a rifle at any other person after that?" Panzon asked.

"Yes, one time. I thought I hated him—but God loved him. And He would not let me fire. He covered my target with a grey mist."

Panzon leaned forward, his eyes wide, "A grey mist? Really?"

"Yes. And I've never seen anything like it again."

"So what happened?" Panzon asked. "What did you do?"

"I just walked away. Well, I walked away eventually. First I took a couple of chickens from that fellow's flock…"

"So," Panzon interrupted. "You have stolen a few chickens yourself?" He was smiling.

"Guilty as charged. Then I took the rifle back to the store where I stole it and gave that man his rifle and one of the chickens."

"And that man you wanted to kill—with your stolen rifle—what happened to him? What did he do that made you want him dead? And what was the grey mist anyway?" Panzon asked the questions rapidly. His smile was gone.

"That man?" Federico asked. "That man is you! For seven years I hated you—or the memory of you. Now I can no longer hate you because God showed me that he has a purpose for your life. That's what the mist was; it was the Holy Spirit keeping you alive." Federico stopped speaking and looked down at the floor. After a moment, without looking up at Panzon, he said, "You ate my food drank my coffee…"

"All the guards had orders to starve the prisoners into submission."

"It was inhumane treatment!"

"We were following orders."

"Si! Si!" Federico's voice became loud. "We were both following orders weren't we?" He paused for several moments. The veins at his temples turned thick and blue. They pulsated. "But they were orders that we should have questioned—and disobeyed."

"Disobeyed?" Now Panzon's voice had a tremor. "In the Revolutionary army? We would have been executed on the spot. I think you know that!"

"Wait. There's more to the story. Why did I hate you? You took a letter I wrote to my mother. You took it and read it to the other guards. Then you kept the envelope and found my mother. You brought her wine—and lies. You wanted to seduce her. Instead, with your lies, you killed her. She died of a broken heart. She thought I had died and that belief killed her. Can any man have more reason than that to hate another man?"

"Are you going to punish me?" Panzon asked.

"No, of course not. I don't even want to judge you."

"I am sorry, sir. I never wanted her to hurt—much less kill her. What can I do to make it up to you? Tell me how can I make amends?"

"Do you realize those were sins against people and God Himself?"

"Yes, certainly."

"Can you say you are sorry for all of your sins? And say it with a truthful heart?"

"Yes. I am truly sorry for my sins. I hope to never sin again."

"Do you mean it?"

"Yes, yes!"

"You have taken a gigantic step forward, Panzon."

"Yes, but what can I do to pay the price for my sins? A three day fast? A novena? A hundred rosaries? What can I do for penance?"

"You ask me what you can do. I will tell you Panzon. You knew the prisoners called you Panzon, right?"

"Yes. I knew. Everybody knew that."

"Alright Panzon. This is what you can do. Sit there. And listen. We are going to have a discussion. Listen carefully. It may be the most important information you have ever heard. You may never have the opportunity to hear it again. We never know. So listen. That is what you must do now. Agreed?"

"Yes, of course."

"Are you aware that all men have sinned?" Federico asked.

"I was five years in the revolutionary army," Panzon said. "I have seen every sin possible. I am aware of sin, yes."

"So you have seen sin. And you yourself have sinned. In looking back at sin, where does that leave you? How do you feel about it now?"

"I wish I could change the past," Panzon said. "But what's done is done."

"Ah," Federico said it with a sigh. "Maybe <u>we</u> can't change the past, but there is one who can change it for us."

Panzon looked across the room at Federico. "Yes? Go on."

"Our Lord, Jesu Christo. He's the only one who can save anyone."

"No. It is not possible," said Panzon. "How can I go to God when he is the one who knows about all my sins? God must hate me."

Federico smiled then. "It's just the opposite," he said. "God loves you so much that he sacrificed his only Son so that you could have eternal life."

"He can change the past?"

"He can make it right. You see, the price has already been paid."

"The price?"

"For all the sins of the world—including yours."

"It must have been some high price," Panzon said.

Federico answered, "It was out of this world."

Panzon's eyes began to fill with tears. He closed his eyes and said, "When you close your eyes you probably see godly things. When I close mine, I do not see God at work."

"What do you see?"

"I see—and I feel—that I am slipping down, down, a dark hole. I am falling straight down, and there is nothing that can stop my fall. I reach out, but there is nothing to grab on to. I feel alone. And what I see is that it is getting darker and darker. And I am alone."

"What you see," said Federico, "is your life—a life of sin—the burden of un-confessed sin. And," Federico paused and smiled, "you can change all of that—right now."

"How?"

"Tell me. Who are you?"

"A man who has lived without God," Panzon said. "And a chicken thief."

"Then what are you?"

"A sinner."

"Who is responsible for all those sins?"

"I am."

"They can be taken away right now," Federico said. "If you ask."

"You can do that for me?" Panzon asked.

"Not me," Federico said. "You ask God for forgiveness, and the burden will be lifted."

"Me—ask God? I have never been further away from God than right now. The pit I am in is bottomless. No person can reach me where I am."

"I agree. Because no person can do that. But God, the Father, and his Son, Jesus can do that—and more. They created the universe together, and they can take their creations out of sin. Do you understand that the dark hole you are in is real?"

"Yes, I know that."

"Do you understand that you are in that hole because of sin?"

"Certainly."

"Are you willing to turn away from sin?"

"Yes, yes, of course."

"And do you understand that Jesus can close that gap that now exists between you and God, and He can bring you into a life with God?"

"Yes, I understand. Only Jesus can do it."

"That's right, only Jesus can do it."

"And do you agree now to turn from sin?"

"Oh yes."

"Good. Then tell God of your decision. Tell Him right now."

"Lord God. I am so sorry," Panzon said. "I have sinned my life nearly away. I choose to turn away from sin right now. I hope to sin no more. I put that life behind me. I can see how it has kept us apart. I don't want us to be apart. Please help me."

"And do you understand who lifted that burden of sin from your shoulders?"

"It was Jesus—by dying on the cross," said Panzon.

"This would be a good time to thank him."

"Thank you, Lord Jesus. Thank you for dying on the cross to pay my debt. Thank you for letting me know the price has been paid."

Federico stood up and moved across the room. He sat down next to Panzon. "How thankful are you to Jesus?" he asked.

"He died in my place," Panzon answered. "I am very, very thankful."

"Thankful enough to turn your life over to him?"

"Yes. Oh yes."

"Tell him—not me. Tell him so he can hear it."

With his eyes closed, one hand raised above him, Panzon prayed, "I need you Jesus. In every part of my life. Sweep me clean. Keep me from sin. Fill me, Lord, with your Spirit. With your new life I see you as my new Savior, new Lord, and new Life. You are my hope. Come into my heart and soul. I accept your sacrifice, your love and…"

"Your grace," added Federico.

"Your grace," Panzon repeated.

Federico put his hand on Panzon's arm and asked. "Did you feel Jesus coming into your heart?"

"I felt relief from sin," said Panzon. "And then I felt joy in my heart. I feel like a child again. It's something like starting over."

"All pure again?"

"Yes. With lots of energy. The air I'm inhaling has no dust in it. And the joy—the joy—seems to be filling me," said Panzon.

"That's the joy of knowing eternal life—for the first time. And it is the Holy Spirit in you. Rejoice in that. Know that when you die you will be taken up into Heaven. No purgatory. No penance. Just joy."

"For a time, your eyes were closed," Federico said. "What was it? What did you see just then? Can you describe it?"

"Yes, my friend. Yes. I had been in that dark hole for so long. And there was nothing to stop me from falling further and further down into it. Nothing to grab onto," he said. "But I looked up and there was a light above me. And it was like a magnet. It pulled me up and up until I sort of flowed out of the hole and into the brightness of joy. It was wonderful. I still feel it.!"

"Almost like a birth canal, right?"

"Yes. Almost," said Panzon. "But this was a birth of the heart and body—not the whole body."

"That's called being 'born again', said Federico. "And in this new life, you are going to be what God wills you to be. You have been reborn into a new life with a new journey. Enjoy it, my friend, enjoy it."

The two men stood up, shook hands—and suddenly embraced. Each man hugged the other with one arm and slapped the back of the other with his free hand. They grinned at each other. Then Panzon said, "It feels like I have returned from the dead."

Federico added, "I know. I know. And no more calling you by your old name of Panzon. From now on you are to be known as Brother Forgiven. Okay?"

"Okay," he said. "And another thing—no more stealing chickens for either of us."

They hugged and laughed together.

Chapter 13
Fourth Meeting of the
X-Treme Book Club

Clayton talked with Jackson. Laura paged through her book. Jerry dropped into one of the stuffed chairs while he kicked his backpack under the chair. Suddenly, Jerry jumped up and shouted, "Look everybody. Look who is trying to sneak in unnoticed. Nice shades Emma."

With a trace of a smile Emma sat down quickly. "Thanks for announcing my late entrance."

"Oh, they all noticed," said Jerry. "I'm the only one rude enough to yell it out. The glasses new?"

"No." Emma took off her sunglasses. "Sorry to interrupt," she said. There were dark shadows under her eyes. "Where were we?"

"Laura just informed us that a sincere confession is necessary," Jerry said. "But I'm thinking that your eyes always look so tired. I bet you work in a cubicle with poor lights, and you are too shy to ask for better lighting. Either that, or you are getting a glare off your monitor screen. Am I right? Which is it?"

"Jerry," Emma said. "I never know whether you are trying to help—or not." She squinted at each person in the group. "My problem has nothing to do with lighting." Her voice was soft. "My problem is lack of sleep."

"Guilty conscience?" asked Jerry.

"I should be so lucky," Emma said. "My problem is just a lack of sleep."

Clayton looked intently at Emma. "Most people suffer from insomnia at some time in their lives. Common problem. Difficult to treat. Numerous causes…" His voice trailed off.

"Hey Doc," Jerry said. "Fix her. Don't just sit there mumbling. Help her sleep. Get the red out. Cure her. And hurry up before she bleeds to death out of her eye sockets!"

"Sleep disorders require a specialist," Clayton said.

"Doc, just do it!"

"I guess I can try," Clayton said. "So Emma, this insomnia, is it the kind where you fall asleep at first but then wake up and are unable to get back to sleep? Or is it the kind where you can't get to sleep in the first place?"

"I wake up and can't get back to sleep for hours afterward."

"You are awakened by a dream then?"

"More like a nightmare."

"Same, or similar, dream over and over?"

"Same. Over and over."

"Reoccurring dreams are usually the subconscious telling us that something is wrong. The dream uses symbols that may be difficult to interpret. I'm not the kind of doctor that does that."

"Show us how you heal people," Jerry spoke slowly. "Emma is an important part of our little group and right now she has a problem, so won't you try to help?"

Clayton looked over at Jackson. "Shouldn't we be discussing the book?" Clayton asked. "That's what we signed up for, you know."

"As long as you asked me, I'll tell you. I think when one person in our group has a problem—then we all have a problem," Jackson said. "Emma is willing to share it with us. I believe she is wise to do so. And if you think you can help her, then that's exactly what you must try to do. The book can wait."

"Hey, I haven't agreed to share anything," Emma said.

"That's alright," Jackson said. "It's your call. Just think about it before you decide. I have found that when I share, I invariably learn more about myself. We are social beings. I think we were designed to share."

"That could be," Emma said. "Except that I'm embarrassed by all of this."

"Don't worry," Laura said. "We want to help."

"But I'm afraid," Emma said. "When I tell you about myself—you guys are all brains—you'll see how stupid I really am. That's what I'm scared of."

"Emma, Emma," Laura spoke in a whisper. "We all have that same fear. But we can ease it by opening up to this group. That's because you are among friends. Friends don't judge. They help."

Jerry stood up and slowly walked over to Emma. He stood directly in front of her. "I won't laugh," he said. "I promise. Okay?"

Emma looked up at Jerry. "Okay," she said. She did not squint.

Without a word, Jerry returned to his seat.

"It's the nightmare," Emma began. "Two or three times a week. 'Scares the stuffing out of me. I wake up sweaty, heart racing, and hands trembling."

"Okay," Jackson said. "Keep going."

"It starts with fear. Fear and frustration. It's the fear that I will fail the test and frustration that I won't even be able to take the test." As she spoke, Emma's hands began to shake.

"You see, I can't move my feet. They're stuck in some thick, sticky mud. So right off, I get this feeling of being trapped—held down. And I'm late for the test. Everything depends on the test. I haven't studied enough for it. And it is being held in a room that is usually locked so even if I find the room I probably can't get into it. I'm late for it already. I'm not prepared to take the test, but if I don't pass it—I know something terrible will happen to me. Then I will never be able to make it right, and I will have failed forever."

"Forever is a long time," the moderator said.

"I know," Answered Emma. "And that's what makes it so scary. It's like the message is: 'Pass the exam—or be doomed'. So I expect to fail, and when I do, my mother will be disappointed. She will never forgive me. I wake up shaking and can't get back to sleep for a long, long time, but when I do get to sleep, I wake up every ten minutes. It takes me a long time to calm down. A long time."

Emma paused, then and the room was silent. "Well, that's my reoccurring nightmare. Any of you guys explain it? Can you make it go away?"

"And this nightmare, you say you have it two or three times a week. Is that right?"

"Yes, Doctor," said Emma.

"But you also have other dreams, right?"

"Very rarely. And they don't bother me. This one scares me and wakes me up and keeps me awake!"

"Okay, okay," Clayton said. "Now don't be offended, but I think I need to ask a personal question. Is your father part of your life? You know, close? Do you talk—get together—see each other?"

"No sir. I never met my father. He left my mother when I was a baby."

"And again, a personal thing. Is your mother what we might call 'bossy'?"

Instantly Jerry sat up and said, "Is that the latest psychiatric terminology? Bossy?"

"Oh yes," Emma said. "My mother calls me incessantly. She leaves about ten messages on my answering machine every day. She wants to know everything I do or say—or even think."

"So you sometimes feel she is judging you?"

"Constantly. The truth is, I can't do anything right in her eyes. That's why I have my own place. I can't live with her." Emma's eyes filled with tears. "Sorry," she whispered.

"No need to apologize. Your feelings are quite normal. Do you have any brothers or sisters?"

"No. None."

"And you had your mother's full attention?"

"Yes. I suppose so."

"And were there other men after your father left? A second marriage? A close male friend? Anything like that?"

"Yes and no. There were a few. But never anything that lasted very long. For a while my aunt Tilly—mother's sister—came to live with us. But they weren't good friends. I think it was just to share expenses."

Clayton stroked his chin with one hand and held his other hand up, palm out—to Emma. "Okay, okay. I think we have enough to work with here," Clayton said. "Your father left sometime soon after your mother came back from the hospital with you. In her mind, his leaving was at least partly—your fault. You may not remember it, but your subconscious remembers the effects of it—like being scolded for getting mud on your shoes. The test you fear is the test of whether or not you can meet life's challenges and a critical mother can give you the idea that you will always fail that test.

In your nightmare, you are locked out of the room where the test is on-going because you were made to feel as if you were not good enough to be part of the family. Your mother's life did not turn out the way she wished, and she had only you to blame. You lived your most impressionable years learning to doubt yourself. You were given signs—verbal and non-verbal—that you drove father away and ruined your mother's life. When judged by your mother, you failed. Now when you are judged by your sub-conscience, you fear failing."

"Yes," said Emma. "You could be right."

Clayton looked around the room and smiled. "That's how I see it", he said. Then he again looked at each member of the book club. Laura was the first to speak. "There you have a typical lesson in modern psychology," she said. "Blame the mother."

Clayton stopped smiling.

"I suppose that's a good analysis," Jerry said. "But Doc—now do something for Emma. Tell her how to cure what's wrong. Right now, Emma is left hanging. That's worse than before. Come on man, do the follow-up. Write the prescription. Speak the cure!"

Clayton looked at Jerry but said nothing.

"Doc, how many years did you study in Pre Med, then Medical school, then your residency program with majors in bill-bundling and estate planning?" asked Jerry. "All that education! Now do something with it."

"Give me a break, kid," Clayton said. "I was trying to figure what would be best for the patient. It's not easy to undo the damage of a critical parent. One idea might be to do a self-congratulatory scrapbook.

"Emma, go to an office supply store, get a fresh notebook and a package of gold stars," Clayton said. "In the notebook write down every success you experienced since high school, every project you worked on and your role in it. Quote all the compliments you received. Yes, and set up some boundaries for your mother and implement everyone."

"Right there," Jerry said. "That's good."

"Fill up the notebook," the doctor continued. "Put gold stars on the stories that give you the most pleasure— your highest achievements. Then read through the notebook every night. Aloud. Read the ones with the gold stars twice. Enjoy yourself—your success. Take credit for all of it. Get the idea? Including college—list the sororities that wanted you and you turned down. List every course in which you received an 'A'. Quote every praise you received from your counselors. That's the stuff that will pick you up. Make it required reading for every night. Yes, that's what you should do. That's my recommendation."

The group returned to silence. Emma slowly pulled out her sunglasses and slipped them back on.

"I don't get you Doc," Jerry said. He spoke slowly pausing between every word. "You have under-estimated our Emma. Even If she agreed with your scrapbooking idea, her sub-conscience would never buy it. You should know that." Jerry's face was flushed and his speech became more rapid. "What's wrong with you Doc? Is this a bad hair day for you? Can I get you a cup of coffee? Or a glass of water? Or maybe a nice bowl of hemlock? Although I don't know where I could score hemlock at this time of night. Or even a bowl—for that matter."

"Jerry! Jerry!" Laura called out. "I agree with what you are saying, but don't think it's doing any good. So, let me try a different interpretation."

The group became silent. Emma sat forward. With one hand she twirled some of the hair on the back of her head. With the other hand she waved wide circles as she spoke.

"Can't you see," Emma said. Her voice was barely audible. "I'm done. Beaten. There's no place left for me to turn."

"How do you mean?" asked Laura.

"The nightmares." Both hands were making circles in the air. "I used to be tired in the mornings. Lately, I get mad at that dream. See, it's wearing me down. I'm afraid it's turned everything into some sort of a duel."

"Duel?"

"Yeah. Some kind of contest. An important contest. And I'm losing now."

"You have gone from insomnia to fear. Is that right?" Jackson asked.

"I have a dream sort of like that," said Jerry. "There's this big dog chasing me. And every time I look back he's gaining."

"You don't get it Jerry," Emma said. "This nightmare isn't about getting a dog bite." She dropped both hands into her lap. "I give up," she said. "If I don't fight it, I'll lose and if I do fight it—I'll still lose."

"That's not so," Laura said. "You just need a little help. And I'll help you. Together—we are going to finish your dream."

Emma looked at Laura. "If I finish the dream I'm afraid I might die."

"No, no," Laura answered. "When we finish it, you will live—live as never before."

Emma looked at Laura. "How do you think you can help me?" she asked. "Don't you see I've been struggling with this thing for ten or twelve years?" Emma stopped speaking then but continued to stare at Laura.

"You always get so scared, that you wake yourself up without finishing it." Laura said. "The thing is, I had the same dream for many years. I finally decoded it. Now I can help you because I know how it ends."

"You do?"

"Yes—and it's so good."

"Then tell me. Tell me now."

"Well, that mud your feet were stuck in, it represents the earth—or the world. Your subconscious wants you to find true answers—the solutions to your problems. It wants you to find spiritual answers. It knows you tried some of the 'world's' paths. But you found those things only work for a short time. Then they pull you down and keep you from moving ahead. They are never enough."

"That's true," Emma said. "I think I need the spiritual answers. Like Federico found with that silver cup."

"Hang on, girl," Laura said. "The best part is yet to come."

"Interesting," Jackson said.

Laura continued, "Emma that fear you feel was the fear of missing out. As if the results of one test would determine your place in this life—and the next. The fear was the terrible fear of missing out on eternal life, and there was no chance for you. You couldn't pass the final examination on your own. You couldn't even get into the room where the test was given. You were the 'outsider'; and once in a while, did you think you could hear the sound of singing coming from that locked room?"

"Yes, yes, I could. Not always; just once in a while," Emma said. "And that choir sounded so joyful."

"Oh, I know," Laura said with a smile. "And at other times, you couldn't hear anything. Right?" Laura's smile faded.

"That's is so, so right," Emma said. How could you know?"

"I'm not sure," answered Laura. "Maybe my feet were in the mud-hole right next to you. But I can remember the panic I felt because I was on the outside. I was afraid I would be outside forever."

"That's about where I usually wake up," Emma said. She pulled her sunglasses off to wipe a tear. "I wake up out of breath like I am suffocating with fear. Like death is near, and I have nothing to hang on to. Nothing."

"But you know that the door to the room is just ahead of you, right?"

"Yes. I can see it."

"Listen to me, Emma. On the other side of that door is the answer."

"I knew someone was there, but I didn't know who," Emma said.

"You know the answer is there," Laura said. "And that knowledge gives you just enough strength to pull your feet out of the mud and get to the door. The instant you get to the door it swings open, and the man who opened it stands there. He says, 'I've been waiting for you."

"Emma, that man is Jesus, and when he invites you to enter that room—that room of salvation—you accept his invitation. He is the only one who can let you in. He is the key. There is no other path to heaven. And you will feel loved and safe; you might even join the choir. And that man will look at you with the most amazing eyes you have ever seen. He will look through you, but he will say to you, we are going to have some interesting talks. Then he will start to walk away, but he will stop and turn back to you and say, 'We have eternity, you know.'"

"And when he's gone, another man will welcome you. He has sparkling eyes. And you will ask him, 'Who was that man?' and he will answer, 'That's my Son, the Messiah, the Redeemer, and the Christ.'"

"Now here's the best part, Emma. Listen carefully. That's when you will ask, 'How can I be allowed to stay here? I didn't pass the test. I didn't even take it.' And the man with the sparkly eyes will look at you, and he will say, '*My son—took the test—for you.* He paid the price. For all eternity. When he paid the price with his life, he took your test. Now enjoy the heaven that was planned for you from the beginning.'"

"Yes," said Emma. "That's it isn't it? That's it."

"Sure is, girl. You're out of the mud, and you accepted the invitation to go through the door. Your future, your spiritual success is secure. You are in God's hands. Understand?"

"Yes. That's what I've been looking for all along. The Federico experience," Emma said.

"I think I would call it the salvation experience."

"I guess I could use some one-on-one tutoring," Emma said "Would you help me?"

"You ready to do that right now?" asked Laura.

"You bet."

"Then let's scoot over to the coffee shop and grab a booth. Excuse us, guys. We're going to settle something—now—for eternity."

Clayton watched the two women depart. "That seemed pretty intense."

"Blame it all on Abbot Federico," said Jackson. "Reading about him brings out some intense reactions."

Jerry glanced at the two men and quickly looked away. "So you guys feel it too?"

"Feel what?" Clayton asked.

"Change. Everything is changing," said Jerry. He took off his cap and scratched his scalp. "Now that it's just us men, I was wondering if you guys noticed it."

Jackson said, "Define what you mean by 'it'?"

"Well I don't know if I'm growing up or being brain-washed."

Jerry's eyes narrowed. "You guys—the over 30 crowd—and the book we're reading—it's all—going strange. It's like mind games, and I'm being pushed around. Ya know?"

"Before you open your mouth again," Jackson said, "Think. Then explain what you are thinking. And Jerry, be specific."

"Oh sure, be specific," he says. "It's not easy for me," Jerry said, "There's a new feeling inside of me. And with it seems to come an idea that I have never had before. It seems like I'm being asked to give up my self-centeredness. Before tonight I always planned on using my life to accumulate great wealth. Now—there's a new plan. And it's taking over. My goals seem selfish—shallow. Like they would be taking my life and wasting it. Maybe even wasting the time of those around me. All of a sudden I can see the difference between wasting my life and using my life for others. The old way would stand in the way of relationships; the new way would deepen them." Jerry stopped speaking and looked into the distance.

"Well Jerry, we're reading about a man," Jackson said, "a man who becomes a saint. I believe his story has given many readers a transfusion. New blood, you might say."

"Sure, that's a big part of it," Jerry said. "So, I felt like we are witnesses to a higher form of humanity. Maybe that's what literature is all about. Is that it? Showing us other levels of caring for others? Even higher levels of responsibility?"

Jackson smiled and said, "Higher levels of responsibility and self-centeredness are about as opposite as any two life styles can be."

Jackson turned to Clayton. "You've been unusually quiet for a while. What do you think—or feel—at this point?"

"We didn't have any discussion about the book tonight. The discussion was what I came for, not my feelings." Clayton said.

"Interesting, Doctor," Jackson said. "Very interesting. Let's see if that attitude doesn't change over the next four weeks."

"Oh? Why? What's coming up?"

"Well," Jackson answered, "Abbot Federico's story has only just begun."

Chapter 14
The Enemy

"Bring them in," Federico called out. "The brothers are still here—waiting."

The chapel door opened and Brother Mason walked in with a middle-aged woman and a young woman. The younger woman looked like a small version of her mother. Both wore peasant skirts and blouses. Both had thick, straight black hair. The difference, other than the two sizes, was in their eyes. The girl looked around with eyes full of fear. The mother's eyes seemed full of anger. The girl held her mother's hand. She said, "They all saw me, mama, so can we go home now?"

"Maria, Selena," Mason announced, "These are the brothers of our monastery." With a sweeping motion he indicated the group of robed men. "And this is our leader, Abbot Federico."

"You are the Abbot?" the mother asked. "Yes?"

"How may I help you and your daughter?"

"You can scare away evil spirits, yes? She has two voices. Her voice used to be high like a small bird. But the other voice is low. Basso profundo. If she talks with that voice she will say strange things. I do not know the words she uses then. And there are times when she jumps around and bumps into things. And there are other times when she is quiet. Then she cries.

"People in town have told me you can fix her. Is that not so?"

"Please come in," Federico said. "We will ask the Lord to heal her."

As they entered the monastery the mother said, "If this 'thing' in her is an evil spirit please make it go away. You will do that? You fix her so I have my real daughter back. This cannot be my daughter—the daughter I raised for 20 years. This is a different person. My daughter used to sing like an angel. With a high voice. She did not jump around like a crazy animal. Now her voice is very, very low. Many times it sounds like she speaks with two or three voices coming out of her."

"I will do what I can by asking Jesus to drive out the evil spirit."

The mother and daughter walked up to Federico. "She's a good girl. She's a good girl," the mother said. Meanwhile, the girl coughed and twitched. At times she would grimace and sudden strange sounds would erupt from her throat. Her eyes were wide open and fearful.

Mason leaned close to the mother and said, "Abbot Federico is becoming famous for his healings."

Federico heard Mason's comment and said, "Nothing happens by my power. It is only by the power of God." As

Federico spoke a tremor came over the girl and she shook uncontrollably. Federico waited until the shaking stopped and said, "We are happy to see you both here. Please sit down." He pointed at two chairs that had been placed in the center of the aisle. "In a moment or two I will ask all these brothers to pray with me." He paused, "Ah, I'm sorry; what are your names again?"

Immediately Mason answered, "Mother Maria and her daughter Selena."

"And how old are you Selena?" Federico asked.

The girl looked up and away. She did not answer.

Maria said, "She is twenty, and she's a good girl—but thing..." her voice trailed off.

"Our Lord and Savior Jesu Christo told us to not be afraid," Federico said. "He said he would be with us when we gather together in his name. We have just finished hearing the mass—as we were gathered in his name. Now we remain here to pray for Selena—to pray in His name. Fear not. Our Lord is with us."

After several moments of silence Federico said, "Now let us prepare to pray." As men accustomed to seldom speaking, the Brothers sat or knelt in silence. Father Delgado stood behind Federico. Brother Benedict, a short, dark man with massive hands, feet and a protruding jaw, stood alone near the front door. Maria and daughter sat in the two chairs with Mason standing directly behind them. Then Federico knelt before the girl. She continued to cough and grimace.

209

Occasionally her right arm flew upward making a strange salute and her head would jerk backwards. As soon as she could again regain control of herself she would look around the room. Some of the men were watching her. Others had their heads bowed. Her eyes were glistening with tears.

"Maria—named after Mary the mother of God," Federico spoke loudly, "you have brought forth a beautiful girl…" He stopped speaking and remained silent for several minutes. Suddenly, he resumed in the same voice, "and the extra sounds and movements we hear and see today—we fully understand as not a penance, not an evil force, not a sin—but as a tragic disease. We see little Selena here as a child of God—a shy, bright, beautiful creation of God—in the need of our prayers."

The girl's coughing became louder as Federico spoke.

"And that disease we know, was not part of God's intention for little Selena when he created her. That disease had no place in God's mind—at creation   or now."

Then Federico's voice became low and he prayed, "Our Lord, we believe—and know—that you are the creator of the universe. We see the beauty and the perfection of your creation all around us. For this, we thank you. We firmly believe you love your creatures.

"You, who created all of nature, want no part of it to be wasted. You, who created energy, want no energy to be lost." Federico stopped praying, straightened up and looked around the room. "Brothers, are we of one mind about this?"

All of the men nodded silently.

Federico continued, "So look upon us this day Father. See your child as perfect…" His prayer was interrupted by the girl's coughing and twitching. The cough was turning into a barking sound. "See her being made perfect," he prayed, "by the amazing power of your will, by the power of the sacrifice of Your Son and by the power of Your Holy Spirit. Look upon her now." The girl's right arm suddenly flew up over her head nearly lifting her off the chair. For a moment her voice was a low growl.

Federico continued, "We pray that You would look upon Selena as a wonderful part of your great creation. We who gaze upon her here on earth see her beauty. We who humble ourselves in prayer see your love at work in her. But only You, Father can see her nervous system."

The girl's arms were now flinging around with such force that her chair was inching across the floor. Her mother stood up and pressed her hands down on the girl's shoulders.

"Look into her," Federico prayed. "See those neurons that you created—see those making perfect connections to and from her brain and the signals being received exactly as they were sent. Father, set those electrons moving in pure and perfect paths. And let it give You the glory as we also see the beauty of Your creation—all made pure by the blood of your Son."

The girl was beginning to relax. Her arms and head were still. She appeared to be listening to the prayer.

There was a long period of silence during which Federico's eyes were closed, his head was bowed and his lips moved slightly. During this time Selena was also quiet and calm.

"Lord, we believe," Federico resumed praying aloud, "that you have the power to remove any disease from Your sight. We pray that You remove this disease now. We pray that You will see only the perfect result of Your love. Look at your child now. See her through your loving eyes. See only that which is beautiful, good, and perfect. We see Selena as the perfect child of a perfect God. We pray it is Your will and only Your will is to be done here, today."

There was another period of silence. The girl, her mother, and the men neither spoke nor moved. Finally, Federico said, "Amen."

As Federico finished the prayer, he stood up and a collective sigh passed through the room. One brother who had been kneeling was struggling to get back on his feet. Several of the others were smiling.

Suddenly a strange silence filled the room. The sound of chairs being dragged from place to place stopped. There was no conversation. The monks stopped moving. All eyes turned toward Selena.

"Gentlemen," she said. Her voice had become low. Smooth and low. "Can't any of you understand that if you stay here your lives will be coming to an end? Can't you see what lies just ahead? It's change. We all must change as this country changes."

"Hey, girl," Andrew shouted. "What's changing?"

"I'll tell you what's changing. Oil has been discovered. It sits in the sand under us and all around us. It's an ocean of oil. It waits to jump up and be sold to the rest of the world. All that oil is here, under us right now. We are sitting on a world-wide market, and we get the profits. This is your opportunity to renounce your vows of poverty, leave this monastery tonight and celebrate your changed lives."

"Wait a minute," Brother Andrew said. "We take vows quite seriously. We don't renounce anything on a whim. I don't think you know what you're asking."

Selena smiled. "Oh, I know about vows," she said. "But I never had the chance to get out of them. You men don't know just how lucky you are. This is your chance to jump from being peasants to being incredibly wealthy. This is the time to make your move. There is no risk because the oil is here. Under us. Right now. You will be receiving bundles of cash. The oil economy will make many men rich. You can be part of those men. Why choose to be poor when you can have great wealth?

"Do you remember what it felt like to get enough sleep?" Selena said. "At least eight hours every night in a comfortable bed with clean sheets and a soft pillow with a cool cover. Sleep when you want to. Even sleep during the day. There are other things to do during the night. Leave this prison and taste the thrills of the world. A naked woman in bed with you is a gift from god and a woman who wants you is a natural thing. Extreme pleasure can be had from women. Enjoy them as you wish. You can have it all. That's right; you can have it all.

"Do you remember the taste of beef steak with French fried potatoes?" Selena said. "Remember how the steak could be seared on the outside but pink on the inside? Remember how it could be cut up into steaming chunks of flavor? Leave this place. Eat what you wish. Eat as much as you want. And never, never, be hungry again.

"Now let's get to the important part," Selena said. "I'm talking about the recognition you receive when you speak. When you are wealthy and you speak, others will listen. They will follow. Being wealthy will make you famous. Even admired.

"So, don't be afraid," she said. "Step out into the real world. Renounce the vows you took when you were much younger. You are wiser now. Leave this building. Leave the restrictions that have been placed upon you by the Abbot. Stand up to him. Stand up for yourselves and your futures. Leave this place while you can.

"Are you listening to me," Selena asked. "Or did I lose you when I mentioned a naked woman? If that's what you have been thinking about then good. It means you are still alive. But do you call yourselves men? If so, then behave like men. Make manly decisions. Make those decisions now.

Come over here and talk with me. I'll tell you much more about the world you left years ago. And I'll tell you what it will look like very soon. If you decide to stay in this monastery you will regret it for the rest of your lives. Instead of regrets come over here and we can talk. It won't hurt you to get more information. Let's do that now. Plan to free yourselves of the vows of poverty, Selena said. "Show your readiness to become wealthy by departing from this ancient building with its ancient ways of thinking. Great wealth and all the things money buys—they're all yours when you say good-bye to this place."

"Ah, Abbot, sir," Mason called out, "I don't like where this seems to be going. Can I throw this kid out? Maybe even out on her backside?" Several of the monks began clapping.

"No, no," Maria called out from where she was sitting in a corner. "My Selena is a good girl. And what's so wrong with what she's saying? She's not telling you to sin. She's just telling you to take the money from the oil profits."

"Let Selena talk," Federico said. "I would like every brother to hear what kinds of sly attacks we are subjected to. Listen well. Listen how the half-truths are mixed in with the lies."

Brother Francisco, the oldest of the monks cleared his throat and the room quieted down. "Little girl," he said, "If I were to renounce my vows or leave this monastery, it would be like betraying Jesus my redeemer. I cannot betray

Jesus. And I'll not betray Jesus." Francisco paused for a moment and smiled slightly. "That's my bottom line. So, brothers, I cannot betray Jesus because He cares for me."

"Oh, so," Selena shouted. "You won't betray your god. But has he ever betrayed you? What makes you so sure he cares for you?

"You idiots," Selena snarled. Her lips did not move. The words seemed to burst out of her throat. Her eyes were half-closed.

"Am I talking to men? Or are you a heard of sleepy oxen?

"You idiots! Two of your brothers, Julius and Roberto are in the infirmary dying right now. They have suffered for years. Did your god of mercy hear your prayers to ease their pain? Does he care enough to hear your prayers?

"Right now nearly half of your chickens are starving. Watch their agony because you are next. And when it happens will your God care enough to provide you with food?

"Now that World War II is over, the rest of the world is celebrating. They are eating three meals every day. They drink alcohol far into the night. Every night. They have sex until they become so sick of it they invent all sorts of perversions. Does your God care enough for you to invite you to the celebration?

"That war killed off much of the populations of both Germany and Japan. Did your God step in and stop any part of that slaughter? Does your God care about human life? Or your life? Or any life?

"The next generation will be so caught up in taking drugs that half of them will die of overdoses. That will be called, 'the new norm.' Have you seen your God care enough to stop the rising death rate?

"What good have your years of singing and praying done? What good has come from your lives spent in periods of silence, poverty, obedience, chastity, and prayer? Have any of you accomplished anything worthwhile?

"You idiots," Selena shouted. "When you die, nobody will mourn for you. Your God will not weep for you. Your God will not see, hear, or care. When you die, your god won't even notice.

"So abandon your childish fantasies of pleasing your God. Do it now. The future is yours for the asking. Come to me and we'll talk one-on-one. Come to me and find rest. More than rest. Wealth, comfort, gourmet food, wine, sex, fame, respect, prestige, all yours, all that the world offers. Don't be afraid to join in. Choose now—or forever hold your peace."

"Just a minute," Brother Andrew said. "Selena, young lady, the oil under our feet belongs to our country. Right?"

"Si. Right." Her voice was calm.

"And when the profits start rolling in, those profits will be split up and given to the citizens of this country. Right?"

"You are exactly right," Selena said.

"And the monks of this branch of the Benedictine order are citizens. Right?"

"Right. Now can we move on?" Selena spoke quickly. "I have lots to cover yet. Lots of good news."

"No, wait," Andrew interrupted. "Please explain why it is so important that my brothers and I must leave this monastery? It's our home. For many of us it's the only home we've ever had."

At that moment a large, black fly flew into the room. It landed on Selena's cheek. She made no move to make it go away. For several minutes the fly walked over the girl's face. Then it stopped on her chin. As Selena spoke, the fly remained on her chin.

"You all must leave this place," Selena said. "Because the president of the oil corporation, who desires to give you money, wants only team players for his personnel."

Federico laughed. "When the term 'team player' comes up it usually means the 'players' are going to have to go along with a moral decision of the sort that no Christian would ever approve."

"The president of the oil company wants to give you the profits. Okay."

"Hey," Andrew said. "Who is the oil company president?"

"It will be president Garcia," Selena answered.

"Can't you see?" Federico said. His voice was firm. "After the oil rigs are strategically set up and pumping, Garcia will take over as interim manager of the operation. Then he'll be running the country, the oil, and everything else in it."

"Holy cow," Mason blurted, "so that's what nationalizing means. It's taking the industry away from the owners and give it to the people!"

"And it makes the people very happy," Selena said.

"Is it legal?" Mason asked.

"If the government does it, it's legal," Federico said. "It's not moral but it's legal. All that's left then is for Garcia to declare himself Presidente-for-life. That's legal too."

"But that would give him the chance to do away with all elections," Mason said. "It could make him into a dictator."

"Really? What is he now? What has he been for the last thirty years?" Federico said. "He's a wise, immoral man."

Selena glanced around the room. There was no sound and her head fell back as she relaxed. She appeared to be asleep.

"Brothers, we are witnessing the dark side of the supernatural," Federico said. "Remain standing please. It is a form of standing together with me. For now, Satan has taken possession of this little girl. But soon God will bring her back. Pray with me."

"God help me," Maria cried. "Help all of us."

"Yes," Federico said. "God help all of us."

219

Selena did not move.

Federico called out, "Evil spirit, what is your name?"

"Fortissimus," the word came from Selena. A foul smell filled the air. "That's Latin for 'strength'."

"Too bad you weren't given the name for liar."

"Why do you say that?" Selena seemed to be in a deep sleep. Her mouth did not move yet the low voice came from her throat.

"Because your Presidente Garcia has been taking money from this country for years," Federico said. "He has lots of children and all of them have money in Swiss bank accounts. Garcia has said he has no money in Swiss banks or any other banks. That is almost true. He has lots of money in many banks in Ireland, Bermuda and Luxembourg—but not in his name—it's all in his children's names. He has been robbing this country for decades. Why would he change now? You've been telling my brothers that they will receive fortunes just for leaving this monastery.

"When the oil profits start coming in," Federico said, "I don't think Garcia will be giving any of it away to a pack of former monks. That's not his track record. The truth is, he has never given away anything that he could steal for himself. In other words, Mr. Fortissimus, you have been lying to us all along."

"Yes, yes, yes," Fortissimus said. "You see, when men are being tempted they enjoy being lied to. You know that. You hear their confessions. You know these men and you know they are being tempted far beyond their ability to resist. That's how the game is played."

"Most of these men have the assistance of the Holy Ghost to help them with their decisions," Federico said. "They have everything they need.

"You are inside an innocent girl. Is there no end to your evil," Federico asked. His voice was calm, quiet, and firm. "You will have to leave this innocent girl in several minutes. Prepare to depart."

The monks stood in silence. They made small nervous movements and kept looking from side to side, as animals become nervous when they sense a thunder storm is near.

"Are you aware that you are surrounded by men of God?" Federico asked.

The voice of Fortissimus answered, "Are you aware that your men of god are surrounded by a legion of my followers??"

"Yes, and the power that is in just one of my monks is greater than the power that is in you and all of your followers together. We do not fear you because you have often been defeated. It's you who fears us."

The voice in Selena's throat shouted, "You order your followers to sing in the mornings. They are to sing before dawn before they have had that one slice of bread you call breakfast," Fortissimus said. "So your followers drag around all day, sleep-deprived and under-nourished. And not realizing they are being controlled. If they are really men they would throw off your control. They would take command of their lives."

"Evil spirits," Federico called out, "you display your ignorance when you talk about my followers. They do not follow me. They are followers of Jesus Christ, whose death on the cross took away our sins and, with our choice, made us clean enough for Heaven."

Selena's face suddenly twisted into a sneer. "Really?" she said. "Don't be so proud of your men. One of them has already betrayed Christ, betrayed this monastery and betrayed you."

Immediately the silence of the monks was broken. Nearly all were talking. "Who can it be? Who do you think?" "Is it me?" "Why should we believe her?" "It's not me; is it you?" "Who has she been talking to anyway?" "Who has been listening to her?" "She is persuasive." Yes, but whose voice is it?" "When will we know?"

"Don't worry brothers," Federico said. "I know who it is and he will be dealt with."

"Strange isn't it?" the voice of Fortissimus crackled. "Just when you need them, their loyalty begins to crumble." The crackling sound turned into loud laughter.

"I may have lost one out of two dozen," Federico said. "That's about four percent. When you assisted with that treasonous revolt in Heaven, you lost 33 percent. You also lost the entire battle. That was a major loss wasn't it. No

222

wonder you are still angry. It's no surprise you are frightened to go back to Hell and have to report your loss to your superior—Satan. As the saying goes, 'there's going to be Hell to pay'."

Selena moved to the center of the room and sat on the chair that she had occupied earlier. The men all remained standing. None spoke. Then the kitten called 'Little Benny' entered the room. He stood for a moment and saw nothing moving. Then the fly on Selena's chin moved up from her chin to her lower lip. The kitten saw the fly and jumped up on Selena's lap.

With one paw Little Benny batted at the fly. Selena grabbed the cat and hurled him across the room. The cat landed on all four feet, looked back at Selena and walked out of the room.

"Hey," one of the novices yelled. "That's our house pet, named after the founder of this Order. Don't you dare ever touch that cat again. Or I'll throw you across the room. You'll be plastered against that wall. Understand?"

Selena became silent and looked menacingly at the young monk. As if to strike back, the girl swung around and looked at the Abbot.

"Do you men care more for a kitten than you care about yourselves? What kind of people are you anyway?" The voice growled and was suddenly gone. Now it was a low snarling sound similar to a rabid animal's growl. The girl's mouth was not moving. The sound came from her throat.

She stood up. "You idiots make me so angry! Listen to me. This is your chance for all the things that can make you happy!" The girl who had been shy now stood before the men. Her feet were wide apart. Her head was thrust forward and her eyes were full of anger. Her face had turned deep red with blue veins bulging at her temples and neck.

"Were-wolves," Brother Andrew whispered to Federico.

"What?" Federico asked.

"I can see now, why people believe in werewolves."

"Yes. Everything about her changed—in the blink of an eye."

"From human to beast," Andrew said as he watched the girl.

Federico nodded and said, "Whatever she is now, I think it would like to kill us."

"If you are ready for great wealth this is the time to take it and enjoy it," she called out. "But you can do good things with some of your cash. You could set up an orphanage for the community. Or build a new school—with your name on it. Or, be a hero and build a home for unwanted women and children."

Then the girl's face became contorted with a smile. "Or you could have a new home on your estate. Think of it. A large home with a long black Mercedes in front of the house with a cook in the kitchen and a young girl upstairs to grant your every wish. Not enough? Then how about a different girl every night?"

Her smile faded and she said, "You like champagne? Order it by the truck load. How about caviar? Have it flown in fresh every morning. Want to try drugs? When you are seriously wealthy you can get anything you want. DO anything you want. Anything. The phrase 'Party-party', will take on new meaning. You will be so free," she said, "it will seem to you like having been born again."

Quickly Federico answered, "It's interesting how you use religious words and phrases as you try to turn people away from their God."

The girl stood up, stretched, and yawned. Slowly she sat back down. "You heard everything I told you. I explained it to all of you. I want you out of this monastery. Now then, Abbot Federico, can you give me any reason for you and your men to stay in this place?" She leaned back in her chair. "I await your response."

Selena sat on the chair as if it were a throne. "I await your response," she repeated.

Federico scanned the room. It was poorly lit with only two doors and one window facing the courtyard. The window and both doors were closed.

Federico and most of the monks were present. Maria sat alone in a corner.

Selena was near to the center of the room. "Well?" she said. "Mister Abbot, spiritual leader of this monastery, can you make some sort of decision for all of us?"

"Brothers," Federico called, "Pray with me."

In the silence that followed, several monks knelt, others stood with heads bowed. Federico knelt before Selena.

"The eyes of the Lord are on the righteous and His ears are attentive to their cry." Federico prayed in a soft voice. "Holy Spirit, remove this evil thing from our innocent child." This was followed by a long period of silent prayer.

"Jesus Christ, our savior and Lord, free this innocent child from this evil thing." Federico's voice became louder.

"Our Father in Heaven, Jesus our Savior and powerful Holy Ghost—do it now." There was a short moment of silence and the Abbot's voice became very loud. "Wipe this monastery clean of these satanic things. Dispose of them all. Send them back to hell—where they belong—and do it now!

"We pray this by the power of the shed blood of Jesus. Amen."

Federico repeated the prayer two times. Then he stopped praying and listened. Again the room was silent. Federico glanced around the room. "Amen," he said.

Immediately a clash of sounds filled the atmosphere. Selena whimpered softly, made a gagging sound and vomited on the floor. Federico let out a sigh of relief. Several of the monks who had been kneeling during the prayer grumbled loudly as they stood up. Then a new sound slashed through the air. It was the sound of anger as a mass of large, black flies appeared everywhere in the room. They covered nearly every surface, the floor, walls, ceiling, the chairs—and the people. Dozens of flies took over every space. They flew with speed and force bumping into walls, chairs and monks. The buzzing sound became louder as the flies filled the air with their fury.

One of the largest flies landed on the floor directly in front of Selena's feet. It paused there for a moment before rising straight up until it was higher than Selena's head. Then it flew directly toward the window. It bumped into the glass and fell to the floor. Slowly it walked around on the stone floor under the window. Two more flies hit the window; one of them fell to the floor. Then a group of flies angrily hit the glass. At least half of them ended up dazed on the floor. They were followed by groups of flies attacking the window only to join in with the staggering survivors on the floor. Within minutes there was a pile of black, squirming insects on the floor. Most of them were buzzing loudly. Only a few could fly and continue their assault on the glass.

"Mason," Federico called. "Bring that metal bucket, kerosene, the broom and some matches. Hurry."

When Mason returned he was carrying a galvanized pail, a 20 gallon container of kerosene, a broom and a dust pan. He held a packet of matches in his teeth.

"Right there," Federico said. "Right by the window. Sweep them all into the pail. Right away before they can fly again."

Within seconds Mason had the pail buzzing with black, angry, flies.

"Take the pail outside," Federico said. "Don't trip. Don't spill any of them. Okay. Cover them all with the kerosene. Now throw a lit match in there."

Flames shot up into the air. Black smoke curled around the flames.

"So long, Fortissimus," Mason yelled. "So long."

Inside the monastery, Selena slid off her chair and fell to the floor.

Selena opened her eyes. "Is it gone?" she asked. Her voice was the high pitch of a woman. She had been covered with a blanket. She pulled the blanket around her shoulders. "Are they really gone? All of them?"

"Oh yes, little girl," Federico said. "Fortissimus and his followers, they are all gone. Thanks be to God."

Selena continued to look around the room. "They must be gone," she said, "because it is so nice in here. The air is fresh. Everything is clean and the light is finally on."

"You've been resting," Federico said. "Just a few minutes. Are you warm enough?"

"Yes, I am warm enough but the blanket feels good. May I keep it on for a while? And," she looked at the floor, "did I make a mess somewhere around here?"

"Don't worry little one. There was a mess but only for a few minutes. Then it all evaporated into the air."

"Yes, yes," Selena said. "I remember now. The head was rolling around. And those two bright red eyes kept staring at me." Selena looked at Federico. "You dear old man," she said, her eyes growing brighter. I remember it now. As you prayed for me I was able to exhale something bitter. Terribly bitter. It burned on my tongue. And then, when I inhaled, something that smelled sweet filled the room. The bitter had passed away and in its place there was a sweet taste and a sweet smell. It was sweeter than honey. It filled my lungs."

Selena smiled at the Abbot. "You talked directly to God and He made everything good again. It all went from bitter to sweet."

Federico stood up and smiled at Selena.

She smiled back and said, "Thank you. Thank you. Thank you for getting that thing out of me." Then her smile disappeared. "There is something I feel I must tell you."

Federico returned to kneeling on one knee before the girl.

"It was not me you heard during that argument," she said. I don't know what it was or who it was. All I know is it was inside of me. And there was pain from it. Terrible pain.

The pain was not from the voice. The pain came from the thing itself. At first it felt like a fish or a lizard except it wasn't either. But it was alive and it was in me. It was alive and hungry. It had small, sharp teeth. Like an eel or maybe a giant parasite."

Federico stood up again. As Selena stood their noses nearly touched.

"Do you have any idea where it came from? Or how it came to you?" he asked.

Selena looked into Federico's eyes for a moment. Then she quickly looked away. "I don't know how to tell you but the worst pain was when it entered me. My arms and legs were held down by his helpers. It wasn't alone. I could do nothing. They were all so strong. It wasn't my fault," she stopped speaking, took a deep breath and said, "I can't tell you anymore. Talking about it makes me remember."

"That's alright," he said. "You don't have to tell me anything you don't want to tell. Rest for a while. Breathe slowly. Rest."

"No," she said. "I don't want to rest. I need to get this done as soon as possible." She threw the blanket off her shoulders and pulled a chair over to where Federico had been kneeling. She motioned for him to sit down facing her.

"Thank you," he said.

"You are welcome," she replied. As she sat across from him she pulled the hem of her skirt down around her ankles.

"It broke into me," Selena said. Her words came out quietly and rapidly. "It put terrible weight on my most private part. It ripped through that part of me. Do you understand?" She continued to look away from Federico. "It broke into the part of me—the part that is—down there.

"It broke into me. Deep inside. It felt like fire. It kept burning and writhing. I could feel it squirming itself up inside of me from my intestines to my stomach to my chest and then it was inside my neck. I was close to being choked from the inside.

"I was so scared. I thought I would die. I didn't know what to do. I couldn't get away. You know it wasn't my fault? Or was it my fault? How can I tell? How do I know? Can you tell me? And why me?"

Federico did not answer.

"The thing would not let me speak. When it pushed up into my throat it started to yell and curse. I realized it had a mouth and voice. But it was not my voice. It had been doing the talking from inside of me. I think its voice was changed so in the beginning it sounded like me. It was all a lie. Everything it shouted was foul. It was angry like it wanted to kill.

"It cut me off from any communication. It bit my voice box so badly all I could do was growl and cry.

"Every time it yelled anything it smelled bad. Really bad. Like the stench of hundreds of maggots.

231

"It had rows and rows of teeth," she said. "I knew they were small teeth, but they were all sharp as razor blades and they were biting me. Before, when I was jumping around so often I was trying to dislodge the thing's teeth. And all the time, I knew, it was drinking my blood.

"I cannot tell you what words it was screaming. Something about idiots I think. I could hear it and feel all the vibrations of it, but I couldn't understand it. As soon as it had come near my throat it bit me badly so I could not cry or talk or scream. I could not say a word—only a quiet growl. I didn't know if anyone could hear me or not. I felt very scared and very alone.

"I did not think I could stand any more. I wanted to die." Selena stopped speaking. She looked up at Federico and smiled. "Then I heard your voice," she said.

"I think you reached the part in your prayer where you said something like, 'Jesus Christ our savior, free this innocent child from this evil thing. Wipe this monastery clean of these satanic things. Send them back to hell where they belong. Send them back—to hell—now.'

"That was when everything changed," she said, still smiling. "I could tell your prayer was being answered. And I could feel the thing moving up my throat. I was gagging because the scent of it made me want to vomit. I coughed again and again. Part of it was in my mouth but most of it was back in my throat. I coughed. It made me cough. I was gagging, coughing, and trying to spit it out when all my stomach muscles contracted and the thing shot out of me. It felt like I was a volcano erupting.

"There was bitterness in my mouth and the stench was unbelievable. The thing flew out of me and plopped down on the floor, just a few inches from my feet.

"It was at least a foot long. It landed on its side so I could see it. There were scales on its back. They were pale green I think. Most of it was white so I could see sections of red and blue veins and arteries beneath its white skin. It raised its head and looked directly at me. Both its eyes were bright red. And full of hate."

Federico asked: "What kind of creature did it look like? Was it like any sort of animal?"

"Yes," Selena said. "It was like a salamander. It was the ugliest thing I have ever seen in my life.

"Then another strange thing happened. After just a few moments the thing came apart. It broke into three pieces. All three parts were covered with a slimy liquid. They smelled too. It came apart as if it could not live in this atmosphere. The parts were the head with its red eyes looking up at me, the body which was fat and seemed to be gasping for air and then the tail which had one long fin on it. It had four short legs and the feet had brown claws. It flopped around on the floor like a fish out of water. The body and tail both died quickly. The head stayed alive and kept looking at me. It was about the size of a golf ball but not round like a golf ball it was pointed and its lips pulled back and I could see the front row of teeth." She stopped speaking and tried to brush some tears off her cheeks. Federico could see her hand trembling.

"Maybe this is enough for now," Federico said.

"Oh no," Selena said. "I want to end this talk. Let's finish it right away. Then I will never have to repeat any of this again. Ever."

"You sure you want to go on?" Federico asked. "It's very exhausting."

"Well, yes I want to tell the whole story because the next part is about the strangest thing of all.

"See, the head didn't die. It just laid there, mouth open with white, putrid liquid running out of it and its eyes kept looking up at me," Selena said, "Then that ugly head began to shrink."

"Wait," Federico said, his hand in the air. "Say again."

"It's true," she said. "The two other chunks and the slime on the floor, they all dried up and disappeared right away. It took the head longer. It rolled back a few inches, the eyes stayed open and the whole head began to get smaller.

"The head quivered as it shrunk. It became about the size of a marble. Then it went down to something like an ant, then half the size of an ant. Then it was just a speck there on the floor. And then it was only half the size of a speck.

"Then another thing happened. That fly that had been sitting on my chin and later on my lip, flew down by the speck on the floor. He sat there for just a second and flew away. The speck was gone. Did the fly carry the speck away?

The room was filled with angry buzzing. Most of them went at full speed for the window. It was as if they didn't see the glass or maybe had never even seen glass before.

"The entire swarm went for the window," Selena said. "They hit the glass with such force that most of them fell to the floor. I didn't know if they were knocked out or dead. That was when one of the brothers ran out and came back in with a broom, a bucket and a can of kerosene. He swept up the flies and dumped them in the bucket. It was one of those metal pails. He took it outside, poured kerosene in it and threw a lit match in with the flies.

"Black smoke shot ten feet up in the air. Lots of smoke. I could hear splashing from the bucket. Maybe the noise came from the flies. There was also a crackling noise. I couldn't recognize what was making that sound. Then the noise calmed down and the smoke from the bucket turned white.

"I guess that's when I fainted."

"Little girl," Federico said, "Can you tell us any more about the thing? It will help us if you could describe it and maybe a little about how it made you feel. Could you tell us about it while the memories are fresh in your mind? You know you can stop whenever you wish. What do you think?"

"I'm glad it is finally over," Selena said, her voice in a high range. "I owe you so much. I feel extremely indebted to you Abbot Federico and others here. So if you really want to know more about the 'thing' that plagued me, I will tell you."

Selena smiled at Federico but her smile faded the instant she resumed speaking.

"It went on for weeks. I hardly slept during that time. And I couldn't eat much." She paused to clear her throat.

"It was a painful fight. It went on day after day and night after night. You see, I had no way to defend myself.

"It weakened me because it was devouring parts of me. It was torturing me by consuming my spirit. It was inside of me.

"And all that time, I could tell, I knew—that it was drinking my blood."

Several of the monks moved their chairs closer to hear Selena and Federico.

"I could feel it was at least a foot long. It was slimy.

"It was like a giant worm or maybe a snake.

"Sometimes it would not move for several days at a time. Then just when I began to hope it was gone it would make a series of short, darting movements. You see, it knew exactly how to make me want to give up hope.

"Over and over I could feel it slithering around inside of me. It was working its way up. You see, it was heading for my vocal cords. It wanted to steal my voice. To get to my voice, it had to chew through my intestines and lungs. After a while I could feel it chewing on my ribs—like a dog gnawing on a bone.

"I tried to get rid of it by shaking it loose. But I could feel it hanging on with its claws and teeth. Many times I tried to get rid of it by jumping up and down. I thought this might break its hold. But then I would feel it hanging on biting into me worse than before.

"As it grew larger and stronger, I became weaker," she said.

Federico looked at Selena just as a single tear rolled down her cheek.

"Please," Federico said, "let me interrupt for a second. Our God is so powerful," Federico whispered. He closed his eyes. After a silent moment he opened his eyes and said, "Sorry. But now we are ready to look again at what has just happened."

"Okay," Selena said as she brushed her cheek with one hand and pulled her skirt over her legs with the other.

"The evil creature you call 'the thing' used your body as a means to speak for Satan," Federico said. "It was part of Satan's plan to split our country into two nations, both greedy for oil profits. I believe Satan's plan includes a second civil war filled with death and destruction. That could happen yet unless the Lord steps in to prevent it."

Then Federico looked directly into the girl's eyes. "I want you to understand, you played a major role in today's victory over Satan and his followers."

Selena looked up at Federico and asked, "And Satan's plan was to do what?"

"His plan was to close this house of worship and prayer. Had his plan succeeded it would have scattered these

237

monks preventing them from praying together and forming a united stand against him. But now look at what has happened. You, Selena, you came to our door. Your mother Maria asked for prayer to relieve you of Fortissimus and his followers--."

"That's what happened," Maria exclaimed as she joined the group. "That's what I said when we first walked in here. 'Selena,' I said, 'you have evil spirits in you'…"

"Momma. Be quiet. The Abbot it talking."

"I was just saying--."

"Later momma."

"But I just--."

"Momma," Selena said loudly. "Later. Not now."

"We prayed." Federico continued. "Your voice returned and it was the voice of God's will. It was the voice of light."

Two more monks stood and quietly joined the group listening to the discussion involving Selena.

"You no longer jumped around," Federico said. Whatever was eating you—if I can put it that way—was gone."

"Yes, but now I'm afraid all those things will come back to me as memories—or nightmares," Selena said. "Maybe the thing's way of tormenting me will be to keep coming back to my mind." As Selena spoke her eyes darted around the room.

"Selena," Federico said, "you have nothing to fear."

238

"But I'm afraid I'll remember all of it. Maybe those memories will jump back into my mind at terrible times. Like when I least expect them. Or maybe the memories will be so real that I'll experience the pain they gave me, all over again." Her expression was serious.

"No girl," Federico said with a smile. "I can teach you a method to make all the bad memories go away."

"Really?"

"For real. Listen carefully. Trust me."

Federico smiled at the girl. "Whenever the terrible memories start coming back to you, know that you can push them out of your mind by recalling the good parts of your experience. Like when your voice came back. Remember how good that felt? When the thing shrunk down to a tiny speck. That was good. Or like when you spit the thing out and inhaled fresh air instead of his stench. Those are good memories. Think back about when you looked around and the thing was gone. There was no evil spirit left. The room was filled with monks praying on their knees. I was praying too. The room was filled with light. The darkness was gone."

"So, I'm supposed to think good memories?"

"Yes. Only the good. They will drive out the bad."

"But I don't have the power to do that. The bad memories will take control of my thoughts. The bad will have all the power."

"No. Wait," Federico said. "Here's the key to the whole struggle. Just show The Lord your thanksgiving. Tell

Him how glad you are to have Him in your life. Talk to the Lord. Make it a prayer of gratitude. Thank Him for pouring out His grace over you—for hearing the prayers of the men of this monastery—for driving the thing out of you, for taking away your pain, giving you your voice back, letting you be free to give Him your life and your future. Thank Him with a loud voice and be filled with joy. The only joy that lasts."

"So that's it?" Selena asked. "Give thanks to God?" Her brow was lined with disbelief.

"Yes. That's it," Federico said. He leaned closer to the girl. His voice became a whisper. "When your gratitude is perfectly sincere, it's guaranteed to work."

"Have you heard enough from me?" Selena asked. "I'm getting terribly tired. I'd like to go home soon."

"Sure, I understand. Completely." Federico paused for a moment and then said: "I would like you to put into words just a little bit about how it felt when the thing left you. It's important."

"But it is all over now. What's so important that I have to tell you?"

"Trust me. If you can briefly recount, in your words, now, it will be far easier to feel total gratitude in the future."

"I don't understand," Selena said.

Federico, the old Abbot, took the right hand of young Selena. "Understanding will come in the future," he said. "It will make it far easier to feel gratitude in the future. Put the experience into your words."

"Really?" Selena asked.

"Oh yes," Federico answered. "It's a thing we practice at this monastery. You see, when you focus on God, and His communications to us, there is no room for Satan or Satan's followers in our hearts and minds. God drives out evil. You saw that today. Good is victorious over evil. Love drives out fear. Life with Jesus is the victory over all of Satan's threats. When tempted, turn to Jesus. You see Jesus is stronger than Satan and all his followers put together."

Selena looked at Federico. "But when I remember today I'll remember the bad, the thing, and the pain. I don't want to go through any of that all over again."

"Then don't," Federico said. "You can control your memories…"

"Oh really," she interrupted.

"Yes, dear girl. Practice using your memory for good. That's why God gave us memories. And its simple Gratitude is what does it," Federico said, smiling at Selena. "When you thank God for the good—saving you from evil—you literally complete the process. 'Thanks be to God'—becomes the method for wiping out the evil of the past. Focus on our God by thanking Him. Remind yourself of the relief when the evil one left you."

"Yes. It did feel like a relief when it left me," she said. "It became quieter, or maybe weaker, every time you talked about God. It kept shrinking. It was so small that it was only half the size of an ant. And I could spit it out. It burned my tongue as it left me. Then everything became lighter and brighter so when I inhaled, a sweetness filled the air."

"That's it," Federico said. "That sweetness that filled the air—as it filled your lungs—that's what you will be thankful for.

"Re-inforce that positive memory. Make it your primary memory so everything else about today becomes secondary. You don't have to be a prisoner of the negative. Just give thanks to God because all that 'stuff' is in the past.

"Evil things were not your fault. Give thanks. You are innocent. Thank you, Lord.

"You are beautiful. Thank you, Jesus.

"You are loved by our God and loved forever. Thanks Lord.

"And you have every reason to be joyful."

"Imagine the sound of angels singing which is exactly what's going on in Heaven right now because evil has been defeated again.

"You, Selena, you are changed now. Changed in God's love. Understand?"

"Oh yes. I am beginning to understand. You are a wise man." Selena looked up at the Abbot. "And you are a really nice guy."

Selena's voice was suddenly high yet soft. Her eyes rolled back as if she was gazing at the ceiling. "Dear Abbot, the spirit has come upon me. This is the word of God. You have my favor. Use it now. Life is brief; little more than a vapor. Use my favor before that power is swallowed up in useless chatter. Instruct the brothers and pray for them that, through prayer, they may receive the gift of discernment. Help them to see what they have never seen before." She paused for a moment. Her eyes remained unfocused.

"But now be careful. There is one here who is full of evil." Selena's voice became louder as she spoke. "He said he followed Christ but he was lying to himself. So he did not understand that those who follow Satan will receive the punishment of Satan."

"Selena, what has happened to you?" Maria said as she tried to cover her daughter's mouth with her hand. "These are things you must not say to these good monks."

"The girl turned and broke free of her mother's hand. She looked at her mother and said, "Wearing a long robe with a hood does not make an evil man clean. He uses the hood to hide his face from God."

"Selena. I cannot understand you," Maria said. "Are you no longer my daughter?"

"Mama, in this room there is an evil heart with a lying tongue!"

"No, my little one. These are men of prayer—men of God."

"Si, mama. But remember, not all who cry out 'Lord' will be saved. And if a man is here to plan evil for his own profit—then that man is not a man of the Holy Ghost."

Then Selena became still. She was silent. She did not cough. Her arms did not move. She said nothing.

After a time Federico, still close to the girl, said, "Little one, where did you get such wisdom? Where could you have learned such things?"

Suddenly Selena looked up at the Abbot as if she had never seen him before. "I know nothing about what you just asked." She smiled and added, "I only know that I feel good. Very good." Her voice was again the high pitch voice of a young adult.

"But, what do you mean—feel good?"

"I don't know," she said with a shrug. "I just feel good. Isn't that what I came here for?"

Federico smiled. "Yes, little one," he said. "That's what you came here for."

Federico turned and asked Maria, "Would you and your daughter like to stay here for a few moments and pray together? Maybe say a prayer of thanksgiving? I can ask the others to leave if you want."

"I don't know. Does she need more prayer?"

"I think only you can answer that."

Maria looked at Selena. "You are quiet now. Are you feeling alright? No more coughing? No more bouncing around like a jumping bean? You are cured?"

244

The girl ignored her mother and instead looked up at Federico. "Thank you," she said. "Your prayers helped me very much. I am better, thanks. But I am tired. I think we will go home now."

"I can drive you home," Mason offered. "You both look a bit tired. I'll get the car and be in front of that door in two minutes."

"Father Delgado," Federico said, "please go along with Mason."

Maria took Federico's hand and held it without shaking it. "We are poor people," she said. "I have nothing to give you for all your prayers…"

Federico shook her hand and released it. "Please— nothing is expected. God's love is free and his healing is free."

"Yes, she is better. I can see that now. Maybe she is completely healed.

"Come back and visit us sometime soon. I'd like to tell you more about Jesus."   As the mother and daughter slowly walked out of the chapel, Brother Benedict hurried up to Federico. "Interesting meeting today," Benedict said.

"Where have you been?" Federico asked.

"Right around the corner."

"So, you heard it all?"

"Some of us were here out of curiosity. We thought we might hear a message from Satan. Instead, I think we heard from Satan and the Holy Ghost. Right?"

Federico stood looking at Benedict. There was a moment of silence. Then Federico said, "I believe you are correct."

"Then what," asked Benedict, "—what exactly are you going to do about it?"

"I'll let you know after I've prayed about it." Benedict leaned close to the Abbot and whispered, "Who do you think it is?"

"I'll let you know when the time is right."

"Are you saying you know who it is?"

"No. I didn't say that. All I said was that I will let you know when the time is right."

"Oh," said Benedict. "Don't take too long. Because the way it is now—it is uncomfortable." Benedict paused as if expecting a response. There was only a silent moment. Then Benedict said, "The message was clear—at least it was clear to me."

With a slight sigh, Federico asked "And what was that message—to you?"

"Just that somebody left the door open," said Benedict with a trace of a smile, "And soon we will have to adjust to a great change."

"A great change?" Federico said. "Tell me about that."

"It will come crashing in on your monastery like a mountain falling out of the sky."

"It's not my monastery," Federico said. "It's God's."

"Then maybe God will have to change too." Benedict was still smiling.

"Brother Benedict," the Abbot said, "come to see me tomorrow. Make it early morning. It is time we talked."

Chapter 15
Credo

"Yesterday, an evil one was here," Abbot Federico announced. "The meeting room was crowded. He asked some interesting questions. I think it will be wise to consider those questions and formulate our own answers.

"Note that the way Fortissimus phrased his questions, they became temptations. Seeds of sin and disobedience were planted. So how we answer those questions can be extremely important to our spiritual growth.

"I have asked you all to meet here this morning to tell each of you to decide how you will answer those questions when you sense temptation rising within you. Discuss your answers with your spiritual advisor. Don't be proud of your answers but know that you certainly may be stubborn with your rebuttal. Be prepared because there could be future attacks. An evil one was thrown out of here yesterday but he could be lurking just outside our gate today.

"Do you all understand the importance of your answers? They will determine your futures. They are each person's credo—what you believe and what will be the road map of your future.

"So, here are my personal answers that I thought up late last night. I want to share them with you. I hope they will help you.

"Why are we here and why do we stay?"

The Abbot scanned his brothers seated before him. He took a deep breath and smiled. Then his expression became serious.

"The first reason we are all here is because God has asked us here and asked us to stay here. Our God called us here. And we obey our God," he said.

"That's why we are here.

"That's why we will stay.

"Why are we here? It is because this is the place where we belong entirely to God. We are in his hands. Our names are written in the palms of His hands. We belong to Him and not to anyone—or anything—less than Him. Once we understand this we are blessed because we know—we know we are His and He is ours.

"That's why we are here.

"That's why we will stay.

"There are many times when we feel the Lord's emotions resonating within our hearts. That's the Lord sharing His joy with us. At other times we have the joy of seeing other people through His eyes. That's another of the gifts the Lord gives us. We observe people, see them at work and at rest. As we watch them we can feel His love flowing out to those who are growing in grace and in the Spirit and in love. We can feel our prayers being answered.

"That is also why we are here.

"That is also why we will stay.

"Then, being in God's good grace, He invites us to work with Him on His projects. We work with Him, praying and obeying His word, helping to change lives, spreading compassion, empathy, and love and even preventing wars. We are now working to find a method of teaching others how to turn their homes into 'Little Monasteries' in which they may practice mature faith for all.

"This is why we are here.

"This is why we will stay.

"Less than 24 hours ago," Federico said. "This room became a battleground. The battle was between good and evil. The followers of Jesus Christ beat the followers of Satan. And didn't that victory feel good? And why was Fortissimus so insistent that we leave this place? It is because oil has been discovered here. It sits under the sand that this monastery is built upon. Our corner of this desert now seems to be expensive real estate. The evil ones want to provoke a civil war over this patch of sand. President Garcia is ready to march his army into this desert, win the war and claim all the oil profits for the next ten years. But, he fears that our presence here will become an obstacle to his plan. He thinks the people might throw him out of office if his men come in here and burn us out—or kill us off."

Mason raised his hand. "Is the president's hold on his office that shaky?"

"It will be if any of us is killed here," the Abbot said. "People would call it a massacre and demand justice. Even Garcia knows that all the oil in this desert isn't any good to a dead man. But he wants all the oil profits; not just a small share. Now I believe Fortissimus put a plan into Garcia's mind. It is to make us appear to agree to leave so we won't be missed when we are out in the world—getting killed off one at a time. We would appear to have 'sold out', betrayed our faith, received nothing for giving up, then probably over-dosed on something and died."

"Wow," Mason said. "Garcia and Fortissimus are working together—sort of. What's going to happen? What are we going to do?"

"Our prayers must be that our country not be dragged into a civil war," Federico said. "Fortissimus wants war and thousands of deaths. God wants peace, the kind of peace where Brother Forgiven and I can teach mature Christianity. That's exactly what will happen when every Brother in this room prays for peace."

"So, what do we do now?" Mason asked.

"We'll do some extra praying," Federico said. "We'll have a prayer marathon. Twenty-four seven. Three brothers at a time. In this room. Brother Mason, thank you for volunteering. Please make up a schedule."

"Did I volunteer?" Mason asked. "I didn't hear me volunteer."

"No. But God heard you," Federico said. "His hearing must be better than yours. Look at it that way.

"That's why we are here.

"That's why we will stay.

"We know that nothing the world offers can be as good as belonging here and being at-one-with the Lord. Not a bottle of fine wine, not a plate of hot tacos, not even the fellowship of being with our brothers in this monastery. Nothing can be nearly as good as being here heart-to-heart with God.

"That is why we are here.

"That is why we will stay.

"You cannot understand true, lasting joy until you experience God's love being poured out to you as you study your Bible and feel your heart being warmed. Your soul is stirred once you recognize His message is to you and about His love for you. That's God the creator of the universe reaching out to you from His great heart directly to your listening heart. We become filled with His presence.

"That's just a part of what we achieve here.

"That's just a part of why we will stay here.

"To paraphrase our Jesus," the Abbot declared, 'I have told you these things so that in me you will find peace.

In the world you will find tribulation; but be of good cheer for I have overcome the world.

"Brothers, brothers," the Abbot called out. "Spend some time today to think about what you have just heard. Think about it. Pray about it.

"Tomorrow we will have another meeting right here," the Abbot said. "Anyone who has more ideas or comments regarding our beliefs as they were discussed today may talk about them tomorrow. I believe they should be shared with our entire brotherhood. So right after breakfast tomorrow, stop here. And brevity is always appreciated.

"You are now excused to go to your prayer rooms and workstations."

Federico then turned to Brother Forgiven. He waited until nearly all of the brothers had shuffled out of the room.

"Was everyone here this morning?"

"All but four," Brother Forgiven said. "Two in the infirmary, Julius and Roberto. Brother Andrew is sitting with them."

"And Benedict?"

"It's too bad sir," Brother Forgiven said. "Brother Benny came late. He wasn't at breakfast either. Maybe he went into town last night and stayed over somewhere. Too bad."

"No," Federico said. "It's just as well."

"Oh? What do you mean?"

"Ben and I are meeting this morning. It's not a meeting I look forward to. I'll let you know later today. Send up prayer for God's will to show itself—and be done."

Chapter 16
The Fifth Meeting of the
X-Treme Book Club

Jackson leaned against the table. He was silently observing—and smiling. Clayton and Jerry were both talking at the same time.

"Right there is where the whole book falls apart," Jerry said. He was waving the book over his head like a fire and brimstone preacher waves a Bible. "It becomes totally unbelievable. Counter to human nature."

"Right kid. It's unnatural for Federico to forgive Panzon. Can't be done," Clayton said. "Especially between two men. I expected Federico would send Panzon away to starve in the desert."

"He should have," agreed Jerry. "Revenge is necessary. After all, Federico didn't forget any of Panzon's cruelties…"

"Right again," Clayton said. "Starvation would have been such a perfect punishment for Panzon. Slow starvation. Perfect justice."

"Cool irony! The guy who got fat eating the prisoners' food should die from lack of food."

"You guys," said Laura in an unusually loud voice. "So macho with your revenge. But can't you see—it is more difficult to withhold vengeance? I am guessing both you guys read one or two chapters at a time and then come to these meetings and argue from what you remember from your reading."

"If that is so wrong," Clayton said, "What do you think is the right way?"

"It all flows together," Laura said. "Look at the big picture. The knowledge from one chapter provides insights into a later chapter."

"This would be a neat time for an example," Jerry mumbled.

"Remember the action," Laura said. "All the chapters are building up to a profound finale. Federico could not forgive Panzon until he, Federico, remembered his salvation experience."

"You mean that tin cup thing?" Clayton asked. "I thought it was a waste of paper and ink. And a waste of my time to read it."

"Well guys." Laura's voice was softer. "What you call, that tin cup thing, happens to have been the most important event in Federico's life. It changed him forever. Everything was new. And so different it made him able to stand up to Fortissimus. It made him able to work with God to cure Selena. And it gave him the power to forgive Panzon.

"Remember how most of the brothers were befuddled about why they were at the monastery and why they would stay? Federico had answers from God the next morning. They were Holy Ghost answers. What we now call Holy Spirit leading.

"He sort of turned the corner," said Jerry. "He turned his back on his sins. He moved on. He left his past behind him and moved on to accept Christ." Jerry paused for a moment and added, "I didn't like that part, personally. I'm really, really tired of all this Jesus-Jesus stuff. But anyway that's what happened to Federico."

Laura leaned forward. Her eyes were wide open. "This Jesus stuff is what it's about Jerry. Federico emptied himself of the past and of self. Then he was filled with Jesus and the Holy Spirit. And *that* is exactly what this book is about. Repentance and forgiveness. As the old song said, 'you can't have one without the other'."

"Whoa," Jerry said. "You're getting things all mixed up. You can't have forgiveness unless you repent? I can't be forgiven unless I make some sort of confession? In my mind, you're asking a lot."

"Whoa yourself, Jerry," Laura said. "You can't really believe that the cost is too high. Not when you consider the reward—salvation—grace for all eternity."

"Sure. Like Santa Claus will give you more presents if you've been a good girl. You're talking childish, emotional, wishful dreams."

"Oh Jerry," Laura said. "Stop rebelling so you will be able to hear what's being said. I'm not talking dreams; I'm talking experiences."

Jerry paused, pulled his cap off and scratched his head. Slowly he looked up at Laura. "Lady," he said, "you and I must come from totally different parts of town. Cause we sure do talk different languages. And I don't think I'm ever going to understand yours."

Laura drew herself up to answer, but Jerry turned his back on her. Loudly he said, "Hey Doc. Question for you. What's with that girl, Selena? My diagnosis is attention deficit. Am I right?"

The doctor looked up. His expression was serious. "Almost everything is blamed on attention deficit these days. But that's not what that girl had. Her problem was Tourette's disease. Sometimes it's called Tourette's Syndrome."

"As I read that chapter," Emma said, it seemed as if that poor girl did a lot of jumping around. That's Tourette's?"

"Typically it shows up as uncontrollable twitching or tics of the muscles. In some cases there can be parrot-like repetition of words spoken by others as well as other phrases and sometimes even barking sounds or shouts. And it's almost always accompanied by the twitching of muscles."

It's easy to see how in Third World countries it can be looked upon as demonic possession," Emma said.

"Clayton," asked Laura, "is there any cure?"

"It is tricky," said the doctor. "It's neurological you see. Research is being carried out but we still haven't identified the exact part of the nervous system that has gone so completely out of control. Muscle relaxation helps somewhat but we can't call that a cure. So Federico was right when he used prayer to calm her. But—I would guess that over time her symptoms came back."

"I saw a documentary on educational TV some time ago," said Laura. "It was about a summer camp for young Tourette's victims."

Jerry burst out laughing. "Summer camp? Wow. Imagine about 50 kids all trying to make tiny little baskets out of weeds while they are twitching and barking."

"That's not funny," said Laura. "Those summer camps show the children that they are not alone. There are others just like them and life does go on and many do adjust."

"Exactly," said Clayton. "Those summer camps are valuable. Each patient sees others making life work. Some become quite popular. There may be great therapeutic value in seeing other Tourette's patients as positive role models."

"Doctor," Laura said, "do Tourette's people get better—even slightly—as they grow older?"

"Good question. The answer is, in some cases, yes. And that's part of the research that's now going on. You see, some patients do improve with age and some don't. So researchers are trying to determine the cause or causes of that and replicate them."

"Hey Doc," Jerry blurted out, "what's with that monk called Brother Benny'? Is he supposed to be some kind of freak?—or crackpot?—or both?"

261

The doctor automatically patted his chest. His stethoscope was not there. "The author was describing an acromegaliac. Pretty good description too."

"Right!" said Jerry. "Now tell us what that looks like."

"Acromegalia is a disease that some consider to be a form of gigantism," the doctor said. "It is characterized by the progressive enlargement of certain bones. Most often the bones in the head and soft parts of hands, feet, thorax and face.

"Confusing the research is that a few acromegalics present horizontal growth patterns instead of vertical growth. The same bones continue to grow but their direction is different. Such patients end up with bodies four and a half feet tall and four feet wide. Brother Benedict is one of those."

"What causes that?" asked Jackson.

"The pituitary gland," the doctor answered. "That's the gland that regulates growth. For some reason the acromegaliac's pituitary does not slow down as the patient nears adulthood. So some parts of the body keep growing. Facial features especially become enlarged. Forehead, jaw, orbital ridge. The teeth become widely separated as the jaw continues to expand."

"So now we know," Jackson said, "what we have with our 'Brother Benedict'. Right?

"Well, those are just the physical problems," Jackson said. "Often there is a dramatic psychological effect."

"Way to go Doc," Jerry said. "Now it gets interesting. So, don't stop Doc. tell us what happens inside those heads that keep getting bigger and bigger."

Clayton looked straight ahead as if he was trying to recall previously memorized material from medical school. "It's difficult to treat. Very difficult," he said. "The deformities show up in late childhood as accelerated growth. Typically the patient withdraws. He may become resentful— even vengeful. And as adults they are loners which may make them prone to depression and suicide."

"So—"Jerry interrupted, "their faces rule them out of going into politics, right? I mean who would vote for them? Unless they had an 'ugly' party."

"Yes and no," Jackson said. "Most of them sort of go into hiding. They do behind-the-scenes jobs like research. But some go quite public. For example, does anyone recall the professional wrestler called, 'The Swedish Angel'? He was so ugly that it gave him an advantage over many of his opponents in the ring."

"Yeah, yeah," said Jerry. "In one of the old James Bond movies the bad guy was one of those giants. He had gold teeth. He was bad."

"Oh yes" As he spoke, the doctor's fingers again reached for his missing stethoscope. "It often happens that acromegaliacs, in their isolation develop grandiose plans or fantasies that get out of control.

"They usually don't have close friends," said the Doctor, "to provide reality checks. Sometimes their relationships are shallow—if you can measure relationships—so they can switch loyalties for no apparent reason. And there is a tendency to reject any advice that doesn't come from another acromegaliac."

"Then the bottom line," said Emma, "is that he's not a pretty sight."

"Hey guys!" Jerry interrupted. He stood up. His voice was loud. "Check this out. It just came to me." He laughed. "Imagine a summer camp see—but it's for both Tourette's and—" Jerry laughed again— "acromegaliacs. Now, get this picture. You pair them up. One Tourette with one giant guy. So—whenever the Tourette kid starts twitching and barking—his giant beats him up. For the whole two weeks this goes on. Of course the kid's letters home would have to be censored. But the giants who came depressed would go home feeling like they did something good for the world. And the Tourette's kids would go home cured. Bruised all over but no one barking and twitching. A win-win situation." Jerry looked at the group. He was the only one laughing. Slowly he sat back down.

"Your sense of humor is brutal and cruel," said Laura.

"Yeah," answered Jerry, "I know. Isn't it wonderful?"

Jackson took a step toward Jerry, leaned over and looked into the boy's eyes. "Are you high?" he asked.

Jerry's smile disappeared. Suddenly he was angry. "No man! What makes you say that? Can't a guy be in a good mood once in a while? What's the matter with you anyway?"

"I don't know about you," Jackson said. He continued to look at the boy. "But whatever profession in life you choose for yourself, please don't let it have anything to do with children."

"Hey guys, it's not my fault if you never see the humor in any situation." Jerry's voice was loud and deep. "Life is absurd, right? So laugh once in awhile. Okay?" He was not laughing.

"Is there something you want to tell us, Jerry?" Laura asked.

"No way!" Jerry exploded. "When I want to say anything, I say it! Don't you know that yet?"

"Well Jerry, you do sound a bit angry tonight," Jackson said. "If we can help with something—anything—you'll let us know, right?"

Clayton added, "Break up with the little girlfriend?"

Jerry twisted in his chair. He glanced around the room. Then he looked at his feet. Without looking back up he said, "Sometimes I think you guys are more into gossip—than forgiveness. Laura, how does that grab you—you Christian—can you forgive others?"

"Hey, I'm a Christian now too," blurted Emma. "I can forgive. I even forgave my mother."

Laura leaned forward. Her voice was soft. "Oh, Jerry, we can forgive and God will forgive. But that happens after the sinner has stopped sinning. After he has turned away from sin."

"Turned away—what does that mean?"

"As in the sinner saying, 'Never again!'"

"He can't say, like, 'No more for this month'—or something?"

"No Jerry. It's 'Never'—and 'Because I am sorry.'"

"Just seems like it takes a lot of conditions to make this thing kick in. You know I don't like jumping through hoops…"

"But Jerry," Emma interrupted, "it gets you out of trouble."

"Well Jerry," Jackson said, 'everyone in this room knows that you have some sort of a problem. Put it out on the table. I bet you the five of us will come up with at least five good solutions. What do you say?"

"Five good solutions?" Jerry said. "Right. None of you can help me. And I don't expect help anyway. But, well, it's like, there's this guy I know and he's not sure what to do. See lately he's been thinking about right and wrong and how morality is shifting, sort of."

"Could you be a bit more specific?" Jackson asked.

"Sure," Jerry said. "Specifically—is it so terribly wrong to steal from a corporation? A very large, profitable corporation which sets aside a certain amount of their annual budget for shrinkage?"

"What is 'shrinkage'?" asked Emma.

"Shrinkage is that projected percentage of the product," Jackson said, "that is manufactured but does not make it to the point of sale."

"You mean the part that is lost?" Emma asked.

"Yeah," Jackson said. "Lost—or stolen."

"There you are," said Jerry. "If it's set aside to go missing and is expected to be lost—then is it such a big deal when it does disappear? It's a corporation so no individual is hurt by what's lost." Jerry paused and closed his eyes for a moment. "So where does that fit in the new line between right and wrong? And who moved the line?"

Jerry pulled his cap down over his ears. With a frown he stood and hoisted his backpack over one shoulder. He made no eye contact with any of the others. Then he said, "Excuse me now. I have to go home and decide something. I can't say when—or even if—I'll ever be back." As he squeezed between the chairs where Laura and Emma were seated, he said, "You guys have it all so easy. You obey all the laws. So you have no idea of what a problem they can be."

As Jerry left the room, the moderator asked, "Are the laws a problem for any of you?

"I'm planning to go into politics soon. Probably as a state senator." Jackson said, "I'll be writing some new laws and they will be a problem for a lot of people. I'm going to see to it."

"I think Jerry was referring to spiritual laws. Laws of morality, ethics, civility," Emma said. "All things like that."

The teacher glanced at his remaining students and said, "We're moving ahead with our book but it is a struggle. Jerry was in a vicious mood tonight. If we all agree, let's adjourn for tonight, all go home and send up a prayer for Jerry. Okay?"

"Sure."

"Alright."

"Send one up for me too," Jackson said. "I guess I might need it."

Chapter 17
Talk of War

Brother Benedict's sandals left large imprints in the sand as he crossed the courtyard. Slowly he approached the bench where Federico was seated, "Hola Abbot, sir," he said.

Federico opened his eyes and saw Benedict's short, wide frame standing before him. There were dark areas under his eyes. Benedict's smile showed half-inch spaces between his teeth.

"Sit, my Brother," Federico said.

"Thank you," Benedict mumbled as he sat heavily on the bench. "I bring you news."

"We are always thankful for news," Federico said. "Now tell me."

Benedict looked around the courtyard as if fearing to be overheard. "I can bring incredible wealth to the men of this monastery." He paused then and added, "If everybody agrees to a little cooperation."

"Incredible wealth is not what we are looking for. Although ten or twenty more brooder hens would be helpful. What do you have?"

"As we all know—this country will soon be at war."

Federico looked at the brother and said, "I pray not. I don't believe war is in God's will."

"Yes, well, realistically," answered Benedict, "it could begin at any time now. The least little incident will set if off. And it's going to be messy."

"Yes, my Brother. Civil wars are always 'messy'. It means brother against brother, cousin against cousin—and pain upon pain."

"Yes," Benedict said. "But at least it will be a short war. Garcia predicts that we could be victorious within two months. So that's good."

"Two months of killing is good?"

"Yes, sir. And you know the war will be for this desert. The South thinks they have some right to it. Well, we'll just have to show them."

"Nobody wants the desert Benedict. Its miles and miles of worthless sand. The whole truth is both South and North want exclusive rights—to the oil that is below the sand."

Benedict smiled then. His teeth were small. His massively overgrown jaw jutted forward while his dark eyes nearly disappeared beneath his overhanging forehead. "Soon—very soon, oil will be everything," he said. "Better than gold. Those who control oil will rule the world."

"The world is ruled by the Prince of Darkness," Federico replied.

Benedict seemed to not hear his Abbot. Instead he leaned forward and waved his large hands. "Oil will be the end of poverty," he said. Then he added, "For those who

271

know how to market it. The plan is to withhold production so we can drive the price up. Basic supply and demand. The only other commodity with the mark-up of crude oil is drugs. Same strategy. Hold the supply back until consumer demand is willing to pay the asking price." Benedict's smile was gone. "That's why it is so important to be in on the game early. We have to be the producers so that we can manipulate the supply."

As Benedict spoke, Federico slowly stood up and looked down on the brother. "Exactly who is this 'we' you keep talking about?"

"Well," said Benedict. He spoke slowly. "After all the rumors that Garcia wanted the desert, I thought I might be able to help him. So, I contacted him and, to make a long story short, he gave me a job. Sort of. I have an assignment."

"You're working for Garcia?"

"Yes—sort of."

"President Garcia?"

"Yes."

"He's paying you?"

"Well, no. But he did make me a promise."

"And you trust him? What has he promised you?"

Benedict seemed to be shrinking back in his seat. "Well, if I can get the job done, the President has given me his word that I will be considered for the position of Minister of Oil."

"Now you listen," the Abbot said. "I could be wrong but Garcia has lots of grown children, sons, grandsons, and nephews who are in line for the better jobs—and those are just his legitimate relatives. I think he might have you working for nothing."

"Oh no. I believe him. He spoke with me himself. He said I have the inside track."

Federico took one step back from Benedict. He paused for a moment and asked, "And what is the job Garcia has asked you to do?"

"That's hard to explain," Benedict said. He held his gigantic hands up in a slightly protective position. "It's to get you to not be an obstructionist. To get your cooperation. That's all."

"My cooperation in doing what?"

"Could I have a cup of water?" Benedict asked.

"No. Answer the question. How am I to cooperate?"

"To put it in Garcia's own words, he wants this monastery out of the way. To put it another way, Garcia wants the entire desert—all of it—no exceptions."

Federico looked at Benedict and turned to look out of the courtyard at the sand dunes beyond the monastery walls. "This is such a big desert," he said, "Does he have to have this little chicken farm?"

"Well Garcia hired the geologist. And it looks to him like the oil starts right here. Right under our feet."

"Then why didn't Garcia send somebody to ask me if I would agree to being moved?"

Benedict quickly dropped his gaze. He slowly moved his feet in the sand. Without looking up he said, "Probably…" he shrugged, "probably somebody told him that you would never agree to that. And then he said there was no time for drawn-out negotiations. He told me to just get the job done—fast."

"The job. Meaning to get me out of the way—right?"

"Well, that's one way of saying it."

"So, Brother Benedict, in one conversation you have gone from, asking for my cooperation—to getting me out of the way. Is that the bottom line?"

"That is one way of saying it," Benedict repeated.

"And did you try to reason with Garcia? Did you think to look out for the brothers here—your brothers in Christ?"

"My brothers?" Benedict said, "I'm doing all this *for* the brothers. This will be all for their good. They will love it! Don't you see that?"

The Abbot glanced at Benedict. For a time there was silence. Then he asked, "What is Garcia's plan for the monastery?"

"It will be burned to the ground," said Benedict. "Garcia does not want any 'monuments of opposition' left standing."

"And what about the brothers?"

"They will each receive money," Benedict answered.

"Is that the 'incredible wealth' you mentioned earlier?"

"Who can say how much the men will receive," said Benedict. "I'm going to be Minister of Oil. Paying the men will be up to the Minister of Finance—and the President." Benedict saw the frown of Federico's face. "Don't worry. They'll be taken care of."

"Oh, I know how the plan will work. You see, I know the disregard for human life that is part of every Garcia plan. His 'solutions' are usually permanent."

Both men were silent for a moment. Then Federico said, "Let's take this inside. My office please." Together they entered the main door of the monastery.

As they walked down the hallway, Benedict said, "Understand that those Southerners tend to be stupid and lazy. There's a lot of Indian blood in them. They are our peasants and have not earned any part of our oil profits. So, the fewer there are of them, well, the more profit is left for us Northerners."

When they entered the Abbot's office, Federico slammed the door and both men sat down, Federico behind his desk and Benedict in front of the desk.

"Think, man. Think!" Federico shouted. "Where will it all stop? After those people you call peasants are killed—or driven off by war—who will be next? Will the engineers be killed after that—once the drills are in and pumping? And

275

after that, will the army be killed off—once the war is over? And then the journalists—because they know the truth even though they can't print it? And after them, will you want the clergy killed because they know immorality when they see it? Or, think of this Benedict; maybe the Minister of Oil will be killed—once the oil market is manipulated!"

Benedict waved one enormous hand signaling that he wanted to speak.

Federico was not finished. "Somewhere in there, those people who want a democratic vote instead of the dictatorship we have now—they will have to be killed. Then who will be left? Tell me, Benedict—tell me now—where will it end?"

"The Brothers," Benedict said, "have lived here most of their adult lives—in absolute poverty. Now it is time for them to have incredible wealth. Their time has come." Benedict smiled. "My time has come. Think of it; a few years ago the princes of the United Arab Emirates each had one flea-bitten camel. Then they started selling their oil. Now they travel in chauffeur-driven limos—Mercedes limos—when they ride from one palace home to another palace. They have so much money they can't spend it fast enough. Soon they will spend millions of dollars for just one camel. Can you see some of our brothers riding around giving orders to their chauffeurs?"

Suddenly Benedict's speech became soft and low. "And some of the most beautiful women in the world will come here looking to marry wealth. That will put smiles on a few faces. All the brothers need will be a glimpse of real wealth—and what it buys—and they will be happy."

"No!" Federico said. "None of those things will make them happy. They each took vows of poverty because those vows protect them from evil. Christ said, 'The love of money is the root of all kinds of evil'."

"You foolish, old man," Benedict spoke loudly, "you have been here so long you do not remember what the outside world is really like."

There was a moment of silence—only a moment—when suddenly the sound of scratching came from the other side of the closed door. Both looked at each other. Slowly Federico stood up and opened the door several inches. Immediately a small orange-colored kitten trotted into the room and quickly jumped up on the Abbot's desk.

"Ah," said Federico. "Two Benedicts—soft, 'Little Benedict' and 'Brother Benedict'—the challenger. Both of you named after Saint Benedict." Federico smiled then and added, "Neither one of you takes after the original saint." Little Benedict began to purr. Brother Benedict scowled. Federico slowly petted the kitten. After a moment he looked across the desk at the brother. "Why did you come here, to this monastery, in the first place? What did you want?"

"Because I was broke," said the brother. "I had no place to go. And I was so ugly that I had no friends." His voice became a whisper. "I thought I might feel accepted here." He pulled himself up then and his voice became loud. "Now I know better. The answer to everything is wealth. The solution is not handsomeness. I learned that wealth is power. And now is my chance to have it all."

"What you are attempting to do is wrong," said Federico, "but far worse is that you are tempting the others in this monastery. Look at your motives brother. You have made greed your god and now you want others to follow that same path."

"Yes, I suppose that is true," answered Benedict. "I am motivated by greed. I see wealth as my salvation."

"Then are you doing Garcia's work—or Satan's?"

"I can't be bothered to think about that. I know that I will soon forget about poverty. Within weeks I will have no memory of this place. Then—I will be free—to do whatever I wish."

"Is it so easy to forget?" asked the Abbot. "Can you ever forget your vows to God himself? Can you forget the true satisfaction of obedience? And can you forget the sound of your brothers singing vespers in the evening?"

"I will have other things," said Benedict, "many other things to occupy my mind."

"But can you be free of guilt—of shame?"

"Old man," Benedict said, "can't you understand? Then listen carefully to what I tell you now. Where there is no conscience—there can be no guilt."

The Abbot looked sternly at Benedict. "There was a place in you, Benedict." His voice was firm. "You could say that place was in your heart of hearts, or deep within your soul—or even in your spirit. It was an empty place. It was searching. And it was tender.

"God the Father was aware of that empty place, and he offered you a marvelous gift. It was the gift of being able to fill that place," Federico said. "It was the gift of his Son, Jesus Christ, to fill that place and promise you salvation.

"But you rejected the gift—that miracle. And you filled that empty place with the things of the world." Federico's voice became softer. "And as the place was filled with other things—you rejected salvation itself. You rejected God's miracle. Then angels wept. Christ was saddened. And that place deep within your heart became hardened until you no longer remembered what had been offered to you."

"Oh, that's some sales pitch," Benedict said. "But it wasn't what I wanted. I had come here to feel accepted."

"And you could have," Federico said. "You would have felt like a strong link in a chain—a golden chain—that bound the brothers of this monastery to God Himself."

Benedict frowned and said: "Words! Empty words! It's as if you are speaking in some language that I no longer understand. It's over for me. For me—it's all over."

Federico's eyes filled with tears. "Benedict," he said, "If you had accepted Christ as your Lord and Savior—you would have become..." Federico stopped speaking and inhaled deeply.

"What would I have become?" Benedict asked.

"You could have changed—on the inside—you could have become..." Again Federico stopped. He looked up at Benedict. Their eyes fixed on each other.

"You would have become," Federico whispered, "beautiful."

They sat in silence. They looked at each other— Abbot and small giant; saint and sinner; man of God and man of the world.

Benedict spoke first. "An emotional prayer would have changed me?" he asked. As he spoke the question, his lips curled into a sneer so that his features turned even more disfigured. "What kind of nonsense are you preaching?"

"Yes—on the inside," Federico said. "In your heart— the only place it really counts. Yes. You would have become a shining star—positive and beautiful."

"This conversation is over," Benedict said. "Not you, the Father in heaven, his son Jesus or the Holy Ghost can make me believe any of this. I don't have time for any more of this pig slop."

"You have chosen to worship a new god—wealth."

"Damn right!" answered Benedict.

The Abbot bowed his head and quietly said. "Probably."

"Listen old man," Benedict said. "Here's what is going to happen." Benedict's hands had become fists. "I'm going to take this monastery and turn it over to President Garcia. Don't try to stop me. I'm going to do it for the brothers, and I believe they will be with me. I will lead them into the future."

The Abbot smiled as he looked at the brother. "You say you will lead the men? You don't realize that I know you Benedict. You are a fearful man. You have nothing but fear inside of you and now you hope to lead?"

"I am scared of nothing." Benedict said.

"Really?" Federico asked. "Remember when that little girl, Selena was here and the Holy Ghost spoke through her? She said, 'in this room there is an evil heart with a lying tongue.' When she said that –you were scared."

"I was not!"

"Really? The instant she said it—you wet your pants."

"All I remember of that day was that your prayer stunk!"

"And you smelled like concentrated—urine."

"Just shut up, will ya!" Benedict shouted.

"And you are full of fear—now as you were then. You are not a man of God," Federico said. "You are not even a man."

Benedict jumped to his feet. His chair fell over behind him. The kitten flew off the desk and moved to a corner looking at both men.

"This isn't getting us anywhere," Benedict shouted, spit flying out of his mouth with every word. "Just give me the deed for this land."

Federico remained seated. "There is no deed to give you," he said. "It was all settled years before I entered here. It was a verbal agreement. There was no deed because the land had no value."

"Never mind!" Benedict shouted. "I don't need any deed or any Abbot. I'll have some papers drawn up and back-date them so that there will be no confusion."

"That would be illegal. It's ours by the Right of Residence."

"Don't worry, old man. It has to be done. The property is going to be turned over to Garcia. And the sooner the better."

Benedict took one step forward so that he seemed to be threatening the Abbot. "You can't beat me you old fool! All the power is on my side. The power of the President. The power of oil. The power of wealth."

"Yes?" asked Federico. "Any other power you call upon?"

281

"I'm glad you asked. Then you won't be surprised." Benedict said. "I have a company of soldiers on call for my use whenever I need them. Once I point you out to them, they can arrest you and hold you in prison for as long as I think necessary."

"It wouldn't be the first time I was in prison," Federico said.

"Yes—so I have heard."

"You have broken your vows," Federico said. "And those vows could have helped you. Now, you no longer have any part in the brotherhood of this monastery. So—you must leave."

"I leave with pleasure."

"And you have a place in town. Right?"

"I have a room in town. I've been there off and on for a couple of weeks."

"We know. We also noticed that the chapel 'poor box' kept being emptied on the nights you went into town," Federico said. Then he smiled and added "maybe you can pay back those coins sometime when you are chauffeured out here in your Mercedes limousine."

"You talk to me," Benedict said, "like you would speak to a child."

"That's because you think like a child," Federico answered. "But—I will pray for you as if you were a man." Then the Abbot cleared his throat and in a low voice said, "Now get out of my sight!"

Benedict walked out of the office leaving the door open. A moment after he left, the kitten slowly stood up, stretched and walked to the chair that Benedict had overturned. The cat sniffed the chair and looked up at Federico with an expression of interest.

"Yes, little Benedict," Federico said. "That's the scent—of fear."

During the summer of 2008, Sheik Hamdan bin Mohammed bin Rashid al-Maktoum, the son of Dubai ruler, Sheik Mohammed, attended a desert festival celebrating Bedouin traditions in the emerite of Abu Dhabi. There he bought 26 camels for $4.5 million including one female camel for $2.7 million. Source: Associated Press.

Chapter 18
The Sixth Meeting of the
X-Treme Book Club

"Let me teach you something," Jerry said as he walked into the meeting place. The group watched as Jerry walked over to the closest bookshelf. "Note that this backpack is empty," he said as he dropped it at his feet. "You guys like books for their ideas." He removed two books from the shelf, glanced through one and put it under his arm. "Now it's time you learn how some others look at books." Then Jerry turned to the group and showed them the Book in his hand. He read aloud, 'R is for Rose—Reflections from a Passionate Rose Lover by Carolyn Parker!' It's a beautiful book meant to be left out on the coffee table."

As Jerry turned back to the bookshelf, both books slipped and fell to the floor. Immediately Jerry's hands were on his hips in a gesture of intense impatience with his clumsiness. He knelt down on one knee and as he did so he scratched his scalp with one hand. Then he stood quickly and dramatically returned a book to its place on the shelf.

"There are lots of four-color pics in that book," he said. "Brief text. Good use of white space. Just a beautiful book." With a smile, Jerry sat in his usual chair. He sat, empty-handed with his backpack in his lap.

"You have just seen the master book thief at work," Jerry said. "And the book retails for thirty-five dollars." Then he pulled a book from his backpack. He held it up for the group to see the title: "R is for Rose".

"Jerry, what did you just do?" The group members looked from Jerry to the book he was holding.

Jackson said, "I think you took two books off the shelf and only put one back. At least that's what I think. Right?"

"Ah," Jerry said. "Doc is trained in observation. But did you see anything else?"

"No. Tell us how you did the rest."

"What does a magician do with his magic wand when he makes something disappear?" Jerry asked.

"He distracts you with it," Jackson said. "While the audience watches his hand with the wand he does something with his other hand."

"Correct, Mr. Teacher. The teacher gets an A. While you guys were watching my irritation when both books fell on the floor, my foot held the flap open on my backpack. So when I knelt down while you guys watched my left hand scratching my head, my right hand slid this copy into my backpack. And, if security was scoping me out, they would see me put one book back and think nothing of it. See, nearly everybody takes one book out, glances at it and either takes it to check-out or puts it back. But, just one book. That's what security people see most of the time so it becomes what they expect all the time!"

"So, what you are saying," Jackson said, "is that you are a book thief. And now you just taught us how you do it. Jerry, you surprise me more than I can say."

"Maybe this will help," Jerry said. "I am a former book thief. Two days ago I retired. I gave it up forever. Does that help you? I know it helped me."

"Incredible," Laura said.

"Yes," agreed Emma. "So smooth."

"But that's only a part of the deal," said Jerry. "If I tried to go out the door with this book, it would set off an alarm."

"You know I've heard the alarm," Jackson said. "At first I thought it was a smoke alarm."

"Oh no," Jerry said. "That's the alarm for security to stop the person just as soon as he hits the street." As Jerry spoke he held the book by its outspread covers and shook it roughly. What appeared to be a postage stamp fell out of the book. "That's the trigger for the alarm," Jerry said. "As each book gets put into the stacks it gets one of these things. I think they're printed circuits. They're sort of hidden in the books. It you pay for the book, the check-out removes it under the counter. If you don't pay and didn't remove it yourself, it will set off the alarm."

"So, you can just shake them out of the books?"

"Usually. But they are small and very light so sometimes they will stick in between the pages. You have to be careful where you shake the books. Security watches for that. Don't ever try it back in the music department; that's where most of the cameras are. Most of the security people too."

"That is so neat," Laura said. "This chain of bookstores has the technology to stop book thieves—except for our thief who is more slippery than their high tech electronics."

"Thanks for the compliment," Jerry said.

"But kid," Laura became serious, "you were here— you and your backpack—every Tuesday night. With us." Her eyes narrowed. "You used this book club for your cover!"

"Oh no," Jerry said. "I came in here three of four nights every week and I didn't ever take any books on Tuesdays. See, I like you guys."

"How do you sell these books?" Jackson asked.

"I have a crew of guys who take orders for specific titles from other guys. I get them the books their customers have asked for. I take one-third of the retail price printed on the dust cover. And my guys take another third—at least that's what they tell me. And everybody's happy."

"You say you have a crew," Clayton said. "How many people are in your crew?"

"Total of three," Jerry said. "But only one who is any good at it. The other two are sort of their own best customers."

"But you, Jerry," Jackson said, "what becomes of the money? Are you feeding an addiction—or what?"

"No drugs. No alcohol," Jerry said. "I use it for candy. I like sugar. I eat lots of candy."

"You're kidding," Emma said. "You're thin as a rail!"

"I guess I burn it off. Actually, lately I think I have been worrying it off."

Emma looked as if she had been insulted. "When I worry, I gain weight! Stealing for candy. Jerry, you are such a child."

"Yeah, I know," Jerry said. "But what can I do, ya know?"

"The answer to that question," Laura said, "is to grow up!"

"Well, I'm working on that," Jerry answered. "I did repent and I did confess." He smiled then and added, "Since my confessions I don't need so much candy anymore. Funny how that works."

"What kinds of books are you talking about?" Jackson asked.

"Lots of sexy novels," Jerry said. "Sometimes books like the 'Rose' here are ordered for Christmas presents or for

Mother's day. And you would be surprised how many kids give their parents Bibles."

"Oh no," Emma said. "You steal Bibles! Oh my."

Jackson leaned forward. "How graphic are those sexy novels you mentioned?"

Pretty bad. I mean gross-out bad stuff. Most of it probably should never have been printed."

"Listen to him," Laura said, "Jerry has become a moral person."

"That's right," Jerry said. "I have changed. And it's going to cost me. Right now I'm scared silly. I don't know what's going to happen to me. I might have some jail time coming."

"What an experience," Clayton said. "So, where are you with the law at this point?"

"The police have not been called on me yet. Store's doing some kind of inventory to find out how much is missing. And Mrs. Fisher will call her main office to see how they want it handled. Right now—I'm on hold."

"Mrs. Fisher?" asked Laura.

"Oh yes," said Jerry. "I want to introduce you to Mrs. Fisher. Midge Fisher. The manager here. She's been kind of nice to me so far."

"Poor Jerry," Emma said. "Did you have to confess to Mrs. Fisher?"

"I went to my parents first," Jerry said. "My mom threw a hissy. And dad used the word 'disappointed' a hundred times. So it wasn't too bad. Course they don't know how many books I have taken; I rounded off my estimate a bit. Well, maybe a lot—"

"How many, Jerry?" Jackson interrupted. "Can you tell us? Or not?"

"I'm guessing three of four a week for the last eight weeks," Jerry said. "Comes to about twenty-five or so."

"Hey kid," Laura said. "Remember we agreed that what's said in this group stays in this group. So tell the truth, okay? You just said this has been going on for eight weeks. Two minutes before that you told us what your customers were ordering for Christmas—which was five months ago. Want to check your math?"

"How many books did I steal? In all?" Jerry glanced at Jackson and quickly looked away. "I don't know. Never kept any count so I'll see what the store's inventory turns up."

"But are you truly sorry?" Laura said.

"Like big time!" Jerry said. "My parents took me to meet with Midge Fisher. She's the manager here, you know. Dad made me box up some books I had stashed in my room. We brought them to that meeting with Mrs. Fisher. She actually thanked me for what she called, 'coming forward' with what was going on. Let me tell you, going into that meeting," Jerry put on hand on his stomach and the other around his neck, "if I had eaten some candy bars I think I would have puked them up. Anyway, I'm done with candy and I'm done with scoring books. It isn't worth it. I should have known better."

Clayton turned nearly around and looked behind him. "I have the strangest feeling that I'm being watched," he said. "Like every camera in the place is watching us."

"Almost like we're the accessories to the shoplifter here," Jackson said. "Like every security person in the place has memorized our faces."

"What a creepy sensation," Laura said. "So Jerry, for heaven's sake, stick that alarm sensor in the rose book and put it back on the shelf. Please."

Jerry quickly slipped the alarm trigger into the book and rammed the book into its place. "I know that feeling of being watched," he said. "I'm sorry you guys have to put up with it too."

From across the aisle, a woman's voice called: "Jerry, Jerry."

"Hey," Jerry said, "that is Mrs. Fisher. I think she wants to meet you guys. Hi Mrs. Fisher."

She walked directly into the circle of book club members. She was blonde, in her late forties, strikingly pretty yet with a look of authority on her. She smiled at each member of the group. Then Jerry stood up.

"Guys, this is Mrs. Fisher," Jerry said.

"Everybody calls me Midge," she said.

"Let me introduce our group," Jerry said. "This is Dave Jackson, our discussion leader and group brain. And this girl is our Emma who is not afraid to ask questions. The lady next to Emma is Laura; be careful around Laura cause she sees everything through the eyes of Christianity. This is Clayton who is a doctor and we suspect he is also a hair man. And you know me—Jerry the former book thief."

"I'm very pleased to meet all of you," she said. "Now Jerry, if you would leave us for a few minutes I would like to talk with these people—she paused for a moment, then added, "about you."

As Jerry left the group, Midge sat down in his chair. "I wanted to get opinions about Jerry," she said. "I raised two children of my own. I think I know kids and I feel there's a lot to like in Jerry. But you all know him better than I. So tell me. Is he 'save-able'?"

"He's consistently irritating," said Clayton.

"But, occasionally likable," added Emma.

"Your question," said Jackson, "about Jerry being savable. Are you asking whether or not to turn him over to the police? Is that what you are asking?"

"Jerry is an interesting child," Midge said. "I've been in business for many years—most of it retail. I've dealt with many shoplifters. But I've never heard of anyone turning themselves in before they are caught."

"We've been reading about repentance," Jackson said.

"Really? What book are you discussing?"

"Wind, Sand and Hope."

"Good, good, good," Midge said. "Is he getting it?"

293

"I think so."

"We're discussing it?" Clayton asked. "Usually we discuss everything but the book."

"You know he came in?" Midge said. "Came in and confessed."

"That's good," Laura said. "And what did his confession look like?"

"He's plenty scared. He was humble. No wisecracks. No cynicism. And a few tears."

"Tears?" Laura said with a smile. "From our street-smart Jerry? Sounds like you got him right where you want him."

"Yes, I'm letting him hang there for a while."

"Then what's next?" asked Jackson.

"I don't know if you realize it," Midge said, "but this group means a lot to Jerry." She sat with her hands folded and immobile in her lap. "He asked me to stop by tonight and—meet his friends."

"He must really be lonely," Clayton said.

"No, that's not it," said Midge. "He told me he's starting to realize some new things. He sounded sincere. What do you think?"

"He's savable!" Emma said. "Totally."

Midge suddenly stood up. "Thank you all," she said with a trace of a bow. "Mr. Jackson, I'll call you during the week. They're just one or two things to clear up." She turned and gave a wave. "Thanks for your input. See you next week."

As Midge walked away, the members of the book club looked at each other.

"I don't think she cared about anything we had to say," Clayton said.

"Maybe she was looking for evidence," the moderator said, 'to support what she had already decided."

"There was no evidence," Laura said, "only opinions. Big difference."

"Doesn't matter does it?" Jackson said as he stood up and looked down the store aisle. "She's in charge here. Her opinion is the only one that matters."

"I hope she was listening," Emma added.

"Sure," Clayton said. "Like my dog listens for the refrigerator door—listens for what he can get out of it. I think she's going to nail Jerry. And I think he deserves it."

"Oh Doc." There was pain in Emma's voice. "Really?"

"Sure. It was bound to happen."

"Poor Jerry."

Chapter 19
The Discussion

It was a very quiet knock on the door. "Yes, come in," Federico said.

Brother Forgiven stood in the doorway. "Are you going to attend Compline tonight?" he asked.

"No, Mason's covering for me; why do you ask?"

"I've got a couple of question," Forgiven said, "whenever you have a few minutes."

"Come on in. I need to talk to you too. Come in, sit down."

Brother Forgiven walked to the chair in front of the Abbot's desk. He paused, then sat down, took a deep breath and remained silent.

"Yes?" Federico asked.

"It's this mess about a war. The stink of it is in the air. It's coming, and we seem to be in the middle of it. How did this happen?"

Federico looked across his desk at the brother. "How are most wars started?" he asked. "Sometimes it's borders. Sometimes it's about the oil under the ground. What we are facing now is about both."

"I remember the last war," Forgiven said. "I had hoped it would be the final war."

"That seems like a lifetime ago," Federico said.

"For me," Forgiven said, "it was."

"And when that war ended, we had a great motto…"

"Yes—'Two states under one flag'."

"Right," Federico said. "Great motto but a terrible truce."

"I heard that the truce was a fiasco."

"It was indeed," Federico said. "They took the half with El Diablo, the smaller mountain. We got the half with Solidad the larger mountain. They took most of the good farm land. We were left with most of the rocky land."

"But now, this thing with the desert?" Forgiven asked.

"Neither side wanted it then. It was miles of absolutely worthless sand between two mountains. Nobody wanted it. It was never surveyed. It was never even named."

Forgiven said. "I'm beginning to see. Nobody wanted it until six months ago."

"You are so right. Neither state marked the borders. Even the land this monastery is built on was never established as belonging to either state.

"And six months ago a geologist took some core samples and found oil." Federico looked down at his desk and slowly rubbed his forehead with both hands. "The disagreement is about who owns the oil rights. The basic problem—is greed."

Brother Forgiven started to stand and reach one hand out to touch Federico. Instead, he sat back down and said, "I'm sorry, my Abbot. I know how you hate war."

At those words, Federico looked up. He stared at Forgiven. "You know many things," he said, "but you cannot begin to know how much I hate war."

Forgiven tried to smile then. "Maybe they didn't all die," he said. "Maybe their medics stopped the bleeding, and they made it to hospitals in time. At least some of them must have made it to a hospital and lived. Who knows? Some might have lived for years, had full lives…"

"Oh no, my brother." Federico's voice was barely audible. "They died. I saw the impact of every round I ever fired—the impact and the damage. Thanks for trying to comfort me. But they died. All of them."

Both men sat in silence for several minutes. Then Forgiven said, "Ah—what was it you wanted to see me about? You said you wanted to talk to me."

"Yes, my Brother. I need you to go along with Brother Mason and me tomorrow. We're attending the conference. I am giving the opening prayer. Mason will drive. We'll go in the Chevy. Can I plan on you going with us?"

"Yes. Of course. I'm honored. I wanted to hear your prayer anyway."

"I've heard that Presidente Garcia insists on calling it a peace conference," Federico said. He was smiling.

"But the people," Forgiven said, call it the war conference. Anyway—where is it going to be held?"

"Middle of the desert. Close to Solidad."

"Oh, that place," Forgiven said. "I know that place. The people call it, 'The Place of Temptations'. I don't know why they call it that."

Federico stood up and raised himself to his full height by pushing on the desktop with both hands. Then he walked slowly to a cabinet built into the wall under a window. "Would you care for some sipping brandy?"

"Is your arthritis worse?" Forgiven asked.

"No complaints," said Federico.

"But it is spreading isn't it?"

Federico brought a bottle out from the cabinet. "It's trying to envelop my entire body," he said.

"So—more than just your hands and feet, eh?"

"A lot more." Federico walked back to the desk and produced two small glasses from one of the drawers. "I think of it as one of Satan's calling cards. He drops by every morning to make the pain worse. It's not enough to kill me but nearly enough to keep me from morning prayers."

"I'll have a shot of Brandy," Forgiven said, "if you'll join me."

Federico filled Forgiven's glass and then poured several drops in his own glass.

"Thanks," Forgiven said, took a sip and added, "Do we make this stuff here?"

"No, no," Federico said. "I could not trust Mason enough to have vats of temptation here. No. I buy one bottle sometimes when I go into town." Federico did not touch his glass. "Be tactful with Mason," he said. "He's not completely cured. Soon, God willing. Just not yet."

Forgiven finished his brandy. "This is probably not good medicine to be taken on an empty stomach."

"I'm sorry; was today one of your fasts?"

"Yes."

Federico quickly unwrapped a tan linen cloth that had been left on his desk. There was one small biscuit in it. Federico broke it into two pieces and gave one to Brother Forgiven. "This is the cheapest brandy I could get. On an empty stomach it will eat your gut out." Both men broke small morsels off his bread and ate them. Forgiven raised his glass in a salute and drank in silence. Federico did not touch his glass.

After some time, Federico said, "I hope you will look back on this meeting—over the years ahead—and remember it with joy."

"Yes, of course."

"There are a couple more things I need to tell you," Federico said as he re-filled Forgiven's glass. "I'll be leaving soon."

"Where are you going?"

"To a better place."

"Oh, that way," Forgiven said. "Not too soon I hope. We need you right here."

"Now listen," Federico said. His voice was firm. "You, Brother Forgiven, you are to be the next Abbot."

Forgiven looked at Federico. "Oh no. I couldn't. I follow orders not give them."

"Excellent," said Federico. "Follow the orders you will receive from God the Father. He honors obedience."

"I can't. I could never do the job," he said. "So please don't consider me for all that responsibility. Don't plan on me." He gulped his drink.

As if he had not heard, Federico said, "When that time comes—are you listening to me?—when it comes, watch out for Brother Benedict. Understand?"

"Yes, I'm listening, but I don't like it. And I thought he left us. Didn't he?"

"Yes. He's gone," Federico said. "He's no longer a Brother. I think he went to work for Presidente Garcia. I know he has renounced his vows. And I'm afraid he has gone to serve his old appetites."

After several moments, Federico said, "Listen again little brother. This is one of our more important teachings. As the novices complete their first two or three months, one by one, they will ask the same question." Federico paused and gazed out the window.

"Yes, my Abbot. I am listening."

"Yes. As the new ones learn the disciplines, they will ask if it is necessary to live in a monastery to grow in grace." "And the answer is no—not necessary. Right?"

"That's right. Anyone can practice the rules of solitude, silence, prayer—knowing God's will and obeying it. One can learn them anywhere and practice them anywhere." Federico smiled to himself and looked up at Forgiven. "But—there are fewer distractions inside a monastery than outside in the world. And that's part of the theology you will have to use."

"One more thing," Federico said, "when you become the Abbot, don't expect the brothers to give you much respect."

"Why is that?"

"It's because you are the one giving the orders. It usually produces resentment over time."

At that instant Federico's office door was flung open. Mason took one step into the room and said, "what time..." looked around the room and added, "oh, I didn't know you were having a meeting."

"See what I mean," Federico said. "Mason doesn't take the time to knock."

Brother Forgiven smiled and nodded silently.

"I just need to know what time you want the car tomorrow," Mason said as he looked around the room.

"We need to leave by 10 o'clock," Federico said.

"Are you guys drinking instead of going to vespers?" Mason asked. He looked at Brother Forgiven, "I never get anything to drink when I meet with the Abbot."

"Let's not bother my Brother with that right now," Federico said. As he spoke the orange kitten walked cautiously through the open door.

"Sorry, I let Little Benedict in," Mason said.

"Never mind the cat." Federico paused and added, "Just be ready at 10 tomorrow. Thank you Brother Mason. You may go now and close the door will you? One cat is enough."

Brother Forgiven sat in front of the desk. He held his empty brandy glass. A slightly dazed look crossed his face. "Isn't there anyone else you would rather see in line for the job?" he asked.

"You are the chosen one," Federico answered. "Would you like a bit more brandy?"

"Yes. I would. Thank you."

"So, my brandy isn't such bad medicine anymore, eh?"

"No sir. Not at all—ah sir? May I simply refuse the office of Abbot? Would you go along with that?"

"No. But I think we should both finish our bread."

As both men ate, the kitten slowly crept up to Brother Forgiven. He seemed to be stalking Forgiven's sandals. As the cat slowly moved closer, Forgiven suddenly sneezed which frightened the cat who jumped straight up and landed on all four feet. The fur on his back stood up. Both men laughed at the kitten's exaggerated reaction.

"And what exactly did we both witness?" asked Federico.

"That cats can fly—sometimes. Is that it?"

"Well, I was thinking of something else. Remember his name is Benedict. Named after Saint Benedict," Federico said.

Forgiven became serious. "I give up. What did we both witness?"

Federico was laughing. "That was what I would call nothing less than—a Benedictine retreat."

Brother Forgiven joined in with Federico's laughter— momentarily. Suddenly Forgiven was aware that the Abbot had become extremely serious. "There's more you want to tell me. Right?" he asked.

Federico sat straight up and looked across the desk. "Now this is some of the most important information I can give you. You will need to make sure every person here spends time with his Spiritual Director every two weeks. A brother can get way off track in two weeks. So everyone must check in. And don't blame every attack on Satan. Usually when a brother starts to waver about spiritual things it is the result of loneliness."

Federico sat back in his chair and looked intently at Forgiven. "The Spiritual Directors are vital to the success of this monastery. Therefore you must supervise them constantly. Do you want to write some of this down? I have paper and pens right here."

"No. I'm still hoping this is all going to go away."

"Well then remember what I'm about to tell you now," Federico said. "You must see to it that the Spiritual Directors meet with each other once a week. Friday mornings are what they are used to now. They have to compare notes and talk about their own problems. Occasionally sit in with them. Do that unannounced. Give them the benefit of your thinking. Keep reminding them to pray for their directions." The Abbot paused and looked at his Brother. "Do you understand the importance of what we have covered so far?"

"Yes sir. It's a lot, but I understand."

"I know it's a lot to spring on you in one sitting," Federico said. "But when each test comes along—you will not be alone. When you go to prayer God will guide you."

"Yes sir. I hope so."

"Most of this information you know already. I think you have a good idea of most of this—stuff." Then Federico smiled again. It was a long, joyous smile and he said, "You're doing quite well—for an old chicken-thief!"

Both men laughed. Federico poured Forgiven another brandy and both laughed again.

Brother Forgiven stood up and walked to the window. He looked out but night had fallen. He could not see anything but darkness. "Now I have a question," he said, "that only an Abbot could answer."

"Then this is the right time and place to ask it."

"What is the reason for the rule that says the brothers are not allowed to speak of their own spiritual experiences?"

Federico said, "The traditional answer is that such experiences are private, personal matters—between God and one person. If God had intended for the entire group to have the experience—then that is what would have happened. But when God chooses to work with one person it should stay with that person. That is the rule."

"But that's not the main reason for the rule is it?" Forgiven asked.

"No. It's not."

Forgiven returned to his chair before the desk. He sat down and asked, "Then what is the real reason?"

Federico smiled. The smile turned into a laugh. Then Forgiven began to smile. "I think I know," Forgiven said as he began to laugh along with Federico. "It's to avoid competition between the men isn't it?"

"Of course," Federico said. "Look at it like this. We have no women here so there is no one to impress. We live in poverty so we own nothing—which keeps us from gambling. The food is all over-cooked so there's nothing to look forward to on that score. It's a serious life style so there is not much for entertainment. So—spiritual experiences could become a form of competition." Federico was still, quietly laughing.

Brother Forgiven's face was deadly serious. "You mean like one brother might be 'visited' by—say, Saint Thomas Aquinas. So somebody with a competitive attitude could claim that he was visited by Aquinas accompanied by fifty angels. Something like that?"

Federico continued laughing softly. "The angels would have to be really, really little ones," he said, "because the cells are too small to have fifty-one visitors."

Forgiven continued to laugh. "Unless," he said, "unless they are the kind of angels that dance on the head of a pin."

"Just consider what we have here," the Abbot said. "We live in a community of stringent rules, due to our prayer schedule we suffer from sleep deprivation, there is the total abstinence of sex—at least as far as I know—and loneliness—we only speak for a couple hours every day—and then there are always some impressionable ones who are, shall we say, open to suggestion." Federico laughed again and added, "These things can come together at the same time and produce false or counterfeit experiences."

Then Federico became serious. "You realize," he said, "those are the ones you will have to weed out. And do that when their vows are still temporary."

"But Abbot, if we can't discuss our experiences, how will I know which ones to get rid of?"

"You'll know, little Brother. The Holy Ghost tells you. There will be no question."

"Sir, is there any possible way," Forgiven asked, "for me to get out of this Abbot job? I mean, you are still in good health and making good decisions so there is plenty of time—maybe someone else could be groomed for the job-someone you could personally break in…"

"Little brother," Federico interrupted, "listen to me. This has been prayed over. Prayed about until a sense of peace and finality took over the decision. You are the one. Our Father and I concur. You have been chosen."

"Federico, I can think of no person less qualified." Forgiven stopped speaking then. He stood up slowly and slowly walked to the window. After a moment he turned and looked at the Abbot with a surprised expression. "You and the Father concurred? You wanted me to be Abbot too? This is so hard to believe!"

"Hey, let me explain," Federico said smiling. "Over the years you have become my best friend as well as the Brother I love the most—in an agape way, of course."

"Love?" said Forgiven. "You love me? I was one of your worst sinners. You thought I killed your mother. You wanted me dead." He took two steps backwards. He looked around the room. He looked at everything except Federico. "You thought of me as your enemy." Then he finally looked into Federico's eyes and said, "And you had good reason."

"Ah, little Brother—that's just it." Federico's voice was deep then and his smile covered his entire face. "I prayed more for you than any of the others. And for a longer time too. And I noticed that when I pray for a person over a long time, I end up loving that person—loving in a spiritual sense."

"Amazing!" said Forgiven.

In an effort to stand beside Forgiven, Federico started to rise, however Little Benedict had curled up in Federico's lap. "Please come back here Little Brother," Federico said. "Come, sit down and hear me out."

The Brother returned to his chair and sat across from his Abbot.

"This will be good for you to know," Federico said. "Because I think it has something to do with God's will. I believe that when you pray for one of God's creations long enough, you start to feel for that person. You start to feel—well, as God himself feels for that person. And, I'm telling you—God loves his creations."

"It's amazing Federico. How could you do that?"

"It wasn't me, little Brother. It was God's doing. Purely God. He can take any vessel, empty it of all hatred and re-fill it with love. And it doesn't matter whether the vessel is a tin cup—or an Old man."

"God surely is amazing," Forgiven said. "And you are amazing too."

"And please remember to be kind to 'Little' Benedict here," Federico said as he patted the cat in his lap. "He's one of the purest, most sinless creatures in this monastery."

"Yes, my Abbot." I will remember to be kind to him."

"As well as being spiritually kind to the Brothers here?"

"Who am I," Forgiven asked, "to argue with my Abbot?"

"Then you agree?" Federico asked. "You will be our next Abbot?"

"Yes."

"And you will put yourself aside and follow the leadings of the Holy Ghost?"

"Yes. I agree."

"Good. It is done."

"Easier said—than done."

"Dear Abbot," Forgiven said, "I feel this is the right time for me to ask you a question."

"Then ask it."

"A serious question," repeated the brother.

"Fine. Then I'll give you a serious answer. Ask away."

Forgiven looked down at his feet for a moment. Then he looked up and into Federico's eyes. "I have been at this monastery for many years. And I still don't know. I mean— how am I to think about spiritual experiences?" Then he quickly added, "You know what I mean—what I'm asking?"

"Yes, yes, brother. I know what you are asking. It's a fair question. Nearly everyone who has come here and taken the vows has asked that question—or one very much like it."

Brother Forgiven looked into Federico's eyes without blinking. "Well—so?"

"Every novice has been told that he must not come here looking for spiritual experiences," said Federico, "but instead, to look for God."

"Yes, I know that and I appreciate it. And I believe that I have followed that advice for forty years but during that time you have had the experiences and I have not had any. I've practiced prayer, study, solitude, and silence. Still, nothing has come out of all that."

Federico looked across his desk and smiled. Then he asked, "What do you think you are looking for?"

"You once told me that you have seen many things—ordinary things like an ordinary, beaten-up tin cup—and seen them with extraordinary clarity. Forgiven inched closer over the desk top as he spoke, "and you said it was as if you were seeing those things through God's eyes."

"It was a long, long time ago that we had that conversation," Federico said. As he spoke he pushed his glass of brandy to one side and leaned on the desk. "Since then, I have been able to see more than that." He smiled so that the wrinkles at the corners of his eyes deepened. "Now I can sometimes see the purpose for those things.

"When I crossed over this un-named desert..." Federico paused for a moment. He blinked with the memory of it, and went on. "I fell down at the base of Solidad. I was depleted. There was only nothingness. I was devoid of any life—good or bad—burned out. I was the vessel that was empty."

Federico leaned back in his chair and smiled. "Years later, in the courtyard of this monastery, when I saw that old cup turning brilliant silver in God's sight—I knew it was for me. And it was full! It was meant for me—and it was full."

The Brother looked at the Abbot. "You say it was full. How do you mean that? What was in it?"

"Grace."

Forgiven stared at Federico. "I don't understand." He said.

"I'll explain, as best as I can," Federico said. "I can now see more than the material object—such as that tin cup. Now I can see how God uses that vessel for bestowing life-giving water, or grace, to the person who needs it most." Then Federico's smile faded and he said, "I see more than the object. Now I see for that object—or that person."

Forgiven drew back and sat straight up in his chair. "I have never—never seen anything like that," he said. "How does that happen with you?"

Federico said, "It's a gift. It comes directly from the Father."

"But what I'm asking," Forgiven said, "is what do you do to make it happen?"

"It's a gift, I tell you. I suppose you can ask for it, but you can't control it. It's not up to you. It is from God the Father."

"Then what is all this about? Years and years of vows, poverty, chastity, obedience, silence…"

"Hey, put patience in there too." Said Federico. "That's all preparation."

"Preparation for when it happens?"

"No—for if it happens."

Forgiven's face took a pained expression. "If it happens? So all these years might have been for nothing? Is that it?"

"No," Federico said. "In prayer, solitude and silence we have a time of listening and fellowshipping with Jesus. It is never time lost or wasted. It is time well spent. And if it takes a lifetime then it's a life well spent."

"Yes, but in the meantime, what am I to do? Tell me. This is important. I need to know."

"So, little brother, you need to know, huh?"

"Yes, what am I to do?"

"The answer is simple," Federico said. "I can phrase it in two words. Be ready."

Chapter 20
The Sacrifice

"We should be at the conference site by around noon," Mason said. He smiled as he spoke. He enjoyed driving the monastery car. Next to Mason sat Abbot Federico who had said barely a word. Alone in the back seat was Brother Forgiven.

"What's this conference about anyway?" asked Mason. "I suppose it's all about borders, right?"

"Borders?" Brother Forgiven said. "It's always about borders. At one level anyway. Underneath it all it is really about greed."

The brother's words were followed by several miles of silence. Then he said, "Federico, have you been fasting more than two days a week?" Federico did not answer. "You are so thin lately."

Mason, who had a heavy build, said, "It's not my nature to fast. I know it doesn't work this way but if either of you brothers wants to fast for me, you can take my turn. I won't mind."

The car passed another truck filled with men in civilian clothes. "They're on the way to the conference too," Brother Forgiven said, probably just to see the show." The comment was followed by another interlude of quiet.

"Remember Brothers," Federico said, "The new monastery is to be located in one of the poorest sections of Los Angeles. The city of angels. Sounds good huh?"

"Yes sir," Forgiven said from the back seat. "I'll do exactly as you have talked to me about it. But just know I'm sitting right behind you, and you are still too thin."

"Mason," Federico said, "teach your Brother everything you think he should know about the States. He will help you start the new location." Federico half turned back to face Forgiven. "While you are in the States, if you ever run into a small woman, about my age, blonde and blue eyed—named Olivia, talk to her. Tell her I said she should be a good Christian because I don't think I want to spend eternity in heaven if she's not going to be there too."

"You can think about that at a time like this?"

"Yes, my brother," Federico said. "Because I was meditating on all the beauty of the world."

"You just don't want me to know how much fasting you've been doing."

"At a time like this," Federico said, "what does it matter?"

Mason glanced at the other men in the car, he asked, "What do you mean, 'at a time like this'?"

"This desert is familiar territory," Federico said. "I've faced Satan out here before. Sometime today I'm going to do that again. I'm going to do today, much of what I was created to do."

316

Cautiously Mason asked, "And what exactly, is that?"

"I'm going," Federico said, "to say a prayer with the boys."

"Well okay," Mason said, looking straight ahead as he drove around another truck. "I guess we are going to pray for the soldiers." The car sped up slightly. "I'm getting some strange feelings here. They're kinda giving me chills. Why is this conference being held out in the middle of nowhere?"

"It could be a bit dangerous to have in the city," said brother Forgiven. "Too many innocent women and children in the city."

"Dangerous?" asked Mason. "Will one of you please tell me what the plan is?"

From the back seat Brother Forgiven answered, "You are a student Mason. So here's a test. What do you think we will be going to today?"

"Okay," Mason said. He was smiling as he drove. "Let me see if I can make a guess." His smile faded. He said, "There are two sides just ahead of us. Both sides waiting for Abbot Federico's invocation. So, there are two armies, representing two different states—each with their own opinion. Each side will be there, probably well-armed to protect each president. And both armies will be ready to go into combat for some of this desert land. And that's because it has oil under it." Mason stopped speaking as they passed a group of people walking. Then he added: "That had better be some good prayer."

"There is some logic behind the problem," said Federico. "This desert was considered worthless land. Neither side wanted it when de la Rosa seceded from the mother country. So no borders were ever agreed upon or marked off. No borders were ever established. There was no need."

"That was before you were even born," Forgiven said to Mason. "But now the land has value and both sides claim it."

"Yes, maybe I'm too young to understand but two entire countries are ready to declare war—over oil?" said Mason. "It seems like a high price to pay."

"Most wars," said Federico, "are about oil—and oil profits."

Mason glanced over at Federico. His voice was low. He said, "There are men with rifles and by this time they are lined up facing each other in a desert of no-man's land. Probably more soldiers on the way." There was a moment of silence. Then Mason added, "And we represent—a third opinion—which is that no land, with or without oil, is worth the kind of warfare we could expect in the near future."

"That's a fair summary," said Forgiven, "except that you left out one part."

"Which is?"

It was Federico who answered. "Both of their sides are motivated by greed. Our side has God with us."

Mason looked at Federico. Neither man was smiling. "I know," said Mason, "that our God is capable of anything.

But there will be hundreds of armed soldiers out there. Maybe two hundred on one side and the other side with at least that many—probably more. And if they are motivated by greed, what makes you think they are going to listen to you—or to our God?"

Federico glanced over at Mason. Then slowly he turned and looked only at the road ahead. "Our God," Federico said, "is going to give you a day, Mason. That day is today—and you will remember it for the rest of your life."

"Sir, I trust you and I trust our God," Mason said. "You know that. I just don't trust all those trigger-happy men in their new uniforms out there—hyped up for war—and loaded down with ammunition."

Federico looked at Mason. "You say you trust," he said. "You know you want to trust. But at the bottom of your heart, there is fear. Today, you will learn to trust at such a deep level that even your heart will be fearless."

As if he had not been listening, Mason said, "Well anyway, here's my idea of the solution. Just declare a twenty minute war. Both sides agree to just one battle. Instead of several years of killing and thousands of dead—call a cease fire at twenty minutes. Whichever side was winning at that moment—that side takes the land. There would be only a few dead and everybody else goes home a hero—after twenty minutes. Right?"

The two older men were silent for a moment.

"You are naïve," Federico said. "You know many things. But you don't know how men believe in lies. Military men believe that force is the answer. Their minds are clouded with it. For them, one battle can never be called a war."

"But if they want to save their own men's lives," Mason said, "wouldn't they want this?"

"Here's where your "One Battle' idea breaks down," Federico said. "The side that wins one battle will get caught up in the joys of the victory and the power that results. The celebrations will include wine, women, and prestige. But all celebrations must come to an end sometime. Then the men of that side will talk of more fighting. They will thirst for more victories and more power. So there will be more battles."

"Now consider the army that lost the 'One Battle'," Forgiven said. "They will believe that they must march into other battles. It will be a decision based on 'honor'. It will call for retaliation for their men who were killed. So their cry will be, 'Our fallen comrades cannot have died in vain!'"

Brother Forgiven laughed at Mason. "Do you think of a military battle like one of your soccer games? After twenty minutes a referee blows a whistle and both sides stop? Having been an athlete you should know that most men see competition as their role. It is their test of virility. So there is no middle ground. There is either the pride of victory of the shame of defeat."

They could see a road block ahead. Trucks were lined up behind it as only one at a time was allowed through. The car came to a halt in the line.

"Sir," Mason said as they waited, "you two Brothers are my teachers. Tell me, what is the way to stop a war or prevent it from happening? And, what are we doing here? If you know God's will, can you let me in on it?" Neither man answered Mason's questions.

Slowly the line of vehicles pulled ahead until the car came up to the guards. Two soldiers looked into the car. One moved to stand in front of the car while the other disappeared into a nearby tent. He quickly re-emerged with a Captain.

Federico rolled down his window. "I am Federico Llanos, Abbot of the monastery de San Juan de Los Cruz. These are two of my brothers. I have a letter from each of the Presidentes, Presidente Emanuel Garcia and Presidente Jose DeVilla."

"The letter from Presidente Garcia," The Captain interrupted, "is of no value today. President Garcia will not be attending as he had more urgent business in the city. However he is being represented by General Garcia."

"But I was asked to give an opening prayer at this conference," said Federico. "Would you please show me where the speakers' platform is?"

"So you are the prayer man," the officer shouted. "You are late!" he said, his voice full of anger. "These men have been standing in the sun waiting for you. They are not happy. Get over there, now.

"There is no platform today." The Captain said. He glanced at each of the three with a look of irritation. "You can't take the car any further. Leave it over there," he pointed to some undefined location. "You can walk from there. Get your prayer done so the conference can begin." The officer glanced at each of the three and added, "The sovereign nation of de la Rosa will not be responsible for any harm that befalls you. Now—move on!"

As the three men stepped out of the car, Federico turned to Brother Forgiven and said, "The prayer is here in my chest pocket. Just in case I don't get to it today."

"Garcia had more urgent business?" Mason said with a sneer. "What's more urgent than this?"

Brother Forgiven, walking next to Federico put his hand on Federico's shoulder. He looked into Federico's eyes as he felt tears welling up in his own eyes. "About your prayer," he said, "we'll see."

The three brothers walked quickly past row upon row of troops. The soldiers on one side of the field were in olive drab fatigues—seemingly ready for combat. The men on the other side were in sweaty khaki uniforms. There were several hundred with rifles, on each side of the field. Neither side was dug in. All were standing at parade rest.

Mason whispered, "The reason Garcia isn't here is because he thought he might be killed. This could all be a trap. General Garcia is the President's grandson. Some President old Garcia is. Some family man. He sends his grandson—when he thinks there might be some shooting. The kid is only twenty years old and a playboy. I don't know—it's all sort of creepy."

Federico scanned the space in the center of the field. "Take me back to the monastery whenever—it is finished," he said.

The three men walked across the open space of sand and heat. Mason tried to slow the other two and said, "Does anyone else see it? There's something wrong here. Something bad."

Federico continued walking. Forgiven slowed down with Mason.

"Do you see it?" Mason asked. "That front rank. There isn't a Latin face among them. They look like the Irish national soccer team. And they are all in new uniforms."

"What do you mean?" said Brother Forgiven.

"They're not standing at a true 'parade rest' with 'eyes front'. Their eyes are watching everything in the area. Those guys are all paid mercenaries, paid killers, soldiers of fortune. They're all sweaty and ready to kill," Mason said. "Which is what they are paid to do. And we're walking right into the space between them. We'll be in the cross-fire."

Brother Forgiven stopped walking.

Mason said, "We gotta get out of here. Now!"

Suddenly Federico stopped walking. He turned around and faced Brothers Forgiven and Mason. He was smiling. "Today, at this moment," Federico said, "I am more deeply in God's will than ever before. It is very, freeing," he said. "You see—finally there is no option."

Federico looked up at the sky. A solitary buzzard floated high above the desert. "Give my best to the other Brothers at home," he said. "And Mason, all your questions will soon be answered. As an older brother loves a younger brother—so I love you." He stopped speaking and looked again around the desert valley. Then Federico turned again to Brother Forgiven. "My Brother," he said, "we were like twins. What one of us didn't think of, the other did. Together we held a monastery together. Thank you. I look forward to our reunion."

Then Federico walked away from his two Brothers. He walked to the center of the clearing between the two armies waiting and watching him. Finally he stopped walking. He stood still and broke the silence.

"Brothers, are you looking to do battle?" He paused and the men on both sides stared at him. There was no movement.

"Many of you are quite young. Have you ever been in combat?" Federico turned from side to side as he spoke. "Do not be quick to kill and be killed. You say, 'I will do this, God willing' or 'I will do that, God willing.' I ask—are you truly seeking God's will?"

A soldier's voice called back, "A religious nut!"

Another voice said, "And a coward too!"

A new voice was suddenly heard, "Can I shoot him now?"

Immediately an authoritative voice responded, "Hold your fire!"

"Don't take life so casually," Federico said. "And don't take life away so easily." His words were carried in the dry air. The men stood watching and waiting.

"You know," continued Federico, "you are asking in your hearts, can we avoid this war? Your officers have told you this will be a just war because the land is rightfully yours. And your officers have told you there is oil beneath this sand. But think men. Think. Will any of you privates and corporals be wealthy when this war ends? Will you share in the new wealth?"

A voice called out, "My children have been hungry all their lives. And we are standing on oil. Black gold. The wealth of our future. Men, let's win this war and our children will never starve again."

"Do you believe your children will eat well," Federico said, "after you die? Will they eat well on a widow's pension? You know that in your hearts you are asking, can this war be avoided? I tell you—yes. You cannot have a war if there is no enemy. When you are facing your cousins, who is your enemy? Why would you kill those who think just as you think? You say, the other side wants what belongs to our side.

325

But I tell you join both sides together and share it. Do this without killing and being killed."

As Federico spoke, a pack of stray dogs came on the field. Three of the dogs separated from the pack and approached Federico. They moved slowly toward him and finally laid down near his feet.

A voice from one of the soldiers called out, "Your monastery is on the Solidad side of the desert isn't it?"

"Silence in the ranks," shouted an officer.

"You guys want all the oil don't you," said the voice.

"Silence in the ranks, I said!"

Then the voice called out again, "With you, we will share—NADA!"

For the first time since Federico started speaking to the men, a slight cheer rippled through both ranks. An officer ordered, "Quiet men," but his voice could barely be heard. At that moment all three of the stray dogs at Federico's feet stood up and sniffed the air. Their ears were folded back and the short hair on their spines rose in a bristle. Quickly they trotted away and disappeared in the rows of soldiers.

"Pero Padre," it was a voice with a slight tone of respect, "how do we avoid this war?"

"Good question mi amigo," said Federico. "The answer is, change your enemies into friends."

"Si. But how do we do this thing?"

"It is so simple," answered Federico. "You pray for the other side. When those prayers of Christians are sincere, those enemies will become your friends. This will happen in your heart—and theirs. God speaks to the heart. This time, let your heart hear. This is not my answer to your question. It is God's answer. It is God's will."

"Es verdad?" (Is this true?)

"You want to know," said Federico, "how to make friends of your enemies." He paused for a moment, drew a deep breath and said, "Let me show you." Federico stood directly between the two groups. He was bare-headed. His thin face was framed by wisps of white hair. From behind him the sun shone through his hair giving him the appearance of having a halo. Federico closed his eyes. Only his lips moved. Through the desert there was no sound. Then he opened his eyes and turned from one company to the other. Suddenly in a loud voice he called out, "Join with me." The sound of his voice echoed back from the wall of the mountain saying, "...with me, with me."

"Our Father, who art in heaven," shouted Federico. It sounded like a command. The echo repeated, "...art in heaven...in heaven...heaven." Several men could be heard mumbling, "In heaven."

Slowly, Federico went on, "hallowed be Thy name." More voices joined in the prayer..."be Thy name." The mountain wall returned the words, "be Thy name...Thy name... name."

Then Federico, with his face toward heaven called out, "Thy kingdom come..." At that instant one shot cracked

327

through the desert air. As Federico called, "Kingdom come" it was accompanied by the echo of the rifle shot—and Federico's body was flung backward by the impact of the bullet.

There was a second of stunned disbelief followed by dozens of voices crying out, "Oh my God!"—"Who fired that shot?"—"Good shot and good riddance"—"Don't let this happen!"—"Hold your fire!" and then a question, "Who shot the holy man?"

Federico lay sprawled on the sandy ground. He was on his side with his legs tangled beneath him. Brother Forgiven was the first to reach him. He saw that the bullet had entered Federico's chest and come out his back. The brother took a handkerchief and pressed it into the hole of Federico's back. The hole was nearly the size of a man's fist. The handkerchief was immediately soaked with blood. Some blood ran down Federico's chest. Much more blood ran out of his back. It quickly disappeared into the dry sand.

From both companies of soldiers the voice of officers could be heard calmly saying, "Stand fast," and "Hold your fire." The officers slowly walked between the ranks of their men as they repeated the commands. Then a strange quiet enveloped the desert as two armies of men and officers watched the wounded man before them.

Federico looked up at Brother Forgiven with half open eyes. "I will miss you," he whispered.

Then Mason reached Federico and Brother Forgiven. Mason flung himself down by the two. "Don't worry," said Mason. "A medic is on the way. I think you are going to be alright."

"I can feel my blood leaving me. It's God's will," Federico said, "but there's no feeling in my hands or feet." Then Federico looked into Brother Forgiven's eyes. "Not a long vigil—you do the funeral. It was—a clean shot—I will die quickly."

"No, my Brother, no." the Brother said. "You can't die. There is still so much to be done. We need you here."

Then Brother Forgiven noticed an expression cross the face of Federico. He could not tell whether it was a smile or a grimace, "Are you in pain?" Forgiven asked.

Slowly Federico answered, "There is a beauty in this place. Never—I never saw it before."

Brother Forgiven looked at Federico's closed eyes. "Can you see?" he asked.

"No," said Federico. "I feel it."

"What is it you feel?"

Federico's breathing was labored as he said, "It is a soft and silent beauty. It is a presence. It is joyous." He struggled with another breath. "It is from deep in that great heart of God." Federico's eyes remained closed. "It is what I wanted all along."

The Brother waited a second and asked, "Does it give you peace?"

"Yes."

Suddenly Federico moved his hand across his chest. "The prayer," he whispered as his hand fumbled with his shirt. "The prayer I was going to read today. My hand can't feel it," he said. "You take it now and read it at the funeral." He inhaled and added, "I didn't get to it today."

Forgiven reached into Federico's breast pocket and took out a folded sheet of paper. It was smudged with blood. "Don't talk about any funeral," the Brother said. "We wouldn't know what to do without you."

"Don't worry," Federico said. His voice was soft. His lips had turned extremely pale. "You will know what to do." He stopped for a deep breath and said, "Now pray with me."

For a moment Federico's eyelids flickered. Then he said, "Father of forgiveness—forgive them—for they know not yet—what they do." Brother Forgiven took Federico's right hand in both his hands. He glanced at the blood flowing from Federico's back into the sand beneath him. Then the brother was surprised to see a medic kneeling beside him. The medic was a young man who was trying to feel a pulse in Federico's left wrist. The medic looked at Brother Forgiven and gave a slight shake of his head. Brother Forgiven's eyes filled with tears.

Federico's voice came from low in his throat. "Our Father…" His voice was less than a whisper, "who art—in heaven." He did not open his eyes. "Hallowed be Thy name." The skin over his forehead seemed to be translucent. "Thy kingdom…" he fought for a breath, "Thy kingdom come…" he inhaled deeply. "Thy kingdom—earth…as…in…"

Federico's hand fell away from Forgiven's hands and one, shallow breath slipped from his lips. When the brother reached for Federico's hand, he saw that the blood had stopped flowing. Brother Forgiven bent over the body. He held Federico's hand close to his own chest. By the time Forgiven had finished the prayer, Federico's hand, sticky with blood, had become cold.

Brother Forgiven silently wept.

After several moments, two officers emerged from the men still standing at parade rest. From one side a Captain walked out to the center of the field. A general quickly marched out from the other side. The two looked at each other and talked for a few minutes. The one nodded to the other and announced the conference was postponed until further notice, the officers were to order all their men back to the trucks, to return to their barracks immediately, and they were to have the rest of the day off from any duty.

The body of Federico Llanos, Abbot of the Santa Juan de la Cruz monastery, was laid out at the monastery for three days and three nights. On the first night of the vigil, fewer than fifty people came to mourn. On the second day, nearly two hundred mourners came to pass by the body of

Federico. On the third day, people came from both De La Rosa and the mother country. The mourners numbered well over one thousand. The line of mourners moved very slowly past the body. Some called it a miracle that the Abbot appeared to look like a young man. All the wrinkles of his face had disappeared. His hair seemed to be dark again. Some of the mourners said it was as if he had been given a new body. The people filled the chapel and lined up outside the building.

On the third day, several reporters attended the vigil. They did not wait in line. They walked around writing their impressions in small notebooks.

At the funeral service, the choir of monks sang a requiem. Then Brother Forgiven, now Abbot Forgiven, gave the eulogy. At times his voice was too soft to be heard. At other times during the speech, Abbot Forgiven's words were drowned out by the weeping and wailing of the older women.

Because so many of the mourners could not fit into the monastery itself, a crowd stood outside while one of the Brothers stationed himself at the door and repeated phrases that he was able to hear from the eulogy. "We are all Brothers…the family of man…" and several times he repeated "Love recognizes no borders." Then Abbot Forgiven had to stop speaking in order to wipe away his tears. Finally he concluded by saying: "This was Federico's prayer for all of you." At that point two of the newspaper reporters rushed past the brother at the door and walked up to Abbot

Forgiven and asked to see the prayer. Both reporters copied it down.

Many hours after the service was completed, some of the mourners remained at the monastery in prayer.

One day after Federico's memorial service *El Diaro* carried the full text of "Prayer for the People." The following day *Los Tiempos* also printed the entire prayer. Next to the prayer the newspaper carried a picture of school children who had made up a chanting song based on the prayer. The picture showed the children singing on the street. The cut-line under the picture stated that the children's song repeated the line, "Love recognizes no borders."

Within one week, all newspapers on both sides of the desert carried the prayer on their front pages.

Four days after Federico's memorial service, a new team of geologists came from England to De La Rosa. They took numerous core samples from various strata under the sand of the unnamed desert. After testing the samples the scientists concluded that there was only a, "slight trace of crude (oil) at two locations," and "none whatsoever" at any of the other locations. The scientists stated that their oil company would not be interested in pursuing the matter under any circumstances.

Two hours after meeting with the geologists, the presidents of both states met in private and produced a joint press release announcing that they had agreed to avoid war and would in fact, work together for the mutual safety and security of both states. Any wealth found in the desert—the announcement read—would be shared equally. The release was accompanied by a picture of both presidents, Emanuel Garcia and Jose DeVilla, shaking hands and smiling at the camera.

Throughout the country, the news of "no oil" spread with the force of a volcanic eruption. For several weeks it was the primary topic of discussions…

The young women claimed that the absence of oil was the result of a cruel joke being played on the people by a mean-spirited god.

The angry young men argued that it would be a good idea to go to war regardless of what was—or was not—under the desert sand.

Some of the old men laughed and said, "That fool Abbot died for nothing."

One very old woman said: "Maybe Abbot Federico had to die to show the rest of us how to live."

The school children continued to sing their street song that repeated the phrase, "Love recognizes no borders."

Several days after Federico's memorial service, Brother Benedict was seen leaving his room in town. Witnesses stated that he was walking, alone, into the desert with neither a hat nor canteen. No one made any attempt to stop him. His body was never found; it was presumed that his flesh was eaten by the animals of the desert and his bones were covered by the shifting sand.

Now, some 30 years later, the Monastery of San Juan de la Cruz still stands and is populated with thirty brothers and an elderly Abbot named Mason.

In the cemetery behind the chapel, in the wind and sand, one of the gravestones is etched with the following: Federico Llanos—the Abbot who died for us.

The Prayer for the People

By Federico Llanos, Abbot, The Monastery of San Juan de la
Cruz

Heavenly Father,

It is my prayer that You not let our people go to war.

Instead, where there is wealth, teach them to share it with thanksgiving.

Where there is poverty, work together to overcome it.

Where there is bitterness, help them to replace it with love.

For love recognizes no borders.

We are all brothers and sons of the same mother country.

And we are all brothers and sisters in Your great family of man.

Do not let brother be set against brother.

Let not this desert valley be called the Valley of Death.

Let it yield only life with joy and love.

For love recognizes no borders.

Instead of war, let our sons grow old singing and dancing.

Let them watch their grandchildren grow to adulthood.

Let our men drink wine and argue with their wives.

Let our women live to enjoy the wisdom that comes with age.

Let all our people live to find salvation from Your Son.

Then let the sound of singing echo throughout this valley.

For love recognizes no borders.

So, let there be peace.

Amen.

Chapter 21
The Seventh Meeting of the X-Treme Book Club

"Jerry will be late for tonight's meeting," Jackson announced. "I'll tell you more about that in a few minutes. Midge will be here soon; she has some information about Jerry and wants to ask us a question or two. And I have an important assignment for our next, and last, meeting next week.

Leaving one chair empty, the group sat in their usual places.

"Did you have a good week?" Emma asked the group leader.

"Everything under my control," he said, "came out pretty well. And what I couldn't control came out alright too. So, no complaints. How are you doing?"

"Progress," Emma said. She blushed. "It's a process, and I'm working on it, thank you."

"Everybody else okay?" Jackson asked. "No life or death issues, I hope."

"I deal in life and death issues every day of the week," Clayton said.

"Good," Jackson said. "Our lives are in your hands."

As he walked over to the empty chair Jackson said, "You have all finished reading our book, right? Good. Jerry probably didn't, but we can't help that. Now then, you all remember our first session here? That was just six weeks ago.

"That first night," Jackson said, "you copied down a definition of literature that I put on the blackboard. What was that definition?"

In unison the group called out, "literature equals writing—having excellence of form or style—and expressing ideas—of permanent or universal interest."

As they finished their recitation Jackson added, "Amen."

"It did sound like we were praying," Emma said.

"If that was our prayer," the teacher said, "I don't believe it was answered. See guys, I don't like that definition. I don't agree with it."

"But that definition has been our standard of measurement in this group from the start," Laura said. "Do you have a better definition now?"

"Well, yes and no," Jackson said. "I don't have a new definition. But I do have some new ideas which I would like to see added to the old definition."

The group sat in silence and looked up at the leader.

"Let me clarify," he said. "If we are talking about literature with a capital 'L' shouldn't we expect a lot more from it than what's covered by the old rule?" Jackson stopped speaking and looked at each member of the group. Silence prevailed. "If it's true Literature, then shouldn't we be able to find a deeper understanding of ourselves for having read it? Shouldn't we find some change—for having experienced the book? Shouldn't we know more about the world we inhabit? Or maybe we can find a dramatic playing out of the author's vision of what needs to be done to improve one's self, or one's environment, or one's relations with others, or with self—or with God?"

Jackson's eyes narrowed then. "I believe it is time for us to ask, is it truly literature if it does not move us? Or enlighten us, the readers. What if it's not memorable? Not poetic? Not exciting? And then, if it is not literature—then what is it?"

Suddenly the teacher stopped lecturing and laughed. "And if there is a new definition somewhere in there—aren't you glad you don't have to memorize it?"

Clayton raised his hand and said, "Could you possibly give us some specifics? So far everything you have told us is pretty vague."

"Okay, okay. Here's where I want to go with this." Jackson said. "Next Tuesday night, at our last meeting, I would like you people to bring me your opinions—about literature and especially about 'Wind, Sand and Hope.' How did the book sit with you? There are many levels of Literature; where does this book fall on that scale? What did you learn from it? Where did it take you? Because you went through it, where are you now?"

"Mr. J.," Emma said. "You make my head swirl with your lectures. Can you simplify in terms that I can understand—what is the assignment?"

"You know what makes you a good student?" the leader asked. "It's when you don't understand—you ask. That's why you eventually do understand. So, in simplest terms, the assignment is, tell us what you think is the message of 'Wind, Sand and Hope'—and you can tell us anything else you think we should know about it. Just put the message first. Got it?"

"Got it. Thanks."

"Hello book club!" It was the voice of Midge. "Hello hello!"

As Midge walked into the group, Jackson stood up and offered her his chair. "Thank you," she said. "I'll only take a few minutes, but I need to hear what you think." Without waiting for a response, Midge said, "Jerry has cost this store some heavy-duty money. I mean big money if everything he took would have sold at full mark-up…"

"He must be made to pay it all back," interrupted Clayton.

"But it's about half that amount if I figure only my wholesale cost. So I have negotiated a deal with the corporate office. If I can recover the total wholesale cost, corporate says I can use that figure and then I can let Jerry off. They don't care what I do at this point. Here's the thing," Midge said, "in talking with Jerry's parents, his father wants Jerry to get a job and pay it back by himself."

"That will teach him," Clayton said.

"The father won't pay any of it," Midge said. Then she added, "So my idea is to put Jerry to work here."

"He's been nothing but trouble for you," Clayton said. "How can you trust him?"

"Yes, but do you people trust him?" Midge asked. "You do know him somewhat. What do you think?"

"I would trust him now," Jackson said.

"Me too," Emma added.

"Yes," said Laura, "I trust Jerry."

"Well I sure don't," Clayton said. He spoke slowly and firmly. "Never did. Sure don't now."

"If he can't pay it back," Midge said, "I'll have to turn him over to the police. It's that simple."

"He came forward, confessed, repented," Laura said. "Give him this chance Midge, please."

"What would he do here?" asked Jackson.

"All the really crappy jobs. Scraping gum off the floor. Hauling garbage from the coffee shop to the dumpster, shampooing carpets," Marge said, "and helping security people spot shop-lifters."

Clayton looked at Midge and said, "Have you forgotten Jerry's track record? He's a nasty little thief!"

Midge ignored Clayton's comment and asked the group leader, "Is this book club going to continue meeting through the summer? Jerry thinks of you as his friends. Something tells me that if you showed your trust over the next few weeks it would help him gain more self-confidence. Do you plan to keep meeting?"

"He doesn't need more self-confidence," grumbled Clayton. "He's been a wise ass from the beginning!"

Midge turned slightly away from Clayton and spoke to Jackson, Laura, and Emma. "I would pay him a stipend from his salary..."

"Just enough to keep him in candy?" Emma laughed. "And keep him from temptation, right?"

"He would begin to pay off his debt by the end of next week," Midge said. "By mid-summer he would be debt free so I could put his pay into a savings account. By September he'll have some cash for college."

"But Jerry doesn't want to go to college," Emma said.

"He will by mid-summer," Midge said "By then he'll see the difference a Bachelor's degree can make in a bookstore."

"I bet," Emma said, "it's the difference between working with a computer or a putty knife."

"You are all thinking 'pie-in-the-sky,'" Clayton said. "Better tell him to leave his backpack at home."

"Mrs. Fisher," Jackson said. "Can I get back to you about the possibility of extending our club meetings through part of the summer?"

"Sure," Midge smiled. "I hope you will come to a kind decision. Call me when you know."

As Midge disappeared between shelves of books, Jerry strolled in and sat down. He appeared to be out of breath.

"Good timing," Jackson said. "Here's the assignment for next week. I am looking for a short, prepared statement of what you learned from reading our book as well as the discussions we had. You don't have to back your opinions with facts. Just let your emotions fly. Okay? This will be a good chance to be heard. So take the opportunity."

The teacher stopped speaking and looked at each member of the club. With a forced smile and a lower voice, he added, "You've all finished reading the book. Now you have a week to think about the assignment. Next Tuesday night I hope to hear a lot of feedback about our book. Okay? And nobody will be excused from attending. Got that? Any questions?"

"If I may," Jerry said, "I have a question. Not about the assignment but the book. I finished it and one thing really bugs me."

"Way to go Jerry," Jackson said. "Those are the kinds of questions we like."

"Okay," Jerry said. "Right near the end, after the Abbot's memorial service, there's this old guy sitting at a café or something. And talking about Federico he says, 'That old fool died for nothing because there was no oil out there.'"

Jerry moved in his chair and slightly kicked the backpack at his feet. "So, as I read that part over I thought it negated Abbot Federico's life. See, if that old man was right, then the Abbot did die for nothing." Jerry turned to the teacher and asked, "Was the old guy right?"

Jackson smiled at Jerry. "Good question." His smile faded quickly. "What do you think is the answer?"

"Hey man," Jerry scowled at the discussion leader. "Don't dodge the question. It's too important. Was there a purpose in the Abbot's death? Was there oil in that desert or not?"

At that point, teacher Jackson turned to the blackboard and started writing. The chalk in his hand sounded like a small hammer. "Here's the sequence of what happened." He moved aside so everyone could see. On the board was a three part outline.

1. Oil in desert.
2. Federico's sacrifice.
3. No oil in desert.

He turned to face the group. "There was purpose in Federico's life—and death. Divine purpose," he said. "Because of Federico's obedience, his willingness to be sacrificed and God's acceptance—the oil vanished. All of it. Where there had been oil before, there was only dry sand later."

Jerry grabbed his cap and yanked it off his head. "No way, Mr. J." He twisted the cap in both hands as if he was wringing it out. "You can't have it both ways. Just give us truth. Without contradictions. And keep it simple please."

"Simple. You want simple?" Jackson said. "Let's put it in one sentence. Because the Abbot was willing to pay the price for his people, God accepted the sacrifice, made the oil disappear and freed the country from all those new temptations."

Emma raised her hand and said, "So the Abbot's sacrifice changed God's mind. Is that what you are saying?"

"Not quite," Jackson said. "I think the change came when God's will and the Abbot's mind were perfectly and completely in agreement." Then he held up one hand like a police officer stopping a line of traffic. "Let's not get so carried away with the oil thing that we don't see the other important action: the Abbot's spiritual experience."

"Oh sure," Jerry said. "Move along and leave me behind, I still can't understand the oil stuff, and you're going spiritual. Fat chance I'll figure that out either."

Jackson turned to Jerry and said, "Maybe this will help." Then he faced the entire group. One hand was still raised. "See, there was a moment when the Abbot's heart became absolutely aligned with Gods' will. Federico's heart communicated his obedience to God's plan when he said, 'Thy will be done.'"

345

As Jackson spoke with one hand held up, he slowly raised his other until both hands came together palm to palm. The two hands fit together perfectly.

"That was what lead to Federico's spiritual experience," the teacher said. "And it was a beautiful thing to see and to know. You see, in that ecstatic instant, the great, great heart of God the Father was filled with joy. So much so that if flowed over. It flowed over and into Federico's little, human heart. And they were united. God and man. United in God's will." Jackson's voice was barely a whisper. The members of the group leaned forward to hear.

"It was a moment of the most profound agreement." Then his voice became loud. "Do you know the word for this?"

Quickly he turned to the blackboard and wrote one word across it. It was: atonement. With the chalk he slashed the word into three parts: At/one/ment. "God at one with man," Jackson continued, "and man at one with God."

The group was silent. No movement. The teacher continued, "I believe at that moment, God instantly dried up the oil. Got that guys? Was it a miracle? Absolutely. The desert sand was dry all the way down as if there had never been oil there. It was an answer to prayer. It was God's response to one man's obedience. And the result, instead of war, a nation was given time to think about eternity, salvation—and God Himself."

Jackson paused, the moment of quiet ended with a short laugh from Clayton. "I am a man of science," he said. His expression was a combination of a sneer and a snarl. "So I don't believe in miracles. I am also a doctor. So I've seen a lot of life and death. But I have never, ever, seen any miracles."

"Oh," Emma said. "That's too bad."

"What did you say?" Clayton snapped. "Don't pity me! I think you guys are the pathetic ones to believe in miracles. You can't see that it's your escape from all your petty, little existences."

"Hey guys," Jerry said. "Watch Doc's neck. It's going to get really, really red. Soon."

"I know what I see every day," Clayton said. "That's what I believe in. I cannot believe in what I cannot see."

"Wow," Jerry said. "If you went blind you'd believe in nothing?"

"Could it be" asked Laura, "that you fear the things you cannot see—because you can't control them—so you simply decided not to see them? That would be a form of control you know."

"Hey Doc," Jerry said, "she's got you there. And it hurts doesn't it," he added. "It's hurts because she could be totally right. A real 'man of science' wouldn't turn away from evidence would he? But, is it a form of control—or a case of simple denial?"

Clayton looked up at the ceiling and said, "I don't know what any of you are talking about."

"You guys notice Doc's neck and ears are getting red," Jerry said. "Watch the old blood pressure, Doc."

"It looks like you've locked yourself in some kind of intellectual prison," Emma said. "A prison of your own making. How sad. A prison without windows."

"Why are you all ganging up on me," Clayton said. He took his copy of the book and stood up as if to leave. "What's going on?" His voice was calm but his knuckles were gleaming white. "Is this 'hate Clayton' week?"

"Oh, no way," Emma said. "We don't hate you. We know you—and accept you."

"I don't know why but we do," added Jerry.

"So, you are telling us that the Prayer for the People was answered," Emma said. "Is that it?"

"May I answer that?" Laura asked.

"Of course," Jackson said. "I didn't mean to hog the podium."

"Thank you," Laura began. "I believe the Prayer for the People was answered completely. Big time. Everything changed. Instead of being slaves to the ways of the world, the people of de la Rosa were set free to take a step or two into the spiritual world."

"Oh yes," Jackson said. "Closer to that reality which is the spiritual world. Federico was there already as an example to follow."

Jerry interrupted, "Hang on there. I just heard you say, 'closer to reality,' so, on top of everything else that I don't get, now you say there are different degrees of closeness. Did I hear that right?"

The teacher sighed. "I know Jerry. You want a one-sentence answer to something that has been argued over for centuries. And you want the answer immediately.

"Well, here's the best I can do. Yes, there are different levels of closeness to God. Disciplines exist to teach us how to enter into God's presence and even hold us there temporarily," he said. "But I think the highest level we can achieve in this life is the atonement that Federico had near the end of his life. That moment was nothing less—nothing less—than a preview of Heaven. Man with God and God with man."

In the next moment a silence fell over the entire bookstore. Even the piped-in music temporarily stopped. Every member of the book club looked up at their teacher who stood over them with a serious expression.

"Wow," Jerry said. "There is a world of spiritual stuff out there that I haven't seen yet." Jerry's voice was unusually soft. "I would like to understand more about it. A lot more."

Jackson smiled.

Chapter 22
The Final Meeting of the X-Treme Book Club

"It's called a sheet-cake," Laura said as she struggled to lower the massive cake down to the coffee table at the book club meeting place. She removed the protective plastic top. "I did the decorating myself."

The cake was covered with a white frosting. In large letters of gold frosting were the words, "Thank you, Mr. Jackson" Under that were several bright red hearts. Beneath the hearts, in four different colors, were the names: Emma, Doc, Jerry, and Laura.

"Nice work," Emma said.

"Thanks."

"Think it's big enough?" asked Jerry.

"Normally," Laura said, "this size will serve twenty-five people so there might be some left over."

"Well, I would hope," Clayton said. "There are only five of us."

"Six," Laura corrected him. "Midge is bringing the sodas. Besides, Mr. J is a bachelor so he'll want to take some home."

"Sodas, plates, and forks," Midge Fisher called as she walked in. "Is he here yet?"

"No, but expected any minute now."

"Here he is!" Laura said.

Four voices, in unison, broke out with "for he's a jolly good fellow…" As the words came to, "which nobody can deny," Clayton called out: "Speech! Speech!"

The members of the book club took their usual places as Jackson remained standing. "Beautiful cake," he said.

"I did the decorating," Laura said. "That gold lettering is a tricky mix of orange and yellow."

"Well, it's all very nice," Jackson said. "And the cake looks like it might be enough for this group—unless you have invited another ten or twenty people."

"We thought you should have some to take home with you." Emma said.

"And sodas," Jackson said. "And china cake plates. You guys know how to put on a party."

"But the party can't start," Clayton said, "until the guest of honor makes a speech."

"Ah, shouldn't cake eating come first?" Jerry said. "Cause you know Mister J., his speech might be real long or something. You know?"

"Don't worry, Jerry," Jackson answered. "I didn't prepare any speech so it will be short. Okay?"

"Okay," Jerry agreed. "Let's hear it so we can destroy about five pounds of sugar frosting."

"Well then," Jackson began, "I want to thank all of you. Not just for this surprise party, but for your attendance.

I think we have all learned something. We even improved our listening skills.

"I have been the coordinator and discussion facilitator for several groups just like this one. The problem before has always been over the weeks of discussions," Jackson said, "those talks often slipped down to the lowest common denominator. And that was usually pretty base. But not now. This group's level has been quite intellectual."

"Hey," Jerry interrupted. "So where do you rank us—intellectually?"

"I think," the leader said, "you guys tend to think things over at about the level of University graduate students."

"Well, alright!"

"Oh sure," Jackson said, smiling. "I once had a group of writers who spent half of a semester talking about the elements of a story. They couldn't agree on what was necessary for a story. Like, did it have to include a beginning, middle, and an end—or—an introduction, conflict, and a conclusion—or—if they were talking about the same things. I never knew if they were arguing or just wanted to be heard.

"Now this group," he said, "asked some sophisticated questions and instead of arguing, came up with answers. Big difference!"

Jackson paused as he looked at each member of the group. He cleared his throat and said: "My wish for all of you is that you would keep growing. Keep asking the key questions. Theological questions. And spiritual questions—and keep finding answers. That's my wish. And thank you for spending a part of your Tuesday evenings with me."

There was a moment of silence followed by a polite applause. Then Jerry said: "Can we eat now?"

"Yes, let's have our cake and eat it too." Jackson said. "Because you had an assignment for tonight; remember? You're not getting out of it. We'll do that as we eat. Okay? Okay."

As the members of the X-Treme Book Club ate cake and drank sodas, it was Emma who spoke. "You know," she said, "I just love this club. It's taught me so much. I'm really grateful. So—I move that we get a new book—and meet for another eight weeks!" With a smile, Emma looked at each of the club members. Her eyes stopped when she gazed at Jackson. "Mr J., it wouldn't be the same without you. Can you put up with us for another eight weeks?"

"I'm not sure," he said. "Next semester looks pretty tight for me. Of course I could recommend another doctoral candidate to serve as discussion leader. You don't have to have me."

"Oh no," Emma said. "It will have to be you." Then she glanced at the other book club members. "What do you guys say? One new book right? But the same leader, okay?"

"Not for me," Laura answered in a quiet voice. "I plan on doing some serious reading—but on my own."

"Count me out," Clayton said. "I didn't get much out of the first eight weeks. I'm not coming back."

"But we have to keep meeting," Emma said. She appeared to pout. "My mother likes being forgiven."

Laura laughed softly. "I hope your mother's forgiveness doesn't depend on this book club continuing to meet."

"I don't know," Emma said. Her voice was like that of a ten year-old girl. "I thought it might."

Jerry said, "Tell you what. If you ever do decide to meet again, give me a call. And tell me what you are going to be reading." He pulled his cap nearly down to his eyes. "I'll get the books at no cost." Immediately each person looked at Jerry and saw that he was smiling and his shoulders were shaking. "Just kidding," he said.

"Do we all remember the assignment?" the teacher said. "It was that tonight we are to each tell the group what we think is the message of our book. Suppose we do that now—while we are enjoying this cake and sodas. Who wants to go first? Jerry? I see you have sort of an outline or something written out. Would you like to lead off?"

With a mouth full of cake, Jerry shook his head.

"No? Okay, then Emma how about you? Good. Ladies and gentlemen, our Miss Emma has the floor. Let's give her our attention. Emma, tell us the message you received."

"Forgive me for being nervous," Emma said. "I'm not used to having the attention of four people that I totally respect. So, anyway," Emma said, "There were two important things I learned here and from our book. Remember when you, Mr. Jackson, told us how to talk with our friends and family members? We were supposed to share our ideas of the book with them. Anyway, that assignment really helped me talk with my mom. We just couldn't talk before. But now we are at the point where she has explained how she reached several important decisions in her earlier life. She did not have an easy life, and I respect her for hanging through tough times. And as I listened to her it helped me to get over the feeling that she was imposing her will on me without explaining why she was doing that.

"Please be patient with me," Emma said, "because I really don't know what to say is except to say that I'm thirty-one years old, and I thought I knew everything. And then mom decided to tell me some things I didn't know. Like decisions she made. Some good and even some bad and how much of only the good she wanted for me. I guess what I want to say is, I understand much more now than ever before."   Emma sat back in her chair, fanning herself with her hand. "I'm glad that part is over," she said. "The other part isn't so personal." Then a look of surprise crossed her face. "Or maybe it's more personal.

"In our 'Wind, Sand and Hope' I read one word that has brought great hope into my life. The word is 'yet.'

"It was used by Federico just moments before he died. And it has changed my attitude about nearly everything. Remember when Christ was about to die on the cross, he said: 'Forgive them for they know not what they do.' Got that? When Federico was about to die he said, 'forgive them for they know not yet what they do.' Catch the difference?

"To me, the message is that hope is on the way. The yet of knowing—or understanding—is in the near future. We've had thousands of years of mankind suffering from hatred, greed, selfishness, and pain. And most of it from simply not knowing what we do. But our book tells me that a great awakening is at hand.

"The old Abbot was right and because of that, there is hope for tomorrow," Emma said.

"Has this old world ever needed hope more than right now?" Emma paused long enough to swallow. She continued, "Think, now we have weapons of mass destruction, wars because of hatred, anger in men's hearts, abortions, global terrorism—but Federico gave us the promise of understanding. And the promise of working with understanding to resolve differences, tackle problems, find spiritual solutions. That's our hope. And suddenly the future doesn't look so bad.

"So thanks Federico. And thank you, Mr. Jackson."

"Okay Jerry," the leader said. "You're next."

"Sure but... I wasn't' sure I would be here tonight so I wrote this out as a letter to you. It might sound funny."

"Jerry, if you wrote it as a letter," Jackson said, "then I think you should read it as a letter."

"You sure?"

"Go for it."

Jerry shifted in his chair. "Dear Mr. J. and members of the book club," he began. His voice was strong. "Until a week ago I still thought that I was a sociopath—no conscience and no guilt—because I never felt bad about stealing books or lying. In fact, lying about some things made me feel good. Plus, some lies I told so often that I believed them myself," Jerry read.

"Then it happened. It was when I read Federico's death and then his Prayer for the People. It dawned on me that Federico had a choice. Federico didn't have to go to the war conference. President Garcia didn't bother to show up. But Federico made a choice—knowing it would be his sacrifice.

"And I thought, that idea of having a choice—is really cool. And you know, we all have choices to make. Can you picture me as a smiley face with a light bulb going on over my head? Sure, I realize that there is a lot that goes into making each choice. And I know that I prefer easy answers rather than hard-work answers. So it is going to be tough for me to make right choices. But that is what I will do. From now on. I choose not to be a sociopath. I choose not to be a liar. I choose not to be a thief. I choose to get any and all the help I need to make these choices last through my lifetime." Jerry stopped. He did not look up. He took several deep breaths before resuming his reading.

"So thanks Mr. J. You got me started on something good.

"And I'm going to read 'Wind, Sand and Hope' again this summer. Now that I know how it ends I think I might even understand all the stuff that leads up to the end. Granted, I don't have all the answers yet. Do we ever? But I do know that you taught our class something important."

"See ya, Jerry."

"P.S. I didn't believe the part of the book where Federico forgives Panzon. It was so totally opposite of what I have seen of human nature. But, in the last weeks I saw human nature changing right here in this class."   Jerry smiled as he read on. "Emma found a belief on which she can base her new life. And she has already forgiven her mother. Laura has relaxed. It looks to me like she might forgive Doc for being so smug. When I pay back what I owe this store, Midge has promised to forgive me for all the books I stole. And—I am on the road to forgiving myself for being so obnoxious and a thief besides. So, now I see change going on in ways I never expected.

"You get it? Mr. J., the book you had us read has changed a lot of human nature. Mr. J., you are some teacher, and I guess that's some book."

Jerry finished reading and folded the paper into a small square. Jackson began the applause and was immediately joined by the others.

"You are so on the right road," Emma said.

"Think so?" Jerry asked.

"For sure."

"Thanks," Jerry whispered. He took another piece of cake.

"I didn't realize," Jackson said, "What an observant man you are."

"Wanna know where that comes from?" said Jerry.

"Yes. Absolutely."

"Comes from trying to spot every hidden security camera."

"Hm. Sorry I asked," Jackson said. "But that's all over for good. Right?"

"You got that right."

"Thank you very much Jerry," Jackson said. "Laura. Are you ready?"

"Me? I'm not sure," Laura said. "I know what I want to say. But I'm not sure I can put it all into words. I can't always explain things…"

"Forget about explaining things," the teacher said. "Instead, just tell us what you understand from our book."

Laura sighed. "As I see it," she said, "the message is hope. Federico had hope because he learned where to look for it—where to find it. Our Abbot went from total hopelessness to being filled with hope.

"At the bakery where I work, I have to get the dough in the ovens early. So I'm at the bakery by 5:30 every morning. Some mornings I wake up before my alarm goes off. On those mornings I use that extra time by walking to the bakery even though the sun has not yet risen. It's only four blocks and it is dark because the streets are lined with lots of big, old trees.

"The strange thing is that all the birds are awake at that time. Do I wake them? No. I wear tennis shoes. I am silent. But the birds are awake and have started singing—together. Robins and cardinals and sparrows.

"Their singing in the dark used to puzzle me until I looked up one morning and saw that, in the trees—where they live—the birds were already in sunlight. I was below them in the dimness of pre-dawn but they were already in sunlight. So, I learned to stop and listen to those birds, those tiny creatures of God, and it is always a symphony of singing.

"Above me, the trees are full of music. The birds are full of joy. The world is full of forgiveness. While I am still in the dark, the birds see the light.

"Then I resume walking. Quietly. It would be sacrilegious to make another sound. In the tops of those trees there is nothing but the joy of the morning. The beauty of the day is being exalted. And in my heart…" Laura stopped speaking and swallowed. "In my heart," she said. "I know. I know it is a miracle. The miracle of hope. You see, at that level—where birds live—creation is being renewed. It is the five a.m. miracle and it brings the gift of hope with it.

"Try it for yourself," Laura said. "Open your eyes to the beauty of God's creation. Open your ears to the music. Make room for God in your life. Make room and God will fill that space with His hope. Now understand this: the response to hope—is joy. Joy—joy—joy! And that is the message of Abbot Federico's life. God's joy for all of us."

Laura looked up. Her eyes were glistening with tears. Midge stood up, walked over to Laura, pulled her to her feet and hugged her. Emma joined them and the three women took turns hugging each other.

"Laura that was so sweet," Emma said.

"It was beautiful." Midge said. Then she turned to Jackson. "I had no idea your book club had this kind of insight and talent. Mr. Jackson, you must be very proud of them."

"Yes I am, deeply."

"Laura," Jerry called. "Laura, could you possibly make me a copy of what you just said? I think I could use it."

"I don't know. If I can remember it. I'll write it down for you, Laura said. "Right now I don't remember much of it. It wasn't my brain speaking. It was my heart."

"We know that," Midge said.

"That's what was so beautiful," Emma added.

For several minutes the three women continued to hug each other. Their tears mingled together on their cheeks.

"Clayton, old buddy," Jackson said. "The podium is all yours. We want to hear your answer. The question is: what is the message of the book that we have just finished reading?"

"I can only tell you about the message I received," Clayton said. "See, I'm going to have to re-read the last two chapters. The one where the Abbot instructs Forgiven who only partly understands what the Abbot means. And then the last chapter where Federico dies. See, I'm beginning to get it…"

"Which 'it' are you getting?" asked the teacher.

"All that business about people, In the Prayer for the People, the importance of the individuals."

"That's helping you to change?" Jackson asked.

"Absolutely," Clayton answered. "That is, I'm beginning to change. I'm seeing things from a wider view now. I used to see my patients as nameless sources for stories to tell at cocktail parties. I actually thought that was what made doctors popular. And, I'm ashamed to say this, but I also saw patients as nothing more than income for me; the more the better—for me. I guess I didn't really see them as people. To me they were objects to be used for entertainment and profit. And that's why I must re-read Federico. He didn't care about war; he cared about the victims of war. He was a lot like my wife." Clayton glanced at Laura and said: "My wife's name is Suzy and she cares about others more than she cares about herself."

"Aha!" said Laura. "And now you see Suzy's spiritual beauty. Is that right?"

"Sure. I guess so."

"Good, very good," Laura said. "Now I think that you should tell her about all that—your new viewpoint and seeing her inner beauty. She's going to be pleased."

"Think so?"

"Guaranteed. And it wouldn't hurt, in my opinion, to have your two teenagers there to hear what you have to say to Suzy."

"I'll have to think about that," Clayton said. "But thanks."

"Thanks?" the instructor said. "Did I hear you say 'thanks'? I mean, is that it? That's your entire statement about the message of our book?"

"Hey fella," Clayton's face became dark red as he spoke. "I didn't think the book we read was any top shelf material to begin with. And I'm not a big fan of change just for the sake of change. So yes, that's all I have to say about it. Because that's about as much good as I can find in the thing."

"Hey Doc," Jerry said, "Maybe another piece of cake would sweeten you up a bit."

Clayton scowled at Jerry. "Go swipe a set of encyclopedias," he said.

Jerry's first expression was of surprise. In the minutes of silence Jerry's expression became a slow smile. He said, "Something tells me, that the doctor's big change has not quite, happened yet. My prognosis is terminal bull-headedness complicated by extreme conservatism. I recommend electro-shock treatment to help the man awaken his dormant mental facilities."

"Time out gentlemen," Jackson shouted. "Time out both of you."

Jerry's smile was taunting Clayton whose face was deep red.

Jackson gave the signal for time out. "Questions?" he announced. "Any questions at this point?"

"My question," Emma said, "is where did that burst of nastiness come from?"

"No, Emma" the teacher said. "This is our final meeting. So let's stay on the book and our responses to it. I think that's the most important part. Okay?"

"Hey, that's right," Jerry said. "This class is in the final stretch. This is it. So, if none of you guys has a question, can I ask one?" Without waiting for a reply, Jerry said, "Mr. J. you have been teaching us for eight weeks. We've learned a lot but we haven't heard any of your opinions." Jerry glanced around the room. Then his eyes rested on the partly eaten cake. "What do you think is the message of our book?" He slid another piece of cake onto his plate. "And tell us in a way that I can get my small mind around it, please."

"Jerry, don't ever—ever—think of your mind as small. I see you as having great potential."

"Thanks."

"Welcome. So, the message of 'Wind, Sand and Hope' that the author has laid out for us is that there is—hope for the world," Jackson said. "The biggest obstacle standing in the way of hope is lack of forgiveness."

"This is my last piece of cake," Jerry said. "Am I forgiven if I just eat the frosting?"

"Go for it Jerry," Jackson said. He walked away from the table he had been leaning against and sat in the remaining empty chair. His voice was low. "Lack of forgiveness can wreck your entire life. And it can poison the thinking of an entire nation. In our book, Federico demonstrated that forgiveness is possible."

"Forgiveness was possible for Federico," Emma said, "but is it possible for us? Could you forgive the person you know was responsible for the death of your mother? I couldn't. Could anyone?"

"Oh, it can be done," Laura said. "I know it can be done. But the condition is that you have to be on the same track with God."

"Now God is on a track?" Jerry said.

"It's all in there," Laura said. "Just keep in mind the sequence of the events in Federico's life—and bring them into your life. First, you have to understand the sacrifice Jesus made so that our sins were forgiven. And then accept that forgiveness for yourself and be thankful for it. And enjoy your new life in grace," she said. "And then—somewhere in there you'll discover that you can forgive yourself and others. It's a process," she added, "but it can be done."

"Is that the way to peace?" Emma asked.

"Might be the only way," Jackson said. "Consider this. If we had more forgiveness in our lives it could spread out to other areas that are in need of peace. For example, more forgiveness between individuals would lead to peace between husbands and wives; between parents and children; between different socio-economic levels of society and between races. Now think of forgiveness spreading between bordering nations."

Jackson leaned toward Jerry. "You think it's too idealistic?"

"Well sure," Jerry said. "I was looking for the draft to never being reinstated. So I was looking for an alternative to war. That's what I want."

"Okay," the teacher said. "The alternative to war is to never let it start. Now that's not too idealistic; it's as practical as any peace plan can be."

"It sounds too much like those simple peace plans hatched out by groups of retired nuns and missionary priests…"

"Jerry, Jerry!" Jackson said loudly. "What did you just learn from Abbot Federico? Let me remind you. He saved the monastery from being burned to the ground. He saved twenty-five of his brother monks from returning to the ways of the world. And he kept half the men of two states from being killed off in a civil war."

Jerry looked away from the instructor. He did not say a word.

"We don't have to go to war for what we believe," added Jackson. "We just have to help others see the benefits of what we believe. Can you envision it buddy? A world without fear of being invaded? A world without weapons of mass destruction? Jerry—a world without ever again having a draft?"

"Slogans!" Clayton shouted. "All I hear are feel-good slogans. Words that will fit on placards that a stirred up mob of idiots can wave at rallies. But I want to hear something concrete. Strategy. Give me a plan. Do you have a plan?"

"Suddenly you are interested. Is that right?" Jackson asked.

"Are you able?" Clayton asked. He put another piece of cake on his plate. "Are you able to tell me your plan?"

"Ah," the teacher said, "are you willing to listen to the plan?"

Clayton had a mouth full of cake so he nodded yes.

"In the simplest explanation," Jackson said, "modern society has been caught up in chasing the false gods of power and greed. And those two forces, unchecked, will always lead to conflict. So, to avoid future wars, we can rebuild our world by diminishing our emphasis on competition and what competition leads us into." He stopped speaking and smiled. "Don't worry, I'm not going to test you on this."

Jackson's smile faded and he said, "Since the industrial revolution our society has been driven by production and consumption. Manufacturing and consuming. It has taken us as individuals and as a nation deep into a form of competition. As individuals we compete with our neighbors. And as a nation, we compete with other countries. Just remember that competition leads to comparing—and making comparisons leads to judging."

A pained expression crossed the speaker's face. He said, "Almost always, judging produces either pride or envy and the need to control. Whether it's pride or envy depends on whether you are winning or losing the game. For individuals it means the man who lives alone has to have two cars simply because his neighbor has two cars. For nations it depends on whether our Gross National Product is greater than theirs. This power struggle leads to domination and exploitation. It leaves no room for compromise. Differences are not tolerated. Winning is the only acceptable solution. The only thing that matters is being top dog—and staying there at all costs. That's what international power struggles are all about. See how this view brings about wars? And there is always the contributing factor that wars are extremely profitable for the defense contractors."

"Hey," Jerry said, "this is getting good. We grow up with the same idea in sports. You know? When the coach drums it into us that if you don't win then you are a loser."

"Wait a minute," Clayton said, "none of this is in the book we are reading."

"No? Let's look again at the story," Jackson said. "It's an analogy of Christ's life. He was betrayed by one of his own followers who was motivated by greed. He was arrested, put on trial and suffered an unjust decision. Then a brutal, public, humiliating death. And then, his words lived on after him. Federico's life was a parallel of Christ's life."

"Excuse me," Laura said. "I have to butt in here for a second. See, in my view, Christ's life was all about power. But the opposite kind of power. Power for peace. When Christ died on the cross it was a moment of incredible power. The power to make all things new. The power to take away the sins of the world. The power to release unconditional love. And Christ taught us, 'Blessed are the peacemakers.'"

"Exactly," Jackson said. "Christ's victory was not dominion over others. His goal was peace."

"Wait. Wait," said Clayton. "Maybe define the word peace—as you have just used it."

"Peace," Jackson said, "is not just the lack of war. Real peace is the lack of envy and bitterness in men's hearts."

"Okay. I think I got that," Clayton said. His face was still red. "But come on. Is that what was suggested in our book?"

"Well Clayton," Jackson said, "look at it like this. There are two characters in the book: Christ, who was unseen and Federico whose actions we read about. When Christ died, his absolute powerlessness became the greatest power. Because it brought about a higher level of thinking. Then, when Federico lay dying on the desert floor he also appeared powerless. He was bleeding to death so he was too weak to even open his eyes. But he had the power to stop a war, to prevent mass killing and to give his countrymen time for salvation.

"You see, Federico outlined for us readers the power to *not* be competitive, judging, exploiting, and quick to go to war. His was the transforming power to take the jealousy and bitterness out of men's hearts and replace it with the fullness of charity. Think of that guys, hearts full of Christ."

Clayton took the last bite of his cake and slammed the empty plate down on the coffee table. "You think you can prevent war?" His voice was loud.

"No, we can't. But Christ in us can—and will."

"What? You think you're going to ask terrorist leaders to become Christians? That's your plan?"

"No. But when we behave like real Christians," Jackson said, "those other nations will want to follow along. We won't be asking them to change; they will ask us."

"It will never fly," Clayton said. "Too radical."

"Hold on a second," Jackson said. "Are you saying that the enemies of this country *aren't* radicals?"

371

"No. I didn't say that. I'm just thinking that when suicide bombers blow themselves up just to kill others, well, how do you stop that?"

"With our compassion," Jackson said. "We can teach them the value of human life—all human life. And won't that be a wonderful place to start?"

"This is all crazy talk," Clayton said. "I have been asked to consider taking a leave from the hospital and running for Congress. If I did that and won a term you know what I'd do? I'd draft a bill that would make it illegal to undermine our industrial system like you are talking. You could end up in prison…"

"Would you please!" said Jackson. "Throw me in prison. Nothing would work better to unite all the Christians who think as I do. It would create the largest block of voters this country has ever seen."

"You're talking un-American!" Clayton shouted. "Anti-capitalism!"

"Oh no," Emma interrupted. "He's talking Christian-Democracy. Very American. Sort of like what some of the founding fathers had in mind. You know, when they wrote the Constitution."

Clayton stood up. "You are undermining everything this country has achieved in the last 250 years." As he spoke Clayton crumpled his soda can. "You have to be stopped. We'll rewrite the Constitution if we must to protect our way of life."

"Better sit down Doc," Jerry said without looking up. He was paging through a large travel book that had been left on the table. "Sit down," he repeated, "before you blow a gasket."

"What a crock of crap," Clayton said, "I'm not listening to any more of this nonsense. I'm out of here."

Jerry picked up Clayton's copy of 'Wind, Sand and Hope' and slowly handed it to Clayton who grabbed it out of Jerry's hand. "Keep it up," Clayton said, "and I'll see you in court!"

As Clayton marched toward the exit, Midge said, "That is one un-happy customer."

"That is one un-happy man," Laura said.

"I wonder if I should go after him," Midge said. "Maybe I could calm him down before he tries to drive anywhere."

"No need to hurry," Jerry said. "I think he's going to be up front quite a while."

As Jerry spoke, a large, athletic-looking man ran down the aisle toward the front entrance. Suddenly, a siren sounded. The book club members looked up except for Jerry who had pulled his cap off. He was scratching his head and smiling at the cap.

"When the Doc did the can-crusher thing," Jerry said. I flipped through this book that was on the table. "Know what was in it? One of those printed circuits that triggers the front door alarm." Jerry pulled his cap back on and continued to smile. "So when Doc started to leave and almost forgot to take his book, I handed it to him and that trigger thing must have slipped out of my hand and into his book. I know something just set off the alarm at the front door. I think Doc's talking with a man from security right now."

"Jerry!" Emma said. Her hand flew up to cover her mouth. "You didn't!"

"Wow. The guy who knew everything," Laura said, "just learned a new lesson. A lesson in humility."

"Wait." Midge said. "What if Clayton sues the store for harassment? He didn't really do anything wrong you know."

"Midge, don't worry." Jackson said.

"You sure?"

"He won't cause any trouble."

"How can you be so sure?" Midge asked.

"He'll pay for the book a second time rather than start anything like a law suit. He may be socially inept, but he's not stupid."

"But corporate wants me to avoid lawsuits no matter what," Midge said.

"Listen Midge," Jackson said. "If you're running for Congress, your opponent will have you checked out. And you really, really don't want it on your record that you were caught walking out of a store without paying for a $14.95 book. Even if it was an honest mistake, your opponent can turn it into bad publicity."

"I could go up there and rescue him," Midge said.

Jerry looked up and said, "Or you can let him stew for a while."

"Stew it is," Midge agreed.

A silence fell over the remaining members of the X-Treme book club. The noise of customers walking up and down the aisle as well as the piped in music and the chatter of the coffee shop—all melted deep into the background as the group sat in contemplation.

It was Midge who broke the quiet. She asked: "Mr. Jackson, what you have talked about seems like sort of a new world. I find it difficult to imagine. Would you describe it? Please?"

"You ask me to describe the coming spiritual world," Jackson smiled as he responded. "I would be happy to describe it.

"Understand that our hearts were created—for hope. Our hearts were created to be filled with marriage, family, community—and most of all God. In our next era, our homes will become the new monasteries. By de-emphasizing production and consumption, we will find more time. We will have time to listen to the Holy Spirit teaching us. We will have the extreme pleasure of growing together—in the Spirit. Today's mindless entertainment will be replaced with time for solitude and the maturity that solitude brings. Noise will be replaced with thinking and meditating in quiet—or silence.

Instead of being slaves to materialism we will have our lives based upon sacred disciplines." he said.

Then the teacher looked into the eyes of each person sitting around him. He smiled. "And somewhere in that path of growth, competition drops off, judging disappears, exploitation is no longer needed—and wars become nothing more than a part of history."

"The future," Jerry said and hesitated, "our future—whenever that will be—it sounds so good. But I was wondering, who do you see as being in charge?"

"At this point," Jackson answered, "there are a lot of questions—unanswered questions. I sense that the answers will be supplied when the people of this nation humble themselves, and we become a nation in prayer. Then our prayers will ask the right questions—and God will provide the right answers."

"Hey teacher," Jerry called, "what you are talking about—that is so visionary. It's kind of scary, but it sounds thrilling too. Do you know of a book that we could study that would tell us more about the future. Cause I'd be willing to go with a book like that—you know for another eight weeks or so."

"I think I can come up with material that you would like."

"And you would teach it? I mean lead the discussion?" Midge asked.

"Five minutes ago I refused to lead another series. Now I have changed my mind. But let's not invite Clayton back. Okay?"

"Okay."

Midge raised her hand. "Could I take Clayton's place?" she asked.

Jackson looked at Midge and said, "You know what we're getting into?"

"Yes," she said. "I feel that we are on the cutting edge of everything the future is destined to be. Everything in me says, this is what I have been waiting for."

"She's in," Jackson said. "Agreed? Good."

Discussion facilitator Dave Jackson stood up. He scanned the group. "There is a lot of wisdom in this book club," he said. "Lots of life experiences, many things learned—lots of knowledge. So very briefly, let's share it," he said. "Let's go around the room and give each other the benefit of that learning. Okay?"

All the book club members suddenly had expressions of deep thought. The room was still.

"New member, Midge," Jackson smiled, "Would you share first?"

Midge was silent for several moments. Then she cleared her throat and said, "The advice I would give comes from Jesus who said, 'Fear not.'"

"Thank you," Jackson said. "And I'll go next. My advice to you all is to keep growing."

Laura raised her hand, smiled and said, "Keep listening. Listen to the birds singing, listen to your conscience guiding and listen to our God leading."

Jerry looked at each person. In a quiet voice he said, "The most wonderful words I have ever heard were when Midge said to me, 'By the middle of summer, you will be completely forgiven.'"

There was another moment of stillness during which Emma glanced around the room. Her eyes were clear and bright. "When it comes to what I have learned," she said, "and experienced—I offer you the words of God the Father who said, 'My Son—took the test—for you.'

"There's just one thing," Emma said. "Mr. Jackson, what made you change your mind? It happened so fast. What brought that on anyway?"

"Oh, little Emma," he said, smiling. "Didn't you just see it? Or hear it? This group is good. You're all ready to take it to the next step. So of course, I'll be happy to guide you on that journey—that spiritual journey."

"Well, yes—I guess," Emma said. "I heard words of wisdom from people who weren't all that wise eight weeks ago. But, in the next series of meetings—the journey you mentioned—where are you taking us?"

"We'll be going forward," Jackson said. "We'll be breaking new ground. Emma, Laura, Jerry, and you too, Midge, I am so glad we'll be going together. To answer your question Emma; when you asked where we will be going. The answer is—beyond hope."

Jackson looked past the members of the book club. With narrowed eyes he scanned the bookshelves of the store. "I have some material in mind," he said. The words came out slowly. "It will make you think. It will become a major part of your lives." Then he shook himself as if emerging from a reverie. "I just have to gather it together. Give me a couple of weeks. OK?"

"Meet here in two weeks," Midge said.

"Good. Then we'll meet right here two weeks from tonight. Will that be alright with you Midge?"

"Fine. Looking forward to it."

"Thanks."

"So what should we be doing during those two weeks?" Jerry asked.

"Just get here," Jackson said.

"Anything else?" Emma asked, "that we should do during those two weeks?"

"Sure." Jackson smiled. "In the words of Abbot Federico, 'be ready.'"

Chapter 23
"Preventing War—101"

"This is probably the dumbest question of the entire eight weeks that we've been meeting," Jerry said. "But what happened to all the oil?"

"Everyone can interpret it his own way," Jackson said. "Here's my opinion. It was God's way of 'fixing' the problem. It was 'fixed' so the people of that desert and that town and that region—and those two states—never had to worry about oil again.

"The people had been given a great gift but both sides planned to kill for all of it rather than share *any* of it. Federico reached out to God to fix the problem. And God did just that."

"There was nothing left to fight over," Emma said. "So the war had to be called off. No oil meant no prize for the winning side. I think the question is, did Federico pray the oil away? Or did God work independently?"

"I firmly believe the oil disappeared as the direct result of God's decision to remove it entirely." Jackson said. "God heard Federico's prayer for peace. Federico had become so pure in heart that when he prayed he had the attention of all three forces that make up our Trinity. Federico was willing to be sacrificed for peace. He was sacrificed so that his words would live on after him. The prayer and the sacrifice moved God to fully resolve the problem.

"Sure, I suppose the peace between the two states was uneasy at times. Still it was a form of peace that lasted over the years. The gift of future wealth was taken away in exchange for the gift of peace."

"That is so cool." Jerry said. "Can this be used to prevent other wars? Like right now?"

"Can it be taught?" Emma asked.

"Or can it be tested?" Midge said.

Jackson smiled. "Didn't we just read about the test? God won. The people lived. The peace lasted. The greedy plans were dropped. The people prospered by the work of their hands. I'd say that's passing the test big time.

"There are dozens of so-called 'peace plans'. Some of them work for short periods. Calling both sides to the negotiating table usually prolongs the peace. But nearly all of the plans available at this time have failed. Now then, Abbot Federico's method is the one and only strategy I believe in--."

"Then let's get it in place," Jerry interrupted. "Like present it to our Defense Department, or maybe the United Nations. But let's not just sit on it. We better do something."

"Hold on guys," Laura said. "I'd like to hear more about the plan before we decide what to do with it."

"Great idea," Jerry stood up to speak. "See if you can outline it stripped down to its bare essentials. Tell us about it in terms that even I can understand." Jerry bowed to Jackson and sat down. He pulled his cap off and in a whisper said, "I could give up candy if I was allowed to be part of a project like that."

David Jackson smiled. Very quietly he said, "Hear that? Jerry is willing to give up candy to make this thing work."

"Yeah." Emma raised her hand as she began to speak. "I think when we all understand the plan we'll know Abbot Federico a lot better. So, will you do that—help us understand Federico and his plan. Could you teach us? Like 'equip' us to know enough to see if we can learn it. Maybe it could be our next eight week study. Is that a possibility? Mr. Jackson, sir?"

"Yeah, Mr. J," Jerry said. "This is getting good. So, do we—or do we not—have here a working method for preventing wars? Like what are the ingredients?"

"The ingredients," Jackson said, as he glanced past the listeners before him. "We start with a group of Christian prayer warriors. And their leader—a holy man or woman who does not act like a leader. He, or she, is humble with the purest of motives. Federico was the perfect example of a role model.

"Then there will be a coming together of the group," Jackson said, "all must be seeking God's will. They agree with each other vertically, meaning the entire group agrees with God. And horizontally, meaning agreeing with every person in the group. This is 'unity'. It takes work and time. It has to be taught. And yes, I will teach it.

"Then," Jackson continued. "There has to be on-going prayer. Lots of prayer. Some fasting is a good way to empower those prayers. Also, and this is important, there must be a season of confessions—followed by a season of sinlessness.

"So, by this point in time, the group is unified in agape love. It will be demonstrated during the meetings where members make their confessions. This is when the members make the meetings 'safe' for those confessing. Then the relief and purity this produces in the members' hearts is how the Spirit can fill those members with His presence.

"This all takes place to get the full attention of The Trinity."

"With that many rules, it sounds like you are trying to manipulate God," Emma said.

"Yeah," Jerry added. "Like twisting God's arm behind His back until He says, 'alright, do it your way.' Know what I mean?"

"A lot of people will think exactly the same thing," Jackson said. "But I believe what we discuss tonight is what God wants us to do. We are here tonight looking into the future. And I have a hunch that one of the most difficult parts of the whole miracle will be to give God all the glory."

"Hold it right there," Emma said. "We do all the work but give God all the glory? There won't be any cash reward for a peace plan that works?"

"We don't make the cover of 'Time' magazine?" Jerry asked.

"No cover of any magazine," Jackson said. "We're here tonight to see into the future. It's going to take a lot of hard work. It means change in every area of our lives. But let me tell you…" Jackson leaned forward and whispered, "There will be a reward. A reward such as you have never seen or heard. The reward will be fantastic joy." He continued to whisper, "Joy. Joy. Joy." Jackson straightened up then and loudly said, "The kind of joy—that will last throughout eternity!

"We will do the hard work, because our Creator asks us to do it." He paused and the room was silent. Jackson smiled then and in a voice that could barely be heard said, "When we obey our Creator, He is pleased. Pleased in such a way that His joy overflows from His heart. And flows into ours." Then, in a normal voice Jackson added, "Don't try to understand this yet. True understanding will come, in time. For now just accept that our God will not let us down. The Holy Spirit will join us in the work to be done."

Midge looked up at Jackson and said, "Dave, you are a great teacher—I guess. But could you take another shot at simplifying? Please?"

"You want me to explain it more? I guess I could simplify it by saying it's when a group of Christians meet together; glorify our God; give thanks for past prayers being answered; lay out the petition—or prayer—for God and then pray until the group feels that their will is in total agreement with God's will."

Jackson's voice became barely audible. "God's will," he repeated. "Simplify. Simplify. Easier said than done. Let's say it is about the power of prayer. No. Lots more than that. Let's say it is man's prayer being in total harmony with God's wisdom."

"That's what you call 'simplifying' the story? I can't jump through that many hoops," Jerry said.

"Sure you can, although, getting our wills perfectly aligned with God's will might call for some sacrifices."

"Come on," Jerry blurted. "I'm only 17 years old. If I have to fast it could stunt my growth."

"Maybe it's time for you to forget your physical growth and move on to spiritual growth. There are stages to go through."

"Or do you really mean," Laura said, "stages to 'grow' through?"

"Thanks, Laura," Jackson said. "That's exactly what I mean. Getting to *know* God's will is extremely interesting. And it's not painful at all. Then you move on to *accepting* His will. That's exciting. Next comes *doing* His will. That's a wonderful stage of complete obedience. And then *sensing* His will becomes a reality. It brings great joy.

"If at any point your own will has to be denied, it will take the form of pleasure. Your attitude changes and you find great purpose in working with God and serving him. It's not really a sacrifice. It's love."

Jackson took one step backwards. For a moment, he was silent. The he stepped forward—closer to Jerry and smiled.

"Jerry," he said, "There is one stage where you go through the 'death of self.'"

Jerry sat straight up. His eyes were bulging. "No way." His voice was nearly a shout. "I'm just beginning to live. The death of any part of me is not on my agenda."

"Don't worry Jerry. I'll help you through that part. We might even make it enjoyable."

"Really?"

"It's a simple operation," Jackson smiled. "You remove your own ego."

"What?" Jerry said. "Oh. Now I get it. My ego, huh? Maybe that's not such a bad idea."

"It leaves a lot more time for prayer."

Midge clapped her hands like a teacher calling for attention from a noisy class. "You're rushing into this thing without asking the obvious questions."

"Ask away," Jackson said.

"Well, the plan, as you described it, sounds to me like a prolonged series of revival meetings. That's not my style. Is it yours?"

"Glad you asked. That's not at all what it's like. Most of what I described is practiced in the quiet, often silent act, of listening to God."

"Okay. I could live like that," Midge said. "And I can see a group of men living that way. In a monastery. But what about us civilians in a world with all its distractions? Not the least of which is trying to make a decent living. How can we spend our time in prayer when we have to be in the office or on the assembly line?"

"Good question Midge. You see, as the plan catches on—becomes more common—many Christian homes will become what will be known as 'Little Monasteries.' In those homes, there will be plenty of time for prayer. And that prayer will not be a matter of duty; it will be a form of obedience."

"Okay. Just two more questions and I'll get out of your hair."

"No problem. Fire away."

"The plan seems as good as you present it," Midge said. "But didn't Christ say, 'You will always have wars and rumors of war.'? So—are you telling us to go against Christ's prediction?"

"Sure, Jesus said that. However, saying that was not His approval of warfare. He was just stating the condition of the world. And He," Jackson said. "Was right. There has always been a war or talk of war somewhere—for over 2,000 years. If we become workers to prevent wars and there is one war less—then we will have done God's will."

"I can understand that, Dave. So here is a stumbling block for me." Midge said. "You advise us to use Federico as a role model. You know he does not exist. Never did. He is a fictional character. 'Wind, Sand and Hope' is a novel. It never happened. There was no monastery. Or President Garcia; it was all imaginary. This bothers me."

"Ah, you saved the best for last. " Jackson said. "The short answer is that it's semantics. The long answer is that the book is a form of visionary fiction. Sometimes it is called prophetic fiction.

"I know the author. He was inspired by God to write the book. The scenes came out as God directed. The ending came from the Holy Spirit. After the manuscript was completed, it was put away. For several years. Only two years ago it was pulled out of a desk drawer and published. That was because recent wars have been drawn-out slaughters. It then was the right time for the book—and soon it will be the right time to practice what we learn from it. Yes, fiction is an imagined story. The story of 'Wind, Sand and Hope', was imagined by God. And Abbot Federico is the God-chosen role model.

"Somewhere around this point in our progress, I would expect to face the most ironic temptation old Satan can produce," Jackson said. "Let's call it the, 'slide into pride'. You all know God hates pride. Right?"

There was a moment of silence.

"Right???"

"Right!" The word came out like a shout from a chorus.

"There are many different kinds of pride. The one God hates most is 'Spiritual Pride'. It's where you feel superior to others because you think you're so saintly and are on such good terms with God..."

"I can hardly wait..." Jerry blurted out.

"Don't go there," Jackson said. "But don't worry yet. You're a long way from it. Maybe months—or years away. Anyway, I'll figure some exercise to keep you humble."

"Oh, I bet you will" Jerry mumbled.

"Any other questions?" Jackson said, "And thanks Midge for your participation and good questions. Now—anymore?"

"I don't know," Jerry said. "You're talking about us changing the course of humanity. We are good alright—but that good?"

Jackson smiled at Jerry. Then he looked at each of the people seated before him. "You're right, Jerry. No five people could bring this off on their own. But remember we who pray in the name of Jesus and by the 'Blood of the Lamb' can discover the will of God. Therefore God will be joining with us in our work. By knowing His will we will incorporate God into the plan. Or—more correctly—by God knowing our will we will be working together with Him.

"Think of that Jerry. On our side, we'll have God the Father who created the world and holds it in His hand. God who filled the oceans and scattered millions of stars around the sky to make the Milky Way. We'll have His Son, Jesus, who redeemed the world and we will have The Holy Spirit, who has the power to make all things possible.

"Jerry don't doubt God's power. Come on. Journey in faith.

"And don't worry Jerry. What we are talking about is not a plan to change the world. What it is, is the chance for those who believe in the plan and practice it—it's their chance to obey God directly. They will find the 'great joy'. And that joy will be the result of their obedience."

Jackson stood before the group, his eyes were half closed. With one hand he rubbed his chin. A silence continued for several moments. Then he looked at each of the book club members. "I have some ideas about this niche of theology. Yes, I am interested in holding some discussion-type meetings about it." He paused again, looking at each person looking up at him. "See, you guys know a little about it already. And none of you is scared. At least not yet. But, are you sure? Would you like to meet with me for another eight weeks? Learn much more?   We could call it 'Preventing war—101.'"

"Oh yes. It's fine with me," Emma said smiling up at Jackson. "Remember, it was my idea to keep meeting in the first place."

"Me too," Jerry said, "It means the draft will not be re-instituted. There will never be any reason to draft men into the army again."

"I'm for it," Midge said. "It will be a stretch for me. See, I thought I was a good Christian all along. Because I didn't realize how far someone could go—in this life. It's kind of scary for me. But I'll give it a try."

Very quietly Laura said, "Don't count on me. I won't be able to attend any more meetings. But thank you."

The group turned toward Laura. "What's up? You moving out of town? You ticked off at somebody here?"

"Not angry at anybody," she smiled. "And I will miss all of you, but I'm going to be in a different place."

"I'm going to miss you," Jackson said. "I always had the feeling you knew what I was talking about. You were very important to me and this class. Please stay in touch."

There was a moment of silence. Laura smiled but did not speak.

"Midge, you're good with giving us this meeting place one night a week? For another eight weeks?"

"No problem. You got it."

"Well alright," Jackson said. "Right here. New material coming up. Challenging material dead ahead."

"One more question," Emma said. "Are you doing all this just for our information?"

"No. I'm doing it for me and for God and for all of you. I'm doing it because I'm tired of information without action. And I'm tired of theories. I'm sick of reading new theories. Theories are nothing more than people's opinions and most of them are not what can be called 'new'.

"I want to spend the rest of my life knowing God's will. Knowing God's will directly from His voice—or His heart. See, when we ask God what His will is, He will give us the answer. That's what I want to hear—or feel."

"We've asked God for most of the things we have—which were received from God. So isn't it about time we ask God what He wants from us? He gives us Grace, salvation, the title 'Children of God'—and what does that mean? It means He loves us like mothers love their children. How will He give us what we ask of Him? He will talk to us about it. Our prayers will become conversations with Him. Spending time in those conversations will build relationships and that's what God longs for. That's what we were created for. Remember Federico's letter to his mother when he was in prison? He wrote her that we were created specifically to fill all those spaces that were left in heaven. Those holes were left by the angels that rebelled; they lost the rebellion and were cast into hell. You know nature abhors a vacuum. Well it was God who created that nature. In other words, He's going to fill all the holes. So let us work with him in that goal.

He could do it by Himself if He wished to handle it that way but He wants to work with us—to fellowship with us—to be a big part of our lives. And just what does He want now? I'll tell you. God wants peace on earth. He wants war to end and He wants us to bring it about with Him. Our efforts will produce His joy. And His joy will be shared with us."

"When will it happen?" Midge asked. "And how will it happen?"

Jackson said, "It will happen when we do what God created us to do and it will happen as we become what God created us to be."

Suddenly Jackson stopped speaking. He moved back several steps from where he had been lecturing. He pulled a paper tissue from his back pocket. As he unfolded it, one tear ran down his cheek. "Midge, Emma, Jerry, and Laura," Jackson said, "I have come to love all of you. And I want you along with me on this trip. I want us to be the tiny army that recognizes God's voice when they hear it. Will you do this—for God—with me?"

Emma answered first. "Yes. Of course."

Midge said, "Looking forward to it."

Jerry said, "Count me in."

Jackson looked directly at Laura.

She smiled but remained silent.

THE END...FOR NOW.
A NEW BEGINNING TO FOLLOW.

Manufactured by Amazon.ca
Bolton, ON